Through Hell for Hitler

THROUGH HELL FOR HITLER

A DRAMATIC FIRST-HAND ACCOUNT OF FIGHTING ON THE EASTERN FRONT WITH THE WEHRMACHT

by

Henry Metelmann

CASEMATE
Havertown, PA

Published by
CASEMATE
2114 Darby Road, Havertown, PA 19083

ISBN 0-9711709-1-6

Also published in the United Kingdom in 2001 by
Spellmount Ltd, The Old Rectory, Staplehurst, Kent TN12 0AZ

Printed in U.S.A

Contents

To Monika, Gisela, Mark, Joan and Evelyn
who believed in me.

Introduction

Ihr fuehrt ins Leben uns hinein,
ihr lasst den Armen schuldig werden.
Dann ueberlasst ihr ihn der Pein
denn alle Schuld raecht sich auf Erden.

'You lead us into life and let the poor
become guilty.
Then you abandon him with his pain
for every guilt will be revenged on earth.'

Goethe, from *Wer nie sein Brot mit Traenen ass...*

Born into a poor working-class family, the conviction not to trust my own intelligence but to leave everything important to my 'betters' was a part of my way of thinking since early childhood. The thought of being able to produce something which others might appreciate never entered my mind.

Later in life, though I did not realize it at the time, it was my then teenage son who had more confidence in my ability than I had, who begged me to write for him about my life, and thereby helped to lift this all-smothering deadweight from my mind. Once I had agreed to his request, I had to overcome the restrictive twin problems of time and opportunity. As a poorly paid railway signalman with a young and demanding family to support, I had little choice but to work every hour available in order to make ends meet. But as my signalman's duties included many long weeks of lonely nightshifts, I was able to grab the chance there and then between trains to ponder about my life, to straight away put pen to paper and hold it.

To begin with, doubts about the whole project arose quickly — everything in my life seemed to have been so brutally dull, so uninteresting and without sparkle, and I wondered whether there was really anything worth writing about. The thirties and forties had been such horrible decades that I felt I would have been well advised to leave them undisturbed. I just needed another push, though, and once I had overcome that barrier, and began to unroll the carpet of my past life, I recognized the fascination these two decades would have for those who had not lived through them.

Though I had been very young at the time, I had experienced the tail end of the doomed Weimar Republic, and then over six years in the Hitler Youth and a short span in the SA it gave me great satisfaction, looking back, to be able to place these and important episodes in their political and historical context in my mind. Then, of course, came my time in the Army in the early forties, of which on and off I spent almost three years in Russia. It was only when I started to write about these years that I realized without the slightest doubt they had been the most formative, and certainly the most dramatic, of my whole life. They were years packed with almost indescribable bouts of hope, of joy, elation, sadness, disappointment, suffering, but above all deep human emotions, untidily collected in an energy-laden bundle in my psyche, best expressed in typically German terms, 'himmelhoch jauchzend, zu Tode betrübt' (rejoicing to high heavens, then deadly aggrieved).

Though it was against strict Army Regulation, I had nevertheless kept several very small notebooks as diaries into which I scribbled dates, places and happenings like 'so and so killed', 'Russians attack and blow our cottage up', 'Panzer burnt out' etc. Had I been captured with one of them, I am sure that the mere mention of some of the places alone would have been enough to cost me my life, and I state this with deep shame. But the very fact that I had recorded these events by pen on paper had fixed them so firmly into my memory that I found no great difficulty in writing them out in rough German in notebooks after I had arrived in a PoW camp in Arizona, USA, in the spring of 1945. I still have a couple of them in my possession, the rest got lost or were stolen, but it is largely because I memorized so much from them that I am now able to fulfil my son's wish.

Once I started to write in the many lonely nights in English signal boxes, I discovered to my amazement how relatively easily all those dramatic events of those fateful years came tumbling back from my memory. But as even the original Russian notebooks were very incomplete, with large gaps in between and I am sometimes uncertain about the exact chronological and geographical order of events, I have grouped my recordings largely into two main phases: one our advance into Russia, and the other our retreat. Russia is, of course, enormously large, and four decades having flown by represents a very long time. It also must be understood that the verbatim conversations I recall cannot as such be absolutely correct in detail, and I have therefore saddled the pages with as few as possible. But all of the happenings, feelings and emotions I write about are in essence just as they occurred. About some of the names, whether they were Heinrich or Willy, Helmuth, Igor or Ivan, I cannot be entirely sure any more — and there is one whom I have deliberately misnamed 'Hauptmann Zet', because I fear that he might have a son or a daughter or even a wife still living who mourns him as a fallen hero. Though in no way sharing his ideology, leafing recently through a German book, I found to my surprise that I battled for my life in the same section of the war just west of Stalingrad as the late Franz Joseph Strauss in the terrible winter of 1942/3. Only he reached the exalted position of German Minister of Defence, while I made do with that of an English signalman.

After I had started writing, and after friends thought that it was possible publishing material, my emphasis changed slightly. For with time perhaps getting short, and my generation thinning out alarmingly, I tried to put the emphasis on telling the world what I have done, not because I consider myself in any way important, but because I have got a tale to tell the world, with a warning to not let things slide into a situation where the same horror could happen all over again. At times I muse on what tremendous documentary value it would have had for historians today, had an ordinary soldier of Napoleon's *Grande Armée* complemented Tolstoy's *War and Peace* by having recorded in his own simple words what had happened to him and his comrades on that momentous retreat from Moscow in 1812. Maybe in a small way I can fill that gap as to Hitler's retreat from the gates of that big city 129 years later. When will we ever learn . . .?

1
In early life

On waking up I had difficulty in remembering where I was and what had happened. The temperature in the bunker was still cosy, though the fire and the candle had gone out and it was pitch dark. I felt thoroughly refreshed but dreading the thought of what lay ahead, it took an immense effort to crawl out of my blanket bed and get dressed. The comforting fire was quickly relit, and another, big meal ready in the frying pan, the last hot one, I wondered for how long.

I did not know it, but I had just participated in a great historic event, I had been caught right in the middle of the breakthrough of Marshal Rokossovski's Armies, which within two days trapped Paulus's Sixth Army and consequently led to its annihilation at Stalingrad.

This event was to be the watershed not only of the German invasion of the Soviet Union, but possibly of the Second World War. My only concern for the time being though, was to save my own skin. Where the German lines were after this morning's catastrophe, and how far I would have to walk to find them, I had not the faintest idea. Luckily the sky was clear, and keeping the North Star always to my right, I knew that I was heading westward, and that was where my instinct told me to go.

I took the best rifle and pistol, and packed up ammunition, food, some candles, and a small bottle of best French brandy, which I had found in the Romanian officers' dug-out. I also took a fur coat and hat from there, and later in the evening when I climbed out of my dug-out to start my walk, dressed and booted in elegant furs, I would not have looked out of place in any fashionable winter resort. Only this was for real, not for show. I sneaked over to where I had found the wounded; there was no sound, and all was covered by a blanket of snow. Then I went to each of my four friends, stood next to their bodies and said their names, that was all. And when I walked away I felt like crying, not so much for the others, as for myself.

I walked all night, never daring to go close to a village, as I did not know whether it would be occupied by Russians or Germans. And when day approached I slept in barns, burnt-out cottages, on heaps of straw, or just under some protecting bush. Only occasionally did I manage to make a fire and to warm up some food. For drink, I sucked snow almost all the time while I was walking — and all around me was nothing but an endless white desert. What was perhaps strange under these conditions was that I felt bodily and mentally fit and very alert — in no way was I downcast. But oh, how great the distance from my home and childhood . . .

* * *

I was born on Christmas Day 1922 in the Prussian town of Altona, just across the border from the Hansa City of Hamburg. Had the 1864 War between Prussia and Denmark gone the other way and the Danes won instead of Bismarck's Prussia, I might just as likely have been born a Dane. Such is fate. Father was an unskilled railway worker, and my mother came from peasant stock in the District of Stormarn in nearby Schleswig-Holstein. Tsar Nicholas II had been made an Earl or something of Stormarn, a title given him by the German Kaiser, so mother claimed that we had a Russian connection as well. I was an only child, and loved by my parents who did all they could for me under difficult economic circumstances. We had a flat in a typical tenement block in the working-class quarter of the town. Factories were all around us and there was much smoke and noise — the more healthy green suburbs started further along towards the banks of the River Elbe. The hammering of metal, the grinding and whining of machines, and the ships' sirens from the nearby port, provided the background sounds to my childhood and youth.

Hyper-inflation hit Germany in the first year of my life, before a new currency arrested the slide into a dangerous unknown. Of course, I knew nothing about these upheavals, but remember how as a small child I played with the banknotes and aluminium coins of the old currency. My parents told me that an old lady next door was keeping all the old currency in the forlorn hope that one day it would be brought back, and that she then would be a millionairess.

The era of the Weimar Republic was tumultuous. Revolt was in the air against a background of poverty and mass unemployment. The cities were restless. Working people could not understand the reasons for their poverty, and they began to question the credentials of their self-acclaimed 'betters'. They had found out their Kaiser and had chased him across the border but now, they realized, there were so many new prodding 'Kaisers' greedily reaching for his crown. I watched many a torchlight procession coming from the docks, winding its way past our tenement towards the centre of the town. My parents allowed me to stay up and watch from our fourth-storey window. Most of the marchers were working people of all ages and both sexes, often carrying their children or pushing them in pushchairs. They carried banners which were always red and shouted slogans. 'Work', 'Bread' and 'Peace' were the usual ones, but there were also those of 'Lenin' and 'Revolution'. Police walked on the pavements or stood in groups in the sidestreets, watching and waiting. Mass unemployment and poverty has left a fearful impression on my mind to this very day. Some of my friends could not come to school in winter because they had no shoes, and they must have suffered in addition because propaganda somehow managed to blame the poor for being such. We were sometimes asked by our teachers to bring extra sandwiches for those who had none and I well remember how, with that wrong kind of pride, I strutted to the front of the class to deposit mine for all to see.

I witnessed many strikes and lock-outs in the factories around. Plenty of scuffles took place between police and strikers who tried to keep blacklegs out — whom I once saw fall out of a lorry which was overturned by strikers. It was probably a deep-seated instinct which made us children side with the striking workers. We knew many of them, they lived in our poor streets, and we sensed that their struggle was for us as well.

When I was about seven years old I joined the Christian *Jungschar*, a scout movement largely run by the Lutheran Church which was prominent in our northern part of the country. After Hitler came to power, a law was passed and our lot was taken over by the Hitler Youth. *Ein Volk, Ein Reich, Ein Führer, eine Hitler Jugend* was the key slogan of our time.

I remember the day, January 30 1933, when Hitler was appointed to lead Germany into a glorious future. My father, probably to let me witness history in the making, took me to a celebration in the large square in our town, the name of which was changed on that day from Kaiser Platz to Adolf Hitler Platz. There were thousands of people, and with the torches, the swastikas, the brown uniforms, fanfares, drums and pipes and the shouting, it was all very impressive to me. When the main actors appeared through the large window on the balcony, father whispered to me: 'Exactly as in Kaiser's days; then they fooled us with the Royals, now they have changed into brownshirts.' Then fighting broke out at the back as shouting workers were attacked and chased by the police and Hitler's storm-troopers. Father then took me home, saying that it was a sad day for Germany and the world. But I could not understand what he meant.

On Sundays I sometimes went on walks with Father towards the river. Large villas stood there, in beautiful secluded gardens, and we peeped over the hedges into a strange world of luxury, so unattainable for the likes of us. I knew father had worked hard all his life, and I asked him why we too could not live like that. And when I told him that we had learnt in the Hitler Youth that our Führer would change all those fundamental injustices, he just laughed and said that our damned Führer would make sure that he did nothing of the kind and would do the exact opposite, make the rich richer and the poor poorer; that was what he had been appointed for!

Even though Father hated everything connected with the Nazis, I liked it in the Hitler Youth. I thought the uniform was smashing, the dark brown, the black, the swastika and all the shiny leather. Where before we seldom had a decent football to play with, the Hitler Youth now provided us with decent sports equipment, and previously out-of-bounds gymnasiums, swimming pools and even stadiums were now open to us. Never in my life had I been on a real holiday — father was much too poor for such an extravagance. Now under Hitler, for very little money I could go to lovely camps in the mountains, by the rivers or near the sea.

Then one day a class-mate, Siegfried Weisskamm, was found dead in a gas-filled room with his mother and younger sister. My parents said that it had not been an accident. I was sad, but I could not understand. I was told that Siegfried had been a Jew, but I had not really known; I did not know what a Jew really was, and in any case, what did that have to do with his death?

There was no law to join the Hitler Youth; nevertheless, only one of my class-mates of about forty lads somehow managed to stay out of it. But when I applied to become a locksmith apprentice, the first question I was asked was when I had joined the Hitler Youth.

The songs we sung were beautifully melodic, all about our great race, our *Lebensraum* in the East, and the glory of fighting and dying for the Father-land. I liked the comradeship, the marching, the sport and the war games. We were brought up to love our Führer, who was to me like a second God, and when we were told about his great love for us, the German nation, I was often close to tears. I was convinced that because of the German blood in my veins I was a superior human being. Even in biological terms, I never dreamed of asking what German blood was. I accepted as natural that it was a German duty for the good of humanity to impose our way of life on lower races and nations who, probably because of their limited intelligence, would not quite understand what we were on about. It gave us a great boost when the Duke of Windsor, the former King of England, came to our country to tell us young ones how lucky we were to live in such a great society.

Early one morning before I had woken up, a neighbour of ours, a Herr Eycken, was taken away in a car by the SS and police, it was said. I very much liked him as a man and was greatly disturbed by the whole mystery. He had been a trade union secretary down in the docks, and whenever someone in our street was in trouble, Herr Eycken with his outstanding knowledge and ability was usually called to help. His wife, so the story went, had great difficulty in finding out where they had taken him, and the family had very little money. My mother was too scared to be seen talking to her, we boys did not want to play with his young sons, our former friends, as they were now the children of a traitor, and Father, who had always maintained that the only way to get higher wages was to fight for them, became very quiet and alarmed, and begged me not to repeat whatever he said about the whole Nazi set-up within our four walls. The Eyckens moved away to a still poorer part of town, and I understand that Herr Eycken died several years later of pneumonia in a concentration camp.

I loved it when we went on our frequent marches, feeling important when the police had to stop the traffic to give us right of way at road junctions. The swastika flag, often followed by the large drum, was carried in front of us, and passing pedestrians had to raise their arm in the Nazi salute, to respect the flag. There were some funny sights of old ladies with shopping bags, pulling themselves together and shooting their arms into the air. My father, whenever he saw us coming, usually managed to disappear into a doorway to let the 'brown pest', as he called it, pass by. Mother, not being so quick, sometimes got caught out and I remember how embarrassed I once felt watching her walk past with her arm in the air.

At school and in the Hitler Youth, names like Verdun, Douaumont, the Somme, Flanders and Tannenberg had an almost holy meaning for us. Mud was no mere common substance any more, it was the element in which our heroes had died valiantly at Passchendaele, and our songs extolled them as marching above us in the clouds of a stormy night, still carrying their battle-torn regimental flags towards glorious, final victory. The German soldier, it was drummed into us, was by far the best soldier in the world. We had lost the war because the German workers, led, of course, by Communist agitators, had treacherously put the knife in his back by going on strike while he held the front-line against the numerically superior enemies.

I remember the 'night of the long knives', when a sort of civil war broke out in the Party and SA leaders like Ernst Roehm and Heine were put to death. All we were told about it was that disloyal elements had tried to replace our Führer. A few years later came the *Kristallnacht* when Jewish-owned shops had windows smashed in and were looted, and a number of Jews were killed or drowned. My parents were very angry and sad, and told me that the Nazis were bringing shame on Germany. Father pointed out afterwards that hitherto poor SA men suddenly owned expensive cameras and their wives were strutting around in beautiful fur coats.

Then came the time when we all had to get an *Ahnenpass*, a stamped and signed official document to prove our racial origin. Most of us had great difficulty in tracing our family tree back more than one or perhaps two generations. We had to write and check with church registers, and in many cases the Pastors demanded payment for their labours. What the Nazi authorities were looking for, of course, were Jewish names.

When the battleship *Bismarck* was launched in Hamburg, Hitler came for the occasion with Admiral Horthy, the fascist leader of Hungary. In our Hitler Youth brown shirts we took up position along the main road leading from the city down to the docks. When Hitler and Horthy approached in the black Mercedes, some of us managed to climb into a roadside tree to see better. But because we were too many, the branch was bending down towards the road. The motorbikes were just below us and the whole cavalcade had to stop. Everyone was shouting to us to come down, but all that we could think of was our Führer, the greatest man on earth, the idol of the Germans — there he was, in front of us and looking up at us. After an SS man had managed to climb into the tree and jostled us back, the black Mercedes continued down to the river. We were shouted at, our names were taken and a photo of us appeared in the press with the explanation that four over-enthusiastic Hitler boys had just gone 'over the top' when seeing their beloved Führer. Nothing happened to us. When I told Father in the evening about 'Adolf just yards away from me under a tree', he merely muttered something about 'What a chance!'

Whenever we were led out on a march, it was always into the working class quarters, never into the rich areas of the town. At times we were told that this was 'to remind the workers', but I wondered sometimes what we wanted to remind them of, after all most of our fathers were workers.

Ernst Thaelmann, the General Secretary of the Communist Party, a docker, had lived not far from us along the river's front. Of course at that time he was locked up at Buchenwald, where he was murdered just before the war ended. One day I was holding forth in my all-knowing Nazi way to my father about 'Thaelmann — that Communist!'. Dad, rather unusually, became rather quiet and almost begged me not to believe what the Nazis and the newspapers were telling us about him. He had known him personally and told me that 'our Ernst' was a good and sincere man, and one of the best working-class leaders Germany had ever had. Hitler, he said, was a mere dangerous clown as compared with Thaelmann.

Towards the end of my Hitler Youth days, shortly before I was automatically transferred to the SA, the German Legion Condor arrived back in Hamburg from Spain, where it had fought in the Civil War for General Franco. Our troop went down to the landing stage to line up to greet Hermann Goering, who had a job to get out of his car. The 'Paladin of the Führer', as he was sometimes called, was very jovial and friendly. He chatted to us in a joking way and put his hand on some of our heads. But, though no one said it, there was something distinctly funny about him, waddling along in his self-designed light blue uniform. He had rings on his fingers, and some said that they had smelled perfume on him. Then *Generalmajor* von Richthofen, the leader of the Legion, came down the gangway from the *Wilhelm Gustloff*, followed by all the sunburnt and healthy-looking soldiers, greeted by girls with kisses and flowers. We were all very proud and elated.

Just before the beginning of the war Father had indentured me as a locksmith apprentice to the Railways. When war broke out and I was about to be called up to the colours, or 'the *Preussen*' as we called it, he fell ill and never recovered. Just before he died, Russia was not yet in the war, and only Britain stood between Hitler and 'the New Order'. Father made one final effort to make me come to my senses by giving me what he called loving and all-embracing advice based on the wisdom of his life's experience and observations. Ever since Hitler had come to power, the Nazis had cowed him. As a small boy, I had known him to stand up fearlessly and fight for his right as a human being and a worker, but he had been forced to become submissive. Now that he knew that his life was coming to an end, he was no longer frightened of the 'brown pest'. In spite of all our sad arguments and disagreements, I loved him dearly, and listened attentively to what he said, but I just could not bring myself to believe that his analysis of the situation was correct. He had been a soldier in the 1914/18 War and had fought the French in the trenches in Flanders and the Russians in East Prussia and Poland. On recalling the mass slaughter he had witnessed and been forcibly involved in, his invectives overflowed bitterly. To him, 'patriotism' was nothing but a useful means by which our rulers were able to delude and then exploit the working people as cannon fodder. The underlying reason for the war, he tried to tell me, was that all the big powers involved, being nothing other than large-scale robbers, had fallen out amongst themselves on how the loot from the defenceless world was to be divided between their disgusting greeds. He said I should not believe what the capitalist press was trying to tell me — and all the slogans our Führer was now coming out with; he had already heard from the foolish Kaiser — only then with a different coating on. Like so many of the working people of his generation in Hamburg, he hated the Nazis like poison, but even more so did he hate the paymasters who stood behind them.

When you go out as a soldier, he said, and fight the English Tommy on the battlefield, remember above all that they are ordinary working folk like you. If you could come to know them and their families, you would learn that they are probably also suffering from low wages, bad housing, poor medical care, ever-threatening unemployment, inadequate education and all the other social diseases, all arising out of an outdated social system. And they probably have to listen to the same kind of slogans you are being fed with.

Your real enemy, he tried to impress on me, is not the English Tommy, but the monocled figure in his beautiful uniform and polished jackboots strutting in front of you on the parade ground. For he is the same person who owns the land, the mines and the banks, who lives in the beautiful villas in Blankenese (a river suburb of Hamburg) and makes gigantic profits from investments in armaments, as well as having his fingers in many devious financial pies. He will loudly tell you that your wages should be low for the good of the country, that 'we all' should be prepared to make sacrifices, and that you never should blackmail your employer to back your greed with strikes. The ideas you get from his newspapers are his, they are the very opposite to everything you should stand for in your search for humanism. He will tell you that the nasty Russians are threatening your peace-loving country with powerful armies, and that we therefore must strive to be strong in arms. He wants more police because he fears revolt from the workers in the cities, and above all he is the one who is standing with his bulging wallet behind your pathetic Führer, whom he mani-pulates like a puppet, firmly holding all the strings which make the Nazis dance.

Being so ill, Father's exhortation had tired him visibly. He must sadly have realized that I, his only son, though not arguing against him any more, was unable to see the truth of what he had said. As a philosophical afterthought, more to himself than to me, he said that perhaps it was just as well that the Nazi brainwash had so effectively put a barrier between myself and the truth — otherwise the latter would destroy me mentally by the events bound to come my way.

2
Spiritual preparation

Ich hab' nie mit euch gestritten,
Philisterpfaffen, Neiderbrut!
Unartig seid ihr wie die Briten
doch zahlt ihr lange nicht so gut.

'I have never argued with you,
philistine priests, envious brood!
You are rude like the British
only you don't pay so well.'

Goethe, from *The Pantheist*

Then came the day when I was called up to the Army. Mother was much
depressed to lose me so shortly after Father's death. But I was full of myself,
and now felt able to serve my Führer and Fatherland in a far more significant
way that hitherto. The *Panzerjäger* (tank hunters) were stationed at Harburg,
which is in Hamburg, and most of us, we were all between eighteen and nineteen
years old, were proud to serve in such a modern branch of the *Wehrmacht*,
which had already picked up many laurels during the Polish, French and Balkan
Campaigns. Our barracks, the Dominik Kaserne, had been newly built and
generously laid out against a backdrop of heath and woodland which was convenient to train on. Almost all of us had been in the Hitler Youth, and were
eager to do our bit in the finest army in the world. We were like just grown-up
puppies straining at the leash.

Our training programme was tough and methodical, and we were often driven
to the point of exhaustion. Our officers and Sergeants made no secret of their
aim to mentally and physically break us, in order to remake us in their image
in the Prussian tradition. In the Hitler Youth we had already received considerable elementary military training which meant the Army was able to train us
more speedily. When we were finally let loose on the Panzers, we knew what
it was all about. A firm foundation had been laid to make efficient soldiers
out of us.

Because I had been a locksmith I was chosen to become a driver. At first
came cars, followed by lorries and half-tracks, until finally I drove the tanks,
which at that time were all of the Czech Pz Kpfw 38 (t) type. When I first
drove in column out of the barrack gates, my heart was bursting with pride.

What greater honour could there be than having become a German Panzer driver! It gave me a superb feeling to watch the powerful Panzers roll in front of me, realizing that to the onlookers by the roadside my Panzer was as impressive as all the others.

After several months of training, we were taken into camp on the Lüneburg Heath to receive the necessary mock battle experience. After that we were as good as ready for action — to be let loose on the peoples of Europe. Before that, however, there was to be a spectacular passing-out parade. Special daily parade sessions were organized to provide the necessary polish for the grand occasion. When we arrived at the large *Moorweide* (moor meadow) near the centre of Hamburg in our immaculate parade uniforms with high stiff collars and shiny cuff buttons, we thought we had reached the pinnacle of military excellence. Thousands of people had come to the meadow to watch us.

Countless units of young recruits had come from barracks and training grounds, from all branches of the *Wehrmacht*. Apart from the black of the Panzer troops and the general field grey of the Army, there was the dark blue of the Navy and the light blue of the *Luftwaffe*. As we marched up to form a huge semi-circle, we were proud to show off our pink epaulettes, the emblem of the élite *Panzerjäger*. Everything was efficiently organized down to the last movement, and the short and precise commands were executed with a strongly theatrical touch. We carried our arms with bayonets fixed, and then I looked across the meadow and saw the other units march in from the other side, I could see the reflected sun glitter on the cold shiny steel of their weapons.

It was a crisp, brilliant day, with the sun low above the trees. Many of our trainers had proud expressions on their faces, and after having soaked up their shouting and abuse for weeks on end, it came as a surprise to suddenly be addressed by them in polite terms. So we were human beings after all! Then the military bands marched in from the sides with their pipes, drums, trumpets and fanfares, led by drum majors swinging their shiny golden maces, which they threw into the air and caught with great *élan*, to the joy of the crowds. Everything was sharp and precise, movements were quick and without fault, and there was no slacking anywhere.

A large, low wooden stage had been erected towards the middle of the meadow, around which our huge semi-circle grouped itself. Long red carpets had been rolled out on the grass, leading from the road at the rear where the limousines began to arrive. Out of them stepped the VIPs, some of them, such as the *Burgermeister* of Hamburg, were dressed in morning suit for the occasion. There were church dignitaries, some in Army uniforms but showing their dog collars, while others were in their religious garb. And of course there were the *Wehrmacht* officers of all ranks, including some Generals. They were all in splendid outfits with highly-polished jackboots, while most General Staff officers had red stripes down the outside of their legs. One General wore a black fur cap with plumes on top, right out of the days of Frederick the Great, looking more like a fighting cock than a soldier. Some had brought their wives with them, which added to the atmosphere of a medieval pageant. They all seemed in a good mood, their faces beaming as their chatter wafted towards us across the meadow. There was plenty of introducing and handshaking going on, with the officers doing it in the Prussian military style, clicking their heels and bowing slightly in that carefully nonchalant way. Glancing round, they apparently took stock of the multitudes of young soldiers under arms, and it was obvious that they were well pleased by what they saw.

A microphone was in place on the platform, and loudspeakers hung from trees and posts around the meadow. Then someone waved his hand for general silence. In the wake of rolling drums we stood stiffly to attention as a lone trumpeter blew a silvery, piercing note, 'Ready to Arms', which was followed by a mournful military march in which we presented arms. And then, watched over by our Sergeants, we stood like iron rods, not daring to move even our eyelids. Short cutting speeches were made about the Fatherland, the Almighty, and the Führer, who had given us back our national pride and respected place as one of the most powerful nations on earth. We were reminded that *Gott mit uns* (God with us), surrounding the German eagle holding the Swastika, was inscribed on the metal clasp of our belts — so we had nothing to fear. We were urged to be ready to make the highest sacrifices to guarantee peace through strength, on the basis of German order all over the world.

We were called to swear the solemn oath to follow and obey our Führer for the glory of God and the Fatherland in our time. It was, I think, the Bishop of Hamburg who recited the oath over the microphone: *'Ich schwöre...'* (I swear) and then the Führer and God and Fatherland were again invoked. After every three or four words with our two fingers raised into the air, we repeated the words with a mighty rumble. And at the end of it all came: '...and so God help us!'

Now, after having sworn the oath, we had become real soldiers in every conceivable sense. The Bishop concluded by wishing us well in our endeavours for victory, and announced that anyone who wanted to speak with him after the ceremony should feel free to do so. Fanfares gave a final polish to it all, and we were dismissed. We all started milling around, looking for friends and relatives who had been watching from the sidelines. All the time the cameras were present and the whole show was later presented in the newsreels. With the atmosphere now totally relaxed, I drifted towards the stage and milled amongst the VIPs, some of whom had stepped down on to the grass. I had never seen a General at close range, and suddenly I was in touching distance of several. Their colourful uniforms, tailored from the finest cloth, fascinated me, though some of the figures stuck in them appeared disappointing.

The Bishop was chatting jovially with allcomers and beamed at being congratulated for his fine performance. He was a big man and had a red and happily smiling face. After all, in a way, having said the oath, it was 'his' day. Then I noticed a young soldier whom I knew from the barracks stepping up to the Bishop and asking him whether he could have a word with him. In a halting manner he explained that something deep down was worrying him. In family and at school he had been strictly brought up in the Christian faith and had been taught, come what may, to stick to his religion's principles and above all to the Ten Commandments. He went on to explain that during his training period he had been thoroughly instructed in the art of killing, and could well claim to have become an expert killer. He realized that soon he would be sent to the war, to fight for the country as the Bishop had clearly said. What he now wanted to know from the Bishop was, should he obey the very clear commandment of the Lord not to kill, or should he obey the order of the Captain which, no doubt, would be the exact opposite.

The easy friendly smile had gone from the Bishop's face. His whole demeanour changed dramatically and an intent look came into his eyes as he laid his fat hand on the young soldier's steel helmet, and said in a grave voice (which to me seemed to have the undertone of a threat): 'God bless you, my son...' That was all. No other word was spoken either by him or the lad; and while the latter still stood there like a reminder of a conscience, the Bishop abruptly turned away and talked with some officers and their ladies, in whose company he seemed to be much more at ease.

I watched the lad walk away from the stage with an expression of sadness and utter confusion. He had had courage and had asked an absolutely clear question, but he had received no answer. Even I, with my Nazi ideas and patriotic prejudices understood perfectly that the Bishop had acted with supreme hypocrisy.

Several months later, as we battled towards Kertsch on the Crimea, reaping victory after victory, that lad got killed, not yet nineteen years old. Someone said that he had taken a copy of the New Testament out of his breast pocket together with other sparse belongings. Though having received orders to the contrary, I knew he did not want to kill. But neither did the Bishop's blessing protect him from being killed.

3
Transported to Russia

Von Sonn' und Welten
weiss ich nichts zu sagen.
Ich sehe nur
wie sich die Menschen plagen.

'About sun and worlds
I can tell you but little.
All that I can see
is the suffering of humanity.'

Goethe, from *Faust*

From Harburg we were taken through Belgium into France, where we took up quarters in the Tours region, to await further orders and to make up the numbers of the Occupying Forces. What impressed and bothered me most *en route* was that children approached us and begged for bread. That was a side of the war which I had not really thought about. While most of the time we were engaged in rather futile manoeuvres, we were also used in cordoning-off operations, in attempts to round up resistance fighters, which in most cases came to nothing.

When we made ready for further transport in the winter of 1941/42, the rumour was that we were going to join a reserve Panzer unit somewhere in Czechoslovakia. But as with so many things in the Army, events developed quite differently from what we had expected. What good the secrecy did is highly questionable, for it later became very clear that all transcontinental military transports were closely monitored by enemy intelligence. However, even though Czechoslovakia was on our minds, we knew that the Eastern Front was in dire trouble and that it needed soldiers.

Our tanks and other vehicles were loaded, tied-up and secured on flat-bed railway wagons. Next to them came a few covered wagons which contained all sorts of military gear and light weapons, our food and ammunition, not to forget probably the most important item of all, our field kitchen. At the end of the train were three old wooden passenger coaches, probably dating back to the Kaiser's days. One of them had three or four soft second class compartments in which our officers made themselves comfortable. The rest were third class with wooden seats.

Though French railwaymen had been in attendance during the loading, we did most of the work ourselves. To our mind they could not be trusted. Though we had been told in lectures that many French people, certainly those who had money, were on the whole supporting our aim to establish a New Order in Europe, we were also warned about the Communists and others, who would put a bullet through us if given half a chance. We were instructed not to bother too much about the *Maquis*, as there was so much collaboration between the German and French authorities that the whole intelligence situation was rather open. Though it was probably a matter of honour for any respectable French citizen to be a member of the *Maquis*, our people had a good idea who and where they were, and it was only the Communist Resistance whom we could not penetrate and who were most effective. Just before our departure I talked with a Frenchman in a wine-bar in Parthenay who had had a drop too much to drink and probably wanted to appear well-informed. He assured me that in a way he was quite glad that we Germans had come, as he was in no doubt at all that one day we would leave again. Once before, he reminded me, in 1871 when the French Commune had taken power in Paris and the Conservative Thiers was getting ready in Versailles to squash them, Prussian occupying forces had been at the ready around Paris, ready to save France and probably Europe from Communist revolution should Thiers fail in his attempt. I obviously had no idea, he claimed, how powerful the Communists in France had become again, and that probably the main barrier between them and revolutionary power was the German Army. Such were the invisible lines of strange allegiance, outright corruption and incredible confusion in France under the German heel.

Few in our Company, which consisted of less than 200 men, were over twenty years of age. It was therefore not surprising that few of us realized the serious situation we were in; we looked on this journey, if not the whole war, as one great adventure, an opportunity to escape the boredom of Civvy Street, a lesser object being to fulfil a sacred duty to our Führer and Fatherland.

Whenever we passed through railway stations there was pandemonium. We gave those Frenchies plenty of loud mouth and rude signs, wanting to demonstrate the warlike spirit we were in. Following complaints, we were given a dressing down and strict orders to behave as decent German soldiers. We couldn't quite make it out — after all, had not Germany beaten France — and what was so wrong with showing ourselves a bit like victors?

Travelling was fun. There was always a joker and so much to see. The playing cards were out most of the time and several books made the rounds. There was very little space for all of us to stretch out in comfort at night, but with some lying like sardines on the floor, others on the benches and the rest tucked away in the luggage racks, we had to cope. Making a visit to the lavatory at night was always a precarious undertaking and woe to the one — the swearing was unprintable — who clumsily managed to tread on some sleeping comrade.

Some said the winter 1941/42 was the coldest for a century, and much colder than in 1812 when Napoleon's *Grande Armée* had so disastrously been beaten back across the icy wastes from Moscow. Perhaps understandably, Napoleon and Moscow had become a great topic for us. For had he not marched into Russia with all trumpets blowing and then had to come back? And were not our own troops, who a few days before were said to have victoriously reached a Moscow tram-line terminus, now on their inglorious way back? No foreign army had ever managed to conquer Russia, and with that disturbing thought we sat back and each wondered for himself. What also disturbed us were reports that a number of high-ranking officers had been executed for cowardice in the face of the enemy. We knew that it was terribly cold out there, and how many lower ranks had been shot in that disaster was anyone's guess. The rumours went round and round — there was no end to them.

Our journey was extremely slow and there was always the possibility, though rather unlikely, that some Resistance fighter could blow up the line in front of us. In any case the entire transport system was heavily over-loaded: sometimes we were shunted into sidings to wait for a new engine, or for more important military transports to pass. While the overall decisions were made by German transport chiefs, their execution was left to French railway personnel. When I watched signalmen pulling their levers, I sometimes wondered what was going on in their minds. Sure, they did not like us; our army had beaten theirs and we were now in occupation of much of their country. But I was also bothered by the thought that they, after all, were sitting in their comfortable signal-boxes and that they were transporting me towards the icy wastes of Russia. What was all that good about having beaten them?

While our general demeanour, at least in the presence of our superiors, was one of brazen determination to go to the front and fight the enemy, I was well aware that the real gut feeling was very different. Though no one said it, the very thought of Russia rested heavily on our minds. Each one of us knew of someone in our family or neighbourhood who had been killed in Russia, and we were well aware, on our eastward journey, that the statistics of death and survival were not exactly in our favour. My memories went back to 1939 when the war had started and I had been not quite seventeen years old. In those days, irresistibly caught up in a patriotic fervour, I had feared that the war had come too early, and that I would probably be too late to take part in it. Now, in my secret thoughts, how much I would have given to hear that the Red Army had collapsed under our hammer blows, and that there was no longer any necessity for me to go and fight in the snow — only, perhaps, to lord it over them as an occupying soldier.

The snow cover over France was patchy, and though it was cold, our coaches were well heated from the engine. Whenever our cooks had a warm meal ready in their field kitchen, the train stopped somewhere, and we had to jump out quickly to have our mess tins filled. At stops like that, some of us also ran forward with a bucket to fetch hot water from the engine, to wash up and to wash ourselves in.

After about three days we crossed into Germany at Strasbourg in the Alsace. It struck us that winter was closing in, to the east of the Rhine. There were no longer any bare patches, and the snow layer had thickened. For us young Germans the Rhine had a deeply sentimental meaning. We knew many songs about 'Vater Rhein', the most famous being the *Lorelei* and the *Wacht am Rhein*. From birth, our receptive minds had been filled with various notions of hatred and revenge. As to our relationship with France, it was almost screwed into our young minds that the Rhine forever was to be Germany's river and never simply its border.

We skirted the Black Forest to its north, and passed through the city of Pforz-heim. Now, at least, when we waved to the girls, they waved back to us and answered our thrown kisses. When we stopped at stations, people were friendly with us, many expressing gratitude and pride in our going to the front and defend-ing the Fatherland. One elderly woman pitied us and cried, and deep in my heart I understood what she was crying about! Naturally, we were biased, but we found the undulating German countryside very beautiful. Everything in Ger-many seemed so clean to us, so orderly, so much better, we thought, than what we had seen abroad. That discovery lifted our pride somewhat, also giving succour to our always smouldering arrogance.

Evenings in the train back across Germany were cosy. There was no electric light but we hung candles to make the compartments homely. Increasingly our conversations became philosophical. There was that subject of love, for instance, which was very much occupying our minds: we had hardly lived, and few of us had experienced it — and we sensed somehow that we were now rolling away from it, perhaps forever, so we wanted at least to talk about it. There was so much confusion in us, so many misunderstandings. We were perhaps to be called upon to give our lives for our Fatherland and for freedom, western civilization, our Christian religion, but what did it all mean and why did any-one have to die for it? And I thought more and more about what my father had told me about all this. Several amongst us possessed mouth-organs which they played well, and our subdued songs were about home and our loved ones, but also about war and fighting and dying. One evening we sung the *Lorelei*, and someone reminded us that Heinrich Heine, a Jew, had written it and that now all his works were forbidden in Germany, except the *Lorelei*.

And then came Stuttgart, resting handsomely in a natural bowl surrounded by wooded hills. Huge housing complexes and large factories passed by our windows. We remarked on how different city people's attitudes were, as com-pared with those who lived in the country. The hussle and bussle was very pronounced. Nobody seemed to have time for anything, and what we certainly did not like was that no one was showing any interest in us. Stuttgart at that time had not been bombed, unlike other cities more to the north and west such as Cologne, Bremen, and Hamburg. But even so, its people were now living through the third winter of war, and shortages and restrictions were beginning to bite. Though food was rationed, no one was starving. It was well known that black marketeers were doing flourishing business, and those who had the money could buy almost everything. There was considerable bitterness amongst ordinary working people about the unequal load of the war, which gave rise to the feeling that outright corruption had penetrated into the upper circles of German society.

While our train was standing on a siding of the station, a woman came to our wagon and asked whether we had any fat to sell. Of course we hadn't, and when we asked her why she needed it and was it in short supply, she seemed to blow her top. 'Short supply', she said, 'are you joking? Everything is in short supply, no butter, no fat, no nothing — and the rich have got it all! Can you recall fat Hermann [*Reichsmarschall* Goering, who was in charge of the War Economy] making his bombastic speech to the Party Moguls and asking them whether they wanted butter or cannons — and all the idiots shouted cannons! Now *we* have got what *they* asked for, plenty of cannons [and she pointed to ours on the wagons] and I have no butter to cook with.' So we left Stuttgart with something to think about, about Goering, his cannons, and butter.

Nuremberg came next, the city which in those days was famous for its Party Congresses where the Nazis assembled every year. The 1939 Party Congress, probably to convince the world that the Führer's intentions were peaceful, had been named *Parteitag des Friedens* (Peace Congress); but the war came before it got off the ground. One of us remarked on Goebbels' recent speech, in which he had extolled the Führer's foresight and great wisdom of having struck at Russia before Russia could strike at us. He was countered by the simple question of whether he thought that all the other countries invaded by us, like Poland, Denmark, Norway, Holland, Belgium, Luxemburg, France, Yugoslavia and Greece, had also been poised to attack us — and why they had not done so while we had been militarily weak. After that, nobody bothered to argue any more.

Leaving Franconia, of which Nuremberg was the capital, we crossed into the ancient kingdom of Saxony, which had lost its crown during the German Revolution of 1918. Up to then, King August had ruled his subjects from the Zwinger Palace in Dresden, and his other palaces. It has become a part of German tradition that when August was finally forced to abdicate his throne, he shouted angrily, *'Dann macht doch Euern Scheiss aleene ohne mich!'* (Then get on and make your own shit without me!)

Leipzig, with its great industry, all now effectively roped into the war effort, passed us in the night. Then came pretty Dresden in the early morning, with its soft wooded hills all around its many baroque palaces and churches along the pleasantly banked River Elbe. All the time our journey was extremely slow. But we were young and did not mind, it was all fun, there was so much to see, and, surely, Russia could wait for us! From Saxony we ran close to the old Czech border, across which lay the Sudetenland and beyond it Bohemia with its forests and rolling hills. Of course, since the Führer had annexed these lands three years earlier, the Sudetenland had become part of the Reich, while Bohemia was a Protectorate. Central Europe was now firmly under our control — and with it the famous Skoda works near Pilsen, which very conveniently for us made superb light tanks.

When one of us, an ex-Hitler Youth leader from Hamburg, went on and on about our achievements in central Europe, one elderly (in his early thirties) ex-docker wanted to know what all this pride was about; as far as he was concerned Bohemia could belong to Timbuctoo or the King of China, and in any case in his view it was only right that the land should belong to the people who were living on it. He had a married sister living in Brünn (Brno) whom he had visited in 1937 before all the trouble had started and Czechoslovakia was still independent. He liked it there, all the people had been pleasant and he had made many friends. He had gone again last year, after the 'liberation', but his former Czech friends had not wanted to know him any more, nobody trusted him, and his sister had felt very sad and cut off.

When we crossed into the Prussian Province of Silesia which had been annexed from Poland and colonized by the Prussian kings a couple or so centuries ago, some hard-brained Nationalist claimed that in his view it was still an illiterate colony and a fight almost broke out with another lad whose parents had been born there. Because of transport difficulties we stayed in one of the large marshalling yards of Breslau, for a couple of days. It was my personal impression that the further east we travelled, the more depressing the whole atmosphere became. Whether Silesia was actually more drab and glum than the western part of the Reich, or whether it was the knowledge that the wintry Russian Front was creeping up on us which made me see things in more gloomy terms, I could not really say any more.

While our officers gave themselves permission to visit the city, none of us was allowed to leave the railway yard. We found an old worn-out football which we made playable by filling it out with paper, and after having trampled down the snow and marked four goalposts, we played football between two long rows of trains and made plenty of noise. When darkness fell we often settled down to quiet discussions. Most of us agreed that Silesia did not quite seem like Germany any more. Its villages looked quite different from those in the west, and seemed less tidily arranged, the village streets being mostly unmade. When one of the officers remarked that 'the East was showing us its first glimpse', I mentally agreed with him.

Relations with our officers were militarily correct; the gulf between us though, was great. There were four of them in our transport: one Captain and three Lieutenants. Each had a *Bursche* (batman), and though their food came from the same field kitchen as ours, theirs was collected for them in containers by their *Burschen* and we could not help noticing that even the latter had more and better to eat than we, which left an ever-present simmering resentment. There was no connecting corridor between our three coaches, and while some of us dared at times to jump from one running board to the next on the moving train, the officer on duty, making his daily visit to all, changed over whenever the train stopped. They then sat with us and tried to be pally, but it was an unnatural friendliness and cut little ice with us. While they called us by our family names, we had to call them *Herr* and then their rank. When they sat with us they always managed to smother our natural open behaviour and we were always glad when they moved on to the next compartment, and screwed up our faces after them. I played chess with one of the Lieutenants several times during the journey, and whenever I managed to checkmate him he made a face as if something had interfered with the natural order of things. The closer we came to the Russian Front, though, the more we noticed a subtle change in their behaviour, inasmuch as they probably sensed that, apart from our being convenient objects to shout at, they might have to rely on us and share their fates with us in battle.

We passed through Eastern Silesia with its large industrial complex, the second in size after the Ruhr. A massive influx of Polish blood was suggested by the distinctively wide cheekbones of slavic people. The Catholic church seemed all powerful — People went in and out of the churches all day, and it was said that even the Nazi Party had to step carefully so as not to transgress the holy domain of the Church. The Vatican in fact had given the Nazi state much-needed international recognition in 1933 by having signed the notorious Concordat with it, and many of us wondered whether this had something to do with all German Commanders in occupied Poland having to be Roman Catholic. The sprawled-out industrial cities like Kattowitz, Hindenburg, Gleiwitz and others melted into each other without any demarcation or open country between them. The buildings seemed grimy and the dirt and grit belching from the many tall chimneys had a choking effect and made us keep our windows shut. The people looked generally poorer, more working class than in the west, and in our ignorance we liked to make insulting jokes about them and their accents, and back to front sentence structures in this little 'bit of Poland in Germany'

Someone in our coach remarked that it had been here in Gleiwitz, just on the German side of the Polish border, that a fortnight before the outbreak of the war in '39, Polish soldiers had crossed the border, had occupied the Gleiwitz Radio Station and actually shouted Polish Liberation slogans over the airwaves, before they had become overpowered. Having listened to this, our old docker in the corner screwed up his eyes in a challenging manner and pointed out that every one of these Polish soldiers had been killed during the assault, and that Josef Goebbels had made most of this incident and called the nation to arms against this Polish threat. 'So what about them having been killed; what was so wrong with that?', some of the youngsters wanted to know, 'serves those bastards right and teaches all the rest a lesson on what will happen to them if they dare to attack our Fatherland!'

'Yes, right, but was it not a bit strange that not one of them had got away with his life to be presented to the public, to answer questions and be properly identified?'

'What do you mean by "properly identified"?'

'Well,' he said, he had heard in a Hamburg pub at the time of the incident that none of them had been Polish soldiers at all, that they had not even come from across the border from Poland, but were from a German concentration camp where they had been put into Polish uniforms, and had been taken by the SS to the Radio Station building where they had all been shot dead! Now, the card players stopped dealing, curious heads were raised in the back and we all realized that the conversation had drifted into dangerous waters. Someone suggested that this story probably had been put out by the BBC to smear us and undermine our morale. And as soon as the British radio was mentioned, the conversation came to a dead stop, as each of us knew only too well that listening to the foreign radio and spreading its news was punishable by death. And the docker in the corner quietly sucked his pipe and looked out of the window as if all this had nothing to do with him anymore.

Most of us, I am sure, had 'fiddled with the knobs'. I had and I knew that my father had, but none of us, even now, dared to admit it. Thinking back, I remembered that in this way I found out about the German parachute assault on the British garrison on Crete days before the German Radio had announced it. All the time I had been itching to tell my mates — as most likely they had been itching to pass the 'secret' to me.

We steamed on into Lemberg, or L'vov as the Russians now call it. There was neglect and disorganization everywhere. The expression *polnische Wirtschaft* (Polish conditions) was and indeed is part of German slang to describe untidy and dirty conditions. To see Lemberg and Poland generally did much to strengthen our racial prejudices. From Lemberg the newly created *Ostbahn* took over from the *Reichsbahn*, and we heard hair-raising stories about Communist partisans blowing up the line towards the East almost every day. We were shunted into a siding behind the station, and stayed there for several days, but we did not really mind for the reports coming from the Russian Front were anything but encouraging. We watched transports of wounded soldiers coming back; one pulled up next to us and we talked to some of the comrades. What they told us about the icy battle conditions and the hammering they had received from the Red Army toned down much of our arrogance.

After having travelled by then for about two weeks, it was in Lemberg that for the first time we got permission to leave the train and visit the place. Nice as it was to stretch our legs in the snow, we found everything very depressing. Real poverty was evident everywhere, and it did not need scientific knowledge to realize that the harassed-looking people were starving *en masse*. SS, German Field Police and Polish militia were patrolling the streets, obviously working closely together and chasing people on wherever they had collected in groups. Hollow-eyed children, often in rags, came begging for bread. Not having any on us, we were of course in no position to give them any, and though we had been told in special little lectures before we were let out of our train that they were enemy children, dangerous breeds, some of us found it hard to have to shut our hearts. Some who still believed in the basics of Christ's teaching, must have wondered what had happened.

A large part of the population was Jewish who, we were told, lived together in the poorest part of the city, the ghetto. The latter was no German creation, it had been set up by the Polish authorities long ago and walking around the town, we found that the Poles hated the Jews, all of whom, including the children, had to wear the yellow Star of David on their outer garment. We understood that they had to buy the stars at special stores for exorbitant prices, and that the penalty for not wearing them was very severe. Many of us had seen the odd Jew wearing the yellow star in a German city; but this was all so different, so incomparable in scale, and seeing them walking around in their abject misery we did not know anymore whether we should hate these people or feel pity for them.

I went with a couple of friends to a *Soldatenheim* (soldier's hostel and restaurant) across the road from the station. We sat at a small, round table by the window and had coffee and cakes. But then children came to the window, some with yellow stars, and kept staring at our cakes, making us feel uncomfortable, and we shooed them away and drew the curtains. There were many soldiers in the place and the air was thick with smoke and noise. Most were on transit furlough, either coming from or going back to the front. One could almost judge by the degree of misery on their faces which way they were going — and we were forcefully reminded that we were going the same way as the miserable-looking ones.

A couple of elderly transport soldiers joined us at our table and we got into conversation. They told us that to the northwest of Lemberg, somewhere near the town of Radom, lived an old Polish landowner on a large estate, guarded by the SS. His name was Goleniewski and he was no other, they claimed, than the Russian Tsar Nicholas II himself, who with his family was supposed to have been murdered by the Bolsheviks in the Siberian town of Ekatarinburg shortly after the Revolution. Though it was true that no physical evidence had ever been produced to establish the Tsar's death, we did not believe any of the soldiers' story, and laughed, thinking that they were having us on. But then some others joined us and said that it was true. One claimed that without eliminating the Tsar from the minds of the largely illiterate Russian peasants of the time, the Russian Revolution would have fallen to pieces. Of course we knew that ex-Kaiser Wilhelm II had been quarantined on his estate across the Dutch border near the town of Doorn, and had also, until his death the previous summer, been closely guarded by the SS. The strange thing about this was when about three years later, being driven out of Russia through the Lemberg region, we heard the same story about Panje Goleniewski again.

A long train consisting of covered wagons pulled in behind us and came to a stand. We then noticed that there were people in the wagons, most of which had small window openings about six feet above floor level, and from them we were met by staring eyes. Looking closer, we could make out that they were mainly faces of older people, with younger women amongst them — and then we also heard the voices of children. One woman opposite our window said quietly: 'Brot' (bread) and managed to push her hand out. Then two SS guards came walking along the train, each of them carrying a rifle and a pistol in loose fashion over their heavy greatcoats. They looked fed-up and ill tempered, and when we asked them whether we should give the woman any bread, one said: 'To hell, you won't! They are Jews, lousy Jews, and they had their bellies filled to the rim only yesterday!' So we did nothing, just tilted our heads in a half apologetic fashion to the woman and left it at that. When the train later pulled away from us and we saw the eerie, staring eyes from every one of the passing openings, many of us felt uncomfortable, if not guilty, but none of us said anything about that encounter. All of us had heard about concentration camps, but the generally accepted understanding was that only anti-social and anti-German elements, like Communists, homosexuals, Jews, thieves, bible punchers, gipsies and such like, were being kept in there and forced to do a decent day's work for the first time in their lives. Though we were not far from it, I am sure that none of us at that time had ever heard the name Auschwitz.

After Lemberg came the Soviet Union proper, the Ukraine. The temperature had dropped considerably and when we wanted to look out of the windows, we had first to blow little ice holes. All we could see through it was a white and endless waste, a frightening sight. So that was what was generally understood as Russia, and the thought alone of having to go out and fight in this made our hearts shudder. People in the villages were wrapped up like mummies in thick winter clothing, with little children all but disappearing in them. They were watching us all right when we steamed by, but apart from the odd small child they gave us no recognition.

Then disaster struck; all our lavatories froze up and no amount of hot water poured down could thaw them out. From then on, there was nothing left for those who could not wait for the train to stop but to get out on the running board and hang on to the handles for dear life in the icy wind, and face the elements backwards. To do this effectively one had to drop one's trousers first while still in the compartment, and put on gloves. It was no pleasant sight for the other passengers, especially the wiping, which could not be done outside. To the villagers, however, watching the train go by with red and frosty German bottoms sticking out towards them, it must have been a hilarious sight, probably tinged with the revengeful thought, 'serves you right, you bastards!'

We passed a place where a battle had taken place just after Barbarossa the previous summer, somewhere near the town of Ternopol. Shot-up and burnt-out tanks, toppled over or standing forlornly rusting in the snow, gave us a horrible feeling. Our overall impression was as if they were saying to us, 'Where are you going young lads? Don't you see what has happened to us?' Most of the tanks were Soviet, but some were German. Obviously, our interest was enormous, each one of us trying to get to the frozen window. And the sight was so awful that all that could be heard was an almost whispered 'Jesus Christ!' And when I saw one of the burnt-out Panzers exactly like mine, the thought that I could have driven that charred coffin was too much for me. A bolt of fear shot through me right to the pit of my stomach, making me the next who had to drop his trousers and put on his gloves to manure the battlefield. I was only nineteen, and did not want to die.

It must have been in early December of 1941 when our train reached the large industrial town of Dniepropetrovsk and crossed the wide river Dnieper, on a dangerously-repaired bridge at less than walking pace. Not really knowing where the front line was, we were slightly surprised when we travelled on east of the river, until we came to a small marshalling yard.

As soon as we arrived we knew that something somewhere had gone drastically wrong. There was panic all around us, soldiers, officers and all, were running around in a panic, and our Company Commander had to report to the headquarters at once. When he came back we received the order to make ready.

The atmosphere in our compartment was awful, no one wanted to talk, this place had become a mobile home to us, the last place we wanted to leave. Everyone seemed to get into each other's way, and silly little arguments were developing about nothing. Someone outside said that the Red Army had broken through somewhere in the east and was coming for us. It was not a pleasant thought.

The snow was several inches deep, with a temperature of at least minus ten degrees centigrade and a bitter wind blowing. When all our Panzers and vehicles were lined up in column with their engines running, outside the yard, we had to group around a stack of wood on which our CO stood to give us a speech. '*Kameraden!*', he addressed us; he had never done so before, so we assumed that the situation must be extremely serious. Striking a theatrical pose, he told us (as if we did not know) that we were now in *Feindesland* (enemy territory). Never having given anything away to us before, he now confided that we were soon to go into action, that he was confident that we would prove to be brave soldiers, had not forgotten anything we had learned, and were ready to fight to the last drop of blood for Führer and Fatherland. Probably in ignorance himself, he said nothing about the situation we were to encounter. Most of us were standing there impatiently and getting cold feet in our thin leather jackboots, and he must have noticed our growing restlessness. It was close to pathetic to watch him search for suitable words with which to bring his pitiful sermon to an end.

When we pulled out of town in an armoured column it started to snow. Soon the flakes had covered my driver's periscope and I could see nothing. I had to pull out the whole of the periscope cassette, and stare through an open slit with an icy draught blowing snowflakes into my eyes, which made our compartment like an icebox. I had to put on gloves to handle the levers and ask my mate to cover my forehead and throat with something warm. It was extremely uncomfortable.

With morning came a pale winter's sun, rising in front of us, and we took up positions along the edge of a forest from where we had an uninterrupted view into the wide open country before us. There was plenty of dry wood to be broken out of the trees, which enabled us to get a good fire going but one of the lieutenants came rushing over and told us to put the fire out because the smoke could give us away to the enemy. Luckily we were able to convince him that there was no enemy to be seen for miles around, and that without a fire we would soon have frostbite. Grumbling a bit, he gave in and then sat on his helmet in front of our fire to warm his frozen feet. Being sheltered from one side by the forest, we built up low snow walls on the other and with the fire in between made the place quite comfortable. Apart from some forlorn peasant figure trudging away in the distance, we saw no sign of the enemy, nor did we hear a single shot all the time we occupied this first camp. During the first evening, probably to pep up our morale, one of the officers came round and allowed us a good gulp from a Schnapps bottle, which he did not let go out of his hand. That was all we got — one gulp. Later in the night we noticed that our officers, plus the Sergeant Major and several other favoured underlings, sat around their own fire and got increasingly merry. We were only too well aware that the Schnapps ration belonged to all of us, and that one could not get merry from one gulp. A sullen resentment festered all round while they were singing, which boded ill for the future.

After about three days, the silly alarm was called off. By now we had become used to the place, which the continuous fire had made quite comfortable. If this was winter war, we jokingly remarked, we could hold out heroically to the very end. We rumbled back to the town whence we had come, and rolled straight into the railyard. Our train was still there, though at first without the heating engine. We loaded our vehicles and material and soon made comfortable on our wooden seats, feeling almost more protected there than behind our thick Panzer plates. After a longish and not unwelcome stay we steamed back towards Dniepropetrovsk, but we did not cross the river and stayed on the east side to turn south towards Zaporoshye. The Dnieper was very wide and as good as frozen over, though there seemed to be slight movement of ice floes in the middle. A damp mist hung continuously over the river's run, hiding the horizon and smothering everything in a thick gloom which could hardly do other than reflect the state of our minds. We passed a number of derailed wagons which were lying at the bottom of the embankment. Sticking out halfway from the snow, their deadness was overpowering. Had they been hurled down by us during the advance of early Barbarossa, or had they been blown up by partisans, with our soldiers inside? When one joker reminded us that only a short time ago we had been hanging around near the French town of Cognac in the warm sunshine, we told him crudely to shut up.

It took about two more days until we reached very flat, boggy country, with much windswept ice stretching out in all directions. It was desolate and at the same time curiously beautiful. Low trees, all bent in one direction, and whitewashed thatched cottages, showing almost all roof and no walls, ducked close to mother earth to keep out of the wind. Reeds and small islands were everywhere, and multitudes of waterbirds rose into the cold air, alarmed by our train. We had arrived at the Siwash, a watery region to the east of the Isthmus of Perekop which links the Crimean peninsula with the Ukrainian mainland.

After the Revolution, in the early twenties when White Russian troops were still in occupation of the Crimea, strong lines of fortification had been erected across the narrow isthmus to keep the Reds out, but totally ignoring the Siwash as impassable for masses of troops. But then a strong west wind had blown up and had driven the waters of the shallow Siwash out into the open Sea of Azov. The Red Army, standing to the north, had recognized the opportunity and courageously made use of this 'gift of God'. Its mass of troops, together with horses and light weapons, had crossed the 'impassable' bogs of the Siwash, half wading and half swimming through them, probably in the same way as the biblical Jews had crossed the Red Sea two thousand years earlier. Many drowned, but the bulk got across to the southern banks and the Whites, caught from the rear, and probably not knowing what to fight for any more anyway, were wiped out and the whole of the Crimea was won for the Revolution.

We arrived at the railway junction at Djankoi, which we called Shanghai. During our stay there we were badly harassed in a number of daring attacks by the Red Air Force; so the fighting front, we mused, could not be far away. After getting on to the single line south to Simferopol, the capital of the Crimea, we started on what we knew would be the last part of our long trek, and after less than a day we pulled into the final sidings along the loading docks. Our rail journey of about four weeks was over. As in France, here too were local railwaymen in attendance, some of them even in attractive dark blue uniforms. They stayed very aloof, acting only in their professional capacity, and again we did most of the work ourselves. The big difference, we jokingly reminded each other of, was, that while in France we had suspected some of them to be Communists, here we could be sure that all of them were.

When the first light suggested a tentative dawn, we lined-up outside on the road, ready to move. This time the CO did not bother to bore us with one of his rousing speeches. Our journey took us to the east on a rough road and going towards it we heard from far away the heavy rumble of the front. There was much traffic on the road; going with us were the heavily-laden lorries with trailers, which were also coming back empty on the same road. Driving the heavies transport must have been very difficult, and we saw many wrecks which had just been pushed off the road out of the way.

After about twenty kilometres we left the 'highway', turned sharp to our right and entered a lone village which seemed hidden behind earth mounds and scrub-land. There was only one long, unmade street, with a row of primitive mud cottages on either side. The name of the village was Rosenthal, a German name meaning 'rose valley', and I wondered how it had come by that. I knew that Tsarina Catharina had invited German settlers from Swabia to settle a couple or so centuries previously so during the next few days I tried to find out, but apart from a couple of old men and one woman who could understand a little, I could trace no German connection.

Our orders were to occupy one cottage per crew, and to throw the peasants out. When we entered 'ours', a woman and her three young children were sitting around the table by the window, obviously having just finished a meal. She was clearly frightened of us, and I could see that her hands were shaking, while the kids stayed in their seats and looked at us with large, non-understanding eyes. Our Sergeant came straight to the point: *'Raus!'*, and pointed to the door. When the mother started to remonstrate and her children to cry, he repeated *'Raus!'*, opened the door and waved his hand towards the outside in a manner which could not be mistaken anywhere. He gave her five minutes grace to pick up her belongings, and showed her the number of minutes on his fingers. That, to the woman and her children, I realized, was the cold reality of war. Her husband had probably been called up to the army to defend his country and could not now even protect his wife and children from being thrown out of their cottage. Their possessions were few, things were put into bags or rolled into bundles, and it took them not much more than five minutes. Then she put on her dark peasant coat and her thick felt boots, dressed her children, and they all walked out, with the little ones carrying the smaller bundles.

Outside it was bitterly cold, and when I watched them through the small window standing by their bundles in the snow, looking helplessly in all directions, not knowing what to do, I felt strange. In all my life I had never been in such a situation before. When I looked again a little later, they were gone; I did not want to think about it anymore.

We looked around and quickly sorted ourselves out. The cottage had only one large room, with low half walls for partitions. Everything was extremely primitive. The large mud-stove in the middle still exuded a comforting warmth, the floor was a mixture of stones and hard trodden earth, and there was no ceiling, only the inside of the thatch. The walls were thick, made from field-stones cemented together with mud. The door was heavy in two parts, and lead out to a rough porch. The windows were very small, hardly more than a foot square so as not to let in the cold, and when we looked for the lavatory there was none, only a hole outside behind a hedge as wind protection with two boards across to stand on. And we with all our modern weapons had come a thousand miles to fight these poor people and rob them of their possessions!

We arranged our blankets on straw along the wall while our Sergeant tried his best on a ramshackle bed in the corner. The bits of furniture had all been made of rough timber, as if the occupants had made them themselves. For water we had to go a few houses along, where there was a communal well. Our food box was quickly dragged in, and soon the smell of frying rose into our nostrils and the kettle was on the boil. Once we had something warm in our bellies, life seemed much better. We talked about all sorts of things, of home and our loved ones — but none mentioned the mother with her small children who had been sitting here around the same table only a short while ago.

When I finally bedded down next to my mates, I discovered that there was a warm atmosphere after all in this primitive place. I mused that peasants some-how knew about coming to terms with the elements of nature, and that we were only just beginning to learn from them. Our guard came in and put turf on the fire, which he had taken from a heap outside. Only one candle flickered on the table and all around me was peace. I listened to the cracking of the fire, the breathing from my mates and a soft wind which seemed to be catching something in the porch. All sorts of thoughts came tumbling into my mind, I realized somehow that an enormous step had been taken. There was no knowing what the future would hold, not even what the next morning would bring. But we were young, we lived from day to day and we were sure — or were we? — that our cause was right.

4
Crimean interlude

Des Menschen Seele gleicht dem Wasser.
Vom Himmel kommt es,
zum Himmel steigt es
und wieder nieder zur Erde muss es,
ewig wechselnd.

'The human soul is like water.
From heaven it comes,
to heaven it rises
and then down to earth it must go again,
forever changing.'

Goethe, from *Gesang der Geister*

There seemed to be general confusion as to which Division we were going to join in von Manstein's Crimean Army, and when it was decided that it should be the 22nd Panzers which were still in France, we were billeted away from the battle lines, to the north of the Black Sea resort of Feodosia. The Soviets were holed up at Sevastopol and unable, so we thought, to mount any other operation elsewhere in the Crimea. For Christmas we organized a tree in our cottage with real candles and decorations which we made out of silver paper. Most of us had letters from home and some received parcels with goodies, which we shared. The only thing we could not do was give presents to each other. On Christmas Eve we were gathered together outside the CO's cottage, where he gave us another of his sermons. He reminded us of the meaning of Jesus and Christmas, that our task in Russia was a holy one and that we had God on our side. It was strange to hear him talk in quiet, almost fatherly tones, as usually he shouted and bellowed at us. After that we sang an emotionally laden *Stille Nacht*, and he ended it all with a prayer about God and the Führer. We were glad when it was all over and we could troop back into our own warm cottages and celebrate Christmas as we liked. Outside it was bitterly cold and we were not all that sad that we had to wait for our new Division's arrival from France.

It was, I think, shortly after Christmas when out of the blue the night guards sounded the alarm. At first we thought it was a prank due to some alcoholic misunderstanding. But when we had to line up outside and sensed our officers' nervousness, we realized that something serious had happened. Then we heard shooting from the coast, at first from rifles, but then from machine guns and heavier cannons. What had happened, why did no one tell us? As far as we knew the Red Army was nowhere within a hundred miles. And with a sense of growing uncertainty while we pointlessly waited in the cold, we grew restless and then angry. But just when it seemed that we were to move south into the town, there was commotion down the road out of which disorganized groups of our own soldiers emerged. They were out of breath and in a terrible state of excitement, and what they tried to tell us at first made little sense. But with bits of the puzzle beginning to fall into place, it became clear that the Russians had landed from the sea. They had come quietly in boats which they must have paddled, while the guards, it was now generally assumed, had probably had too much to drink. Many of the Russians had worn German uniforms, and only after having quietly knifed most of the guards, did they use their firearms. The panic and chaos had been indescribable. Whenever our soldiers had emerged from their quarters, they had been met by bullets, and the carnage had been dreadful. Before the two heavy howitzers at the port entrance could be brought to bear they had been blown sky high by heavy ships' cannons. Only then was it realized that a Soviet cruiser and one or two destroyers had managed to creep close to the shore in the dark of night. We listened carefully and we could now hear the revving engines of motor boats, which suggested that the enemy commandos were in full control of all strategic points in the town.

We heard loud shouting on the telephone from the CO's cottage, and later we heard that Russian voices had been on the line and had bellowed something rude to our CO in broken German. Within less than an hour we were ordered to load up, start our engines and follow the CO's Panzer. While having expected to move south towards the coast to sort things out down there, we were more than surprised when we started trekking north away from the shooting, steadily continuing that way into the low hills of the eastern Jaila Mountains. While outwardly all of us moaned and complained about this cowardly running away, I remember that inwardly I was quite happy at not having to move into a battle for which I was still not prepared.

When morning rose from over the sea we were well on our way away from it all, and when we had come over the top and descended on to the northern slopes there was a thin layer of snow on the ground and the temperature had dropped dramatically. We drove through the town of Stari Krim at walking speed as if it was the Chief's intention to warn the populace not to get any 'funny' ideas from the Feodosia landing. About twenty miles further on we entered a sprawling village where we stopped. We had received no information from our officers whatsoever, and when one of us asked one of the Lieutenants, he was told contemptuously that we should not try to reason about events which were above our understanding, that we should leave thinking to the horses who had bigger heads. The response angered us — we were fit enough to fight and die and serve as cannon fodder — but not to know what it was all about.

We were told to billet ourselves in the village. The place looked pleasant enough — it nestled in a natural bowl by a stream amidst hills which were wooded on top. The many lanes were too narrow to take our Panzers and large vehicles, which had to be stabled outside the village, on a flat bit of ground. The CO with his batman took the nicest cottage in the centre, where he was protected all around by our presence. And I noticed how pleased he looked after he had managed to direct the field kitchen right next to his quarters. Each crew was to take one cottage, and if its inhabitants were too much of a nuisance, it was left to us to throw them out. Our own cottage was built on a slight slope, from where we could overlook much of the village, and across a valley to the other side. We climbed half a dozen crumbling steps before entering a ramshackle wooden porch which was untidily full of hoes, spades, rakes, baskets and other utensils. I opened a covered trap door to one side, from which a rickety ladder led into an earth hole, where there was a collection of food and garden produce, some of it in sacks and a few jars. From the porch we passed through a heavy and creaking door and into the cottage proper, which was a single room. In the far corner opposite the door there hung an icon. Bits of curtain and cloth were in front of the two windows, and pieces of newspaper had been pressed into every possible cranny against the draught. The only furniture was a bed, a table, a sofa, a bench and some chairs and an obviously home-made sideboard with cups and plates on was positioned along a wall. A large mud-built stove made the cottage warm and cosy, and we decided to stay.

Sitting on the sofa was an almost toothless, ancient-looking woman (though later we found out that she was only sixty years of age) and her son of about 25. From the moment we came through the door the woman did not stop nagging, and had it not been for the fact that her son was crippled, we would probably have thrown them out. The son's legs hung, swinging, as if they had no bones in them. But with quick movements he tied them up under his body with a piece of cloth and was able to walk using his arms and hands, swinging his body between them. Even with his severe handicap he was extremely agile, and moved around at almost walking speed. He could lift himself into chairs, and even managed to climb ladders, with the elegance of a monkey. Unlike his mother, watching us closely, he knew exactly what was at stake and we could see that it was a great relief to him when, without saying so, we decided to let them stay. Of course there was no question of paying them any rent, and after we told them curtly to move into the corner away from the windows and the door and to stay there and shut up, we settled ourselves as comfortable as we could.

Having been there a week or so I came back from guard duty at 2 o'clock in the morning, looking forward to crawling between my blankets on the floor next to the warm stove. Entering through the gate at the side, I was sure that I had heard a noise coming from right in front of me in the overgrown garden. There was no response to my challenge, no movement, nothing. I was tense and not a little frightened, and I had no rifle on me as I had given it to my mate who had relieved me. I pulled my bayonet out of its sheath and held its pointed wide blade towards the undergrowth. I threw a stone at the point I suspected, which seemed to hit something as it did not fall down on to the frozen ground. Had it been an animal, I reasoned, it would have run already. Then

I saw definite movement, followed by a shape. I held the handle much firmer, ready to plunge. Had I had my rifle or a pistol I would have fired at it. Next came a faint voice in Russian out of the long dead grass: 'Genry, [that's how the Russians called me], its all right, don't shoot, its me, Igor!' As the heavy weight of fear fell from me, another emotion, one of sheer fury, took its place. It was our cripple Igor, who in his unmistakable way shifted his body out of the undergrowth towards me. And there he sat now like an ugly miserable toad on the cold earth in front of me, looking up at me, asking by his whole demeanour for pity and understanding.

'You miserable, silly fool, what the hell are you crawling about here for at this hour of the night, don't you realize that I could have shot you on sight? You know very well that there is a curfew for you Russian bastards during darkness!' I spoke in very quiet tones, so as not to draw attention from my mates whom I knew to be very trigger-happy. All that Igor managed to mumble was 'sorry' and 'Genry', and 'sorry' again. I suspected that he had been playing a game of cards at the neighbours, and held my fist in front of his face to indicate what I would like to give him. But then he turned his head rather sheepishly towards the neighbour's cottage, as if to explain. And when I followed the path of his eyes, I saw the reason for it all clearly in front of me! There in the porch stood the neighbour's strapping girl, Dosia. She had a dark shawl wrapped around her, with something white underneath; her long blond hair, during the day always neatly tied up, was dangling down in untidy strands as if someone had pulled it about. Being younger than Igor and perhaps the same age as Dosia, I knew instinctively what had happened — He had been with Dosia. And for that I had almost killed him. Being only a short distance away, she was watching us intently, as she had probably seen me coming. And when she saw me looking at her and realized that Igor was all right, she gave a quick wave with her hand and tiptoed back into her cottage.

I must have had a very stupid expression on my face, for I still could not really believe what I had seen. Igor with no legs, a total cripple — and beautiful blond Dosia, in perfect health and shape. And when he looked up at me, and this time with a slightly roguish grin on his face, I threatened him: 'You dirty devil, you! Get the hell in! And if I catch you ever again, I swear that I will put a bullet through you like through a mad dog!' I followed him up the steps to then reach over him to open the door. My fury had gone now, and watching him shifting himself awkwardly in front of me, I could not help respecting him as another human being. But was there also a touch of jealousy? Beautiful Dosia and the cripple Igor! There was so much yearning in me, I too needed love; but there was no Dosia to hold me. Everyone was asleep when we came in, except his mother who wanted to lash her tongue at him for being so late and I went up to her and threatened to bash her face in if she spoke another word. And for the first time, after he had whispered 'good night' to me, I wished Igor a good night.

In the morning I went out early to get water from the well which was shared by both cottages and as soon as I started turning the windlass, Dosia came and joined me. Though there was a blush on her face, she looked me straight in the eyes and with a human and very earnest expression simply said: 'Thank you, Genry.'

'Thank me, what for?'

'Well, you know. . .!'

'I could have shot him, Dosia, and you as well! You are both fools!'

'Yes, that's what I thank you for. Did his mother tell him off?'

'Yes, why do you ask?'

'Oh, she is always doing that. She is jealous, doesn't want to lose him.'

'Do you really love him, really, I mean, Dosia?'

'Yes, he is a kind and loving man, a human being of flesh and blood like you and me!' And she looked at me in a very firm way, ready, I guessed, to challenge my ancient prejudices. And it was me then who cast his eyes down in embarrassment, not her. And when she walked away from me with her bucket I thought: yes, why should he not have the right to love, nor she the right to choose?

From then on Igor and I became friends. Often in the evenings we played chess together, mostly he won and I did not really mind and asked him to teach me and correct my faulty Russian, which he did whenever we were together. It was he who sometimes mentioned Dosia's name, but I refused to bite.

Throughout the weekdays we soldiers were kept busy. What we particularly hated was the squarebashing in the village street when we were shouted and bawled at and chased around, and ordered to crawl on our bellies. When we later faced our Russian 'landladies' and arrogantly laid the law down to them, they sometimes let us know with a twinkle in their eyes that they had seen us crawling in the village lanes. I liked maintenance duty, for then I could crawl into the deepest corner of my Panzer, let the engine run for heating and do some reading on the quiet. Sundays were generally more relaxed. We were woken up an hour later and saw to our personal needs like washing and mending in the mornings, then had light-hearted singsongs as well as competitions in chess and cards in the afternoons. From time to time we went on manoeuvres and chased around like wild hares in the otherwise tranquil countryside, which might have pleased our officers but seldom made any sense to us. On one of those larks I stopped my Panzer in the middle of a watery hole as my commanding sergeant in the turret wanted time to sort out our next move. When the CO later gave the report to the lined up company, and mentioned that everything had gone well except that one Panzer had managed to get stuck in the mud, he ordered the driver to step forward. Naturally, I stayed in line, as I had no idea that he had meant me. He then stamped his foot angrily and ordered me by name to step forward. When I did so in a rather unsoldierly fashion, shaking my head all the time, he dressed me down for not having come forward in the first place. My Sergeant made not the slightest attempt to intervene on my behalf, and my anger and frustration became so intense that I began to contradict the CO. When he started to shout at me, I must have lost my marbles and simply interrupted him. The outcome was predictable: three days in clink for arguing with an officer. Seldom in my life had I felt so lost and forsaken.

The CO then stepped back to our Sergeant Major, Lange was his name, and had a chuckling conversation with him. The latter with a great smile on his face stepped back in the cottage to emerge with a newspaper, which he folded into a triangle hat. I had to take off my steel helmet to replace it with the paper hat. He then gave me a long stick which I had to put between my legs and ride up and down in front of the company, calling out: 'I am a little Panzer with a return ticket and got stuck in the mud.' I could have cried at the utter degradation. Luckily all my mates, after the initial giggle here and there, realized the unfairness and insult of it all and stood like rods, not moving a muscle or an eyelid. Only the Sergeant Major and the officers gave a dutiful guffaw, which fell decidedly flat. I was marched away to a nearby stable where I was locked up. Sitting on the straw my frustration and fury were so intense that I shouted quietly between clenched teeth and banged my fists on the floor, 'You bastards, you horrible bastards!'

Cooling down a bit, I thought of my father and what he had tried to tell me. He had predicted that either I would get a philosophical understanding of the whole rotten set-up, or the Army would make a pitiful robot of me. And here I was in a stable, feeling like a strangled rat, and slowly I began to understand what my father had meant. After all, what individualism, how much personal freedom had I left for myself! And after having thought of nothing else during those three days in the stable, I realized that when I was let out and had to report to the CO, he had lost all mental power over me. Looking cold-eyed at him, I thought of my father, and how proud he would be of me if he knew what was going on in my mind at that moment.

I always liked the peace and the warm comradely atmosphere of the evenings when we sat together around the table and played cards or chess, with candles as our only source of light. We had two mouth-organs in our crew and after having bedded down on our blankets we played and quietly sang. Even our Russians seemed to like the melodies, for while they were usually arguing noisily about something, they became very quiet once we had started with our music.

One late afternoon I had to walk to the other end of the village to fetch a couple of cans of petrol for my Panzer. An elderly guard was walking on a short bridge keeping an eye on the hills above and the thick undergrowth in the river valley below. Soldiers from other units seldom came to our village and when they did, they always came in a vehicle, never on foot. I was surprised therefore when I saw two soldiers, one in a black Panzer uniform and the other in field grey, walking slowly towards me; they seemed to have come from nowhere. When I passed them on the other side of the road, I said 'hallo'. Their response was a childish giggle to each other, and they merely nodded at me. I put both my empty cans down, made a remark about the weather and pointed to some clouds in the sky. Their reaction was so idiotically strange — they aped my gesture and also pointed into the sky and said not one word — that I simply gave it up, picked up my cans and walked away. Looking back I could make out that they were discussing me.

I mentioned the two to the crew of the petrol lorry, but none had seen them and when I walked back, they had completely gone out of sight and I wondered how they could have done so so quickly. All of a sudden, coming from the hillside, bullets were whistling by my head. There was no sign of anyone anywhere and I dropped my heavy cans and jumped down the bank to hide behind some bushes. I was lying on the wet boggy earth on my belly and was frightened to death and did not dare to move until two of my mates, also carrying cans, came strolling along, wondering what I was doing in the bushes below. I told them what had happened and we looked around but could find nothing. Back in the village I reported the incident; one of the Lieutenants suggested that I 'had seen ghosts', I felt annoyed, withdrew into my shell and said nothing any more.

In the following night there was an explosion. We all rushed out from our cottages, to find a lorry was in flames. Then shots were fired and no one could make out where they were coming from. Suddenly there were two more explosions. One of our Panzers, standing away from the others, went up in flames like a torch, and then a small ammunition dump blew up, starting a great display of fireworks. All of us were senselessly rushing about on a well-lit stage, when a single shot was fired out of the dark surround. There was a scream, but the lad, luckily, was not badly hit. And out of the dark came an insult in perfect German: '*Ihr deutschen Schweine . . .*' (you German swines).

It was about two or three in the morning when all calmed down and the cost assessed. The CO wanted to see me in his cottage. He was very interested now in the two soldiers I had seen, how they were dressed, did they carry weapons, how old they were and did one look like a German. 'Aha', I thought, 'looked like a German, but how does a German look?' But I knew what the CO was after, for it was well known that the leader of the Crimean partisans was a German Communist with the name of Voss. A big price was on his head, dead or alive, and it dawned on me that I might have been one of the few on our side who had seen him. Seeing the CO sitting there behind his oil lamp and scratching his head, I could not quite conceal a crooked rascally smile. 'Serves you right!', I thought, 'you didn't want to listen to me earlier and thought that I had seen ghosts!' And I wondered whether in his report to Battalion HQ he would go so far as to mention me and the two strange soldiers I had met on the road.

Our food supply was not of the best. With the land route from Germany to the Crimea very long and vulnerable, and the sea passage from Romania, due to the Soviets still holding on to the Sevastopol, not yet open, we often felt quite hungry. Usually we had only one warm meal a day, with the nutritional quality seldom rising above a thin cabbage soup with the odd piece of potato; every second day each of us received half a loaf of bread, some fat, a bit of cheese and some hard honey.

Every lunch-time two of us had to fetch a large canister with our section's meal from the field kitchen. Once when it was my turn with my mate, the cook had filled it up for us with a watery rice soup. Carrying it back we had to walk over a bit of rough terrain and had to pass under the road bridge, where no one could see us. We found that the canister lid was not shut properly, and some of the soup was slopping over and running down on the outside. We put it down under the bridge and lifted the lid to then put it back to see whether we could shut it properly. But we couldn't, and what was more, we had known beforehand that we couldn't. It was a shame, we agreed, that such valuable soup should slop over and be wasted like this. And all the time we fiddled with the lid, the smell coming out of the canister was simply delicious! Then we looked at each other — 'well, what do you think — it is such a waste, surely. The cook Arthur has been such a fool to have filled the canister to the brim like this. We must do something about it, but what? and our mates are waiting for us.' As it so happened, we both had a spoon in our pockets — and we lowered the soup level to the safety line about one inch below the rim, so that the soup no longer flopped over. When we arrived where our mates were waiting for us, we could see that they were hungry by the expectant way they looked at the canister. Only one of them mentioned that we had been a long time, and we said that silly Arthur had fiddled about with the lid and that there was much water under the bridge. After that we took our place at the end of the queue and the Sergeant ladled an equal share into our mess tins.

Under Voss's leadership, the partisans bothered us considerably. Whenever someone heard a strange noise, he shouted: 'Voss, Voss!', which, though being meant as a joke, was nevertheless an indication that the partisans grated on our nerves. At night only the towns and villages which we had actually occupied were ours, and everything else belonged to the partisans. Transport operated in convoys only, with machine-gun and sometimes Panzer protection. Burnt-out cars and lorries by the roadside were grim reminders to us of Voss's successes, and as one mate jokingly remarked when we passed one such wreck: 'Well, the trouble is you can't keep those blasted Germans down!'

One dark spring morning our Company had lined up in the village ready to go on *Partisanenjagd* (partisan hunting). We left our Panzers behind and took only light tracked vehicles and a couple of lorries. My reputation as a driver, after having got 'stuck' in the mud, was still low with the CO, and he announced that he would be sitting next to me to keep an eye on me on our trip to the operation point. The road we would take to Stari Krim was said to have been built by the Greeks over 2000 years ago. It wound itself in never-ending curves through the foothills of the Jaila Mountains, crossing several narrow rivers over bridges and sometimes by ford. It was an exceptionally beautiful morning, and driving east, the sun, still hidden below the hills in front of us, lit up the sky in a breathtaking mellow hue. It had rained the day before, and the air was clear and still and the birds were singing. I pointed out to the CO a bluish Venus, sitting brightly in the low sky. The CO looked quizzically at me from the side and asked: 'How do you know that?'. Thick skinned and insensitive, he was probably unaware that he was insulting me. He just cleared his throat and said no more when I told him that my father had told me about the universe and other stars and distances. As it was one of the fields I had always been interested in, I told him about Copernicus, Newton, Galileo and so on. I then became aware that I was the one who did the talking and he the listening — and he did not watch my driving at all, but had slumped back into his seat and said: 'Go on!' And while passing through the magnificent countryside I mentioned to him how insignificant we humans were on this small planet, even if some big-headed people believed that they were all important like gods. Whether he got my 'arrow', I do not know but he asked: 'Have you any thought on who created it all?'

'No, how can I. But I can understand that people throughout the ages have called it — and still do — what is so mystically ununderstandable, God.'

'Are you religious?' he asked.

'No, not in the sense of the organized church and going on my knees and making hocus-pocus.'

'But you nevertheless believe?'

'How can I not when I don't know what all this is about, when I look at all this incredible beauty and simply cannot find an explanation for this creation.'

It is all too much, isn't it, he said and then we passed the first cottages of the old town of Starii Krim which once had been the capital of the Crimea and rumbled noisily over its worn cobblestones to wake up the German soldiery and the populace. We drove into the market place and he directed me next to a ruin of a monument, and he threw off that thoughtful mantle, and was all soldier again.

The ruination of the monument was clearly of recent date. Two life-sized concrete boots, which had probably belonged to either Lenin or Stalin were still sticking to the foundation. Around the monument was a small park with shrubs and low trees, and in the early sunshine it all looked rather charming. As the curfew was just about to be lifted, no townspeople were about, only armed German guards strutting around, watching our arrival with bored interest. Shortly after, two columns of Tartars, each about a hundred men strong, arrived, and lined up along the wall of the largest house on the square, which was probably the town hall. Their leaders brought them rather untidily to attention, then crossed the road to meet an interpreter and report to the CO, who walked along the line to inspect them. 'What a shower! The "Gurkhas of the German Army", someone said, and we all stood back and giggled. The village we were in was populated by Russians, but there were about 400,000 Tartars in the Crimea, and many of the villages around were populated totally by them. Several Tartars, small and swarthy men, then came over to us and behaved as if we were long lost friends, but somehow I could not feel much respect for them, and pondered on what would happen to them if the fortunes of war should take a turn. Some of 'hem received rifles and ammunition which we had brought with us in the lorry, and after a lot of chin-wagging and organizing, the whole lot, led by their pathfinders, set out by foot into the hills.

We drivers had to stay behind to guard the vehicles and even though I did not say so aloud, I was not sorry about this! The sun was now shining warmly and we settled down in the pleasant surroundings of the park, watching the townspeople, who mainly consisted of women and the old. Having diligently learnt my Russian, I tried to talk to some of them, but apart from a hesitant '*Njet*' or '*Da*' (no or yes), they did not respond.

Behind us was a hospital which was entirely taken over for German requirements. It was getting close to midday when I walked round the buildings and coming to one of the outhouses, I could not miss the aroma of beautifully-cooked food. Following my nose, I walked in and along the corridor. There it was, right in front of me, and the large door was open. Placing myself in the doorframe, I tried in my mind to sort out the Russian helpers from the German cook and then tried to make polite and intelligent conversation with him. But he probably knew exactly why I was being so nice to him, and apart from some grumpy response completely ignored me. 'Fat, tight-fisted dictator!' I thought while I still managed to show him a friendly smile. Then an officer came strutting up the corridor from behind and asked me what I was doing there. Well, what could I say, it was all too obvious, and I pointed towards where the nice smell was coming from and told him that as a matter of fact we had been rather short of food for a long time. Though rather officious, he was quite friendly and asked me how many we were, and when I told him that we were about half a dozen, he told me to get them in. I could hardly believe my luck. And when I offered that we would do any job for him in return, he responded that there was no need for it as he had as many Russians as he wanted. When I told my mates that I had organized a decent meal for all of us, they did not ask any questions but grabbed their mess tins and followed me like dogs. Coming up the clean, tiled corridor, the officer was ready for us and in a loud voice announced that each one of us had to take one large spoon full of cod liver oil before the meal. We thought he was joking, but when he brandished a large bottle of golden 'strength-giving oil', as he called it, we all just made large, friendly eyes, not daring to argue with him. I hated cod liver oil at the best of times and when I gulped the treacly stuff down from a far-too-large dinner spoon which he had filled to the rim and kept hold of by the handle, I was almost sick. But he was true to his word, it was all worth it, the meal was delicious and we had as many helpings as we liked. After many treacly thanks and other meaningless assurances, we finally trooped back to the square, where amidst the belching and other noises, none of us dared attempt any quick bending-down movement for fear that the good food would come running out. It didn't take long for all of us to fall fast asleep on the grass and the benches.

In the early afternoon we were rudely woken. Two of my mates with a Tartar had come back from the hills with the order that I should come with my half-track and take back some of the equipment. The mountain track was rough, being little more than a dried up river bed. Having mounted a light machine gun on the structure behind me, the three were ready for any sign of danger. We were only too well aware that we were now in Voss's country. All around us was pure unspoilt beauty and peace and the higher we climbed the grander the view became, looking back towards the picturesque town. Several times we had to clear the path of fallen trees and other obstructions, being well aware of the possibility of a trap having been set for us. We then entered the clearing where our unit had set up camp in what had been the partisans' hiding place. Our CO had arranged for only a few machine guns to be set up around the camp, while most of the unit with the Tartars had fanned out into the wilderness around. The former inhabitants of the camp, as they had not taken their tents and other equipment with them, must have left in a surprised hurry, no doubt thanks to our guides, the Tartars. About an hour after our lot had arrived there, a boy of sixteen or seventeen suddenly appeared from behind the trees. He must have been asleep somewhere, his clothes had all been undone and he had been trying to pull his trousers up. When he stepped into the clearing he had had no idea about the 'change of ownership' and the danger he was stepping into. Before he could find out, a bullet had ended his young life. I stepped over and saw him lying. He had a pleasant face — what crime had he committed, I thought? When his country had been invaded, he had joined his local partisan group and gone into the hills with them — as I probably would have done had things happened the other way. But why did we have to shoot him? While I was looking through some of the literature the partisans had left, a group of Tartars came back and reported the wildest stories. By gestures they pointed out the cuttings of throats and their own heroism, and that all in relation to people they had lived together with in the same area for centuries. After all the raiding parties had come back, we sat in a large circle in the clearing and I listened to the reports. I noted with interest that only those parties which consisted of Tartars alone had had considerable success, all the others seemed to have been on a wild goose chase.

We arrived back at Starii Krim before darkness fell. The Chief thanked the lined-up Tartars and told them that their help would never be forgotten by the Reich. I am not sure whether he paid them. After they marched back to their own villages, waving at us until they disappeared into the sinking dusk, we trundled back on the winding Greek road and arrived in our village in the pitch dark. About a week later we heard that a Tartar village, the one from which our volunteers had come, had been raided in the night. Many had been killed, their houses burnt down and their cattle driven away. Where does right end and wrong begin?

Shortly after, we moved to a Tartar village called Kosy. It was situated in the top end of a bare mountain fold which ran down in a gracious sweep to the Black Sea coast. Its lanes were too narrow to take any of our vehicles; even ordinary walking was difficult and one had to step, even jump from stepping stone to stepping stone. But what an idyllic place the village was. Behind roughly built-up stone walls were the courtyards, in which much of the family life took place. The houses were all built of field stones, and most were two storeys high. The eaves of the house we were quartered in protruded over a narrow flight of stairs along the walls which led straight up to a long balcony, from where a door led into the bedroom. From one rafter there hung a most intriguing 'washing drum' which one filled up with water from the well below, then pushed a long nail which had a thick head, which hung from the bottom, releasing a trickle of water to be caught with cupped hands with which one washed. This primitive arrangement worked remarkably well. 'Our' house belonged to an old hunchbacked Tartar who lived there with three generations of his family. He told me that he was the Mayor of Kosy, and beckoned me one evening to step into a small sideroom on the top floor. Behind the door hung a poster of Adolf Hitler, and he tried to tell me what a great and good man our Führer was, and how bad Stalin was. But though I fundamentally agreed with that analysis, I somehow did not like him for having said that to me. In the family living room was a large table with legs no more than a foot high. A large number of various-sized cushions were placed all along the walls, on which they usually sat. We were all invited for a meal one evening, which was very good, though a bit spicy. The Crimean wine was good too. But sitting on the cushions around the table, I found the position very uncomfortable.

Spring came very early in that part of the world and it must have been in March when the masses of almond trees, standing in the lush grass in the sweep down to the sea, were out in full pink blossoms, a very beautiful sight to behold. Sitting under one of those trees, I discovered my first body lice, which were to accompany me for most of the next three years.

To move closer to the attack, we took ourselves to a village in the eastern end of the Jaila Mountains with the romantic sounding name of Sally, which in a rather untidy but charming fashion had settled itself along both sides of a narrow stream. The picturesque surroundings reminded me of some lower parts of the Black Forest back in Germany. The waters of the stream had cut through sandstone in places, and had made gorges into which they fell from a plateau higher up. There was much wild woodland on the hills, and early spring was showing its promise with the first buds. The mainly one-storey cottages were dotted all over the place, all of them had spacious vegetable gardens, some with fruit trees, and the womenfolk were busy preparing the earth for planting. While the bulk of our Company had settled in the village itself, our crew of four, of which I was the driver, had been billeted in a small cottage on the outskirts up a steep slope near the edge of the woods, which could only be reached by climbing a narrow footpath. The cottage, from where there was a beautiful view into the valley and to the hills beyond, had only one room, and was built against the slope, with a rough stone base and a wooden upper structure. Amongst the trees at the back stood a couple of stables with some goats and sheep in them. Underneath, within the foundations, was a tool-cum-woodshed, and wooden, creaking steps led up to a verandah which stretched along the narrow front under overhanging eaves. It was pleasantly light near the window beside the door, where we organized our blankets, and rather dark at the back where we told our Russians to go, to keep quiet and out of our way. They were a couple well in their forties. The husband, suffering from a chest complaint, had difficulties in breathing, while his buxom wife, with greying blond hair, looked the very picture of health itself.

Just before dark when we were sitting around the table for our *Abendbrot*, the couple's two offspring arrived. They had probably already heard about our arrival, for both appeared excited and a little breathless when they stepped in from the small porch. Looking around at the changes we had made, it was clear that they did not like them. Michael, so he told us in a sullen manner, was sixteen and a pupil in the near-by town while Anna, who was nineteen, my own age, had been in the middle of her teacher's training course in Simferopol when our army arrived. Both were now helping their parents with their smallholding. Even without our presence, their home was already cramped enough. Everything was extremely primitive, even the water had to be fetched from down in the village. After Anna had quietly spoken to her parents, she turned to me, probably because I had bidden her *'dobre vecher'* (good evening) in Russian and asked whether she could talk with me. She came close to the table, rested her hands on it and steadily gazed at me with her mixture of brown-green eyes. Though her movements were gentle, I could easily sense that a flame of anger was burning fiercely deep down. She said that her father was gravely ill and that his doctor had prescribed fresh air and no excitement, and that therefore it was unfair of us to barge in and upset the quiet tenor of their lives. Looking steadily back at her, I very much liked what I saw. I realized that to confront us like this needed a lot of courage. I made it clear to her that we were under orders, that she of course could go to the CO in the village to complain, but I left her in little doubt that I would be surprised if she would be listened to. And when I added that we had noticed her father's condition and would try not to cause unnecessary inconvenience, she seemed to accept the situation, and quietly explained to her father.

During most of the days we were away from the cottage, trekking through the countryside and generally preparing for the coming battle. During darkness one of us was always outside on guard. Starting off, I usually strolled around for a while, walking halfway down to the stream and checking a couple of long strings with tins on which we hung every night from tree to tree, then coming back to sit on the verandah, rifle at the ready, steel helmet off to watch and listen in the still night. When bedtime came, Anna usually asked us to blow out the candles so that she and her parents could undress and get into their beds. My place on the floor was at the foot of Anna's bed, Michael also slept on the floor next to the stove and there was little space for anyone to move.

The preparations for the onslaught on Kertsch were in full swing now. Heavily-laden transporters with trailers were pounding day and night through the village, where altogether we stayed for several weeks.

Anna and I crossed paths several times during the day and I was always much aware of her. She exuded pride and walked with a lovely womanly gait, even while doing menial tasks like taking the goats out to the meadow or walking to the field with a hoe, but we never exchanged many words except the usual ones about the weather, the animals or the happenings in the field. I sometimes noticed how intently and thoughtfully she listened in the background when in the evenings I laid down the law to brother Michael about the superior way of life in Germany. I strongly sensed that often she was angered by what I said, and perhaps that was why I said it, to draw her somehow, but she never took my cue and responded. After dark, except for the guard, we were usually all together. One of us loved to play the mouth-organ and I noticed how much Anna liked the melodic German tunes. When I sometimes caught her humming away to the music and she then felt my eyes on her, she reacted by putting up a stony face and uninterested expression. We *Landsers* (ordinary German soldiers) often played cards, which was always noisy. I played chess with Michael, and though Anna said that she could play, she never once accepted my challenge. As they had very few candles and no oil at all for their large hanging lamp, Anna asked sometimes whether she could sit close to our candlelight with her needle work. I became aware that it was more than by mere chance that she always chose to sit close to where I was sitting. And the jolly commotion around the table, the laughter and the joking, got a bit out of hand, there was always that 'innocent' touch and the momentary meeting of the eyes, which only she and I knew about and which made me play badly so that my partner told me off, wanting to know what was the matter with me.

Being drawn by the opposite sex was a very new experience to me. Naturally, there was 'rough' talk amongst us young soldiers and I mixed with the best of them, but when it boiled down to reality I was very shy indeed and had never had a girlfriend. When war broke out I was seventeen, and from its first day dancing had been forbidden. We were told that dancing around in cheap enjoyment when our Fatherland was bleeding from a thousand wounds was unethical. I suppose I longed for love without being able to properly formulate what I wanted, perhaps Anna too had her longings and her dreams and at some deep level beyond words we somehow vibrated to the same chord. There was always that look, quickly switched off or turned away when unexpectedly caught.

It struck us all as peculiar that Michael and Anna disappeared for several hours on most days. It seemed strange that none of us ever saw them going. I asked Anna several times where she had been, and she showed obvious anger that I thought to have the right to ask her. Her mother told me that she was helping friends with their smallholding in Ossmanschek, and when I pointed out to Anna that the path to that village led right through partisan country, her eyes darkened in a gesture of triumphant defiance and she said that partisans certainly would do *her* no harm. When I warned her that the suspicion alone of being a partisan would be enough to cost her her life, she merely shrugged her shoulders in resigned defiance. We *Landsers* talked about it and wondered whether we should not report our suspicion to the CO, but we had all come to like 'our Russians' on a personal basis. It was partly due to me, being the only Russian speaker, translating to them in a favourable light, what Anna had supposedly said to me, that we dropped the idea of reporting. I sensed somehow that I was running into 'difficult waters' as it is not easy to properly analyse one's own emotions, but I realized that an intangible link was developing between Anna and myself which made me act as I did. My mates remarked on my being unusually quiet, and even moody, but they did not know that inside me all was havoc.

At night when a guard was out we always left the door unlocked. I was surprised one night, therefore, when I wanted to come back in to wake my mate to find the door locked. But when I touched the handle, and well before I had time to make a noise, I heard light footsteps coming quickly across the room. And when the door noiselessly opened, there was Anna. The faint light from the outside shone on her as she stood there in her white nightdress with her brown hair hanging all too tidily over her shoulders. There was no sign on her of having awoken from a deep sleep. No one else seemed awake in the room and we stood there and looked at each other and said not a word. Not wanting to break the moment I indicated that I wanted to come in. But instead of stepping right back to her bed and leaving the shutting of the door to me, she stood back in the doorframe, leaving little space for me and begged me to pass. She did not give me an inch! And when I closely brushed against her, every single fibre in me seemed to be on fire as I sensed her living body softly touching mine. It was like tasting heaven. After having woken my mate and lying down on my blanket only a yard from Anna's bed, I did not sleep a wink that night — and neither, I could hear, did Anna. I listened to her every move, her every breath, but after morning came, neither of us gave the slightest indication of what had happened in the night.

The following Sunday was a beautiful day with spring trying to show its first dressing. The four of us were sitting outside in the grass in the warm sunshine when Anna came down the steps to then cross the meadow and walk down the narrow path towards the stream. She wore an attractive grey-green dress, the colour of the early willows, her long hair was tied together at the back and her legs were covered in white stockings. To me she looked very beautiful and when I saw my mates following her with their eyes, it gave me a feeling of pride. When she passed, she merely gave me a glance but I knew deep down that she was 'talking' to me. Shortly after she had gone out of sight I announced that I was going down to the village, which was in a different direction from where Anna had gone. But as soon as I was out of sight of the cottage, I turned to my left, crossed the meadow at the bottom and arrived at the stream. There was no path at the water's edge and it was muddy. To keep my balance when trying to get round overhanging willows and alders, at times I had to step on to boulders in the stream. I was glad that the growth around me was so thick that I could not be seen from anywhere. I took my time, because in my heart I was sure that Anna would be waiting for me, and when I came round a soft bend I saw her standing by the water's edge, slightly bending over with her hands on her knees as if watching something in the swirling water beneath her feet. She merely turned her head when she saw me approaching and showed no surprise at all. I crossed the stream on boulders to get to her side, dropped my cap into the grass beside her and quietly said: 'Anna, *maja* Anna!' to which she responded with '*Strasdvi*, Genry! That was all we said. We stood very close to each other without touching, and she had a serious look in her eyes which held mine steadily. In me everything was vibrating, it was all too much to grasp! There was Anna and for the first time we were really alone! With our senses fully alive, words were meaningless, my whole feeling, my entire being was only conscious of her. She then stepped back and sat down on a tree trunk while I hunched in the grass before her. I could see that she too was racked by emotional turmoil, and after collecting herself, all the time holding me firmly in her gaze, she said in a hardly audible voice: 'Genry, it comes deep from my heart that I am sad; why is it that you had to come into my country like this?'

'I did not choose, Anna, last year I was called up to the Army, was sent to France after training and then put on a transport going east. I did not know that we were going to the Crimea, did not even really know where that was and that it was part of the Soviet Union!'

That might be so. But do you understand that you and I never can be friends, real friends and perhaps more, I mean, as perhaps we both would like to be to each other. You realize that, don't you, Genry? Ours is such a beautiful country, you only know it as a soldier, it is bathed in peace and I love it with all my heart, so much, in fact, that I would be prepared to give my life for it to protect it — even against you. You have fallen into it with brutal force and have by that made yourself our enemy, my enemy. There never can be peace as long as we have not forced you out, and how ever can you and I express what we feel for each other. Do you understand what I mean, Genry?'

Yes, Anna, I think I can. But I can find no words to explain, yours is a very beautiful country and as to barging into your lives as an enemy soldier, I must confess that I really never once have given it any deep thought.'

There was so much more we wanted to say to each other, but probably due to my at that time very elementary Russian, we were unable to put all these feelings into words. Then Anna, holding a small bunch of flowers and bending her head slightly forward, gently started to cry. Her sobbing gave me pain — but at the same time it did make me very happy because it told me more than her words could have said. When in a loving gesture I touched her foot in front of me, she softly took my hand away and said 'Njet, Genry, njet, you must not do that!' But she held my hand in hers for those precious few seconds longer.

'I must go now!', she said, 'it was good and right that you followed me and that we told each other before you leave - and I will not forget as long as I live!' We stood up and the only sounds around us were those of nature, of the birds and the gurgling water rushing playfully around the boulders and over the clean pebbles. Sadness and joy, darkness and light were all jumbled up inside me into one large knot which I was unable to open or tear apart. As much as I wanted to, I did not dare touch her. I felt I had no right to do that. And all of a sudden, standing slightly higher, she took my head into both her hands and kissed me fully on the lips. Next she was on the boulders to cross the stream and when I set out to follow her she said: 'Njet, Genry, I must walk alone, once I am over the brow, you must walk along the river through the woods and take your time. And you must trust me!' That was all! I watched her step quick-footedly up the steep path through the meadow. Only once did she turn to look back and give me a short wave before she dipped out of sight. I sat down for a while on the trunk on which she had been sitting, and tried to sort out my thoughts. And when I then walked back slowly through the woods, it dawned on me what Anna had meant by trusting her. I was now alone in partisan country with no weapon, not even a knife, but in myself I was sure that I was safe, as Anna otherwise would never have told me to walk that way. I walked through it all as if in a dream and when I arrived back at the cottage my mates were still playing cards in the grass. I could see that they wondered about the direction I was coming from. But none said anything.

Anna was inside with her mother preparing food, and it being such a beautiful day, the door was wide open. Then the mother came out on the verandah with Anna standing right behind her and asked me whether I had liked my walk. And when I said 'yes, the walk was lovely, you live in such a beautiful country, your country, Anna!' And having put the emphasis on 'your', Anna gave me such a loving smile, for she had understood what I meant.

We stayed in Sally for another two weeks, mainly servicing and preparing our weapons and vehicles. Not far from Sally was a large divisional ammunition dump which one night was hit from a low-flying plane and blew up spectacularly. It soon became clear that it had not been a lucky hit, but the end result of a well-prepared plan. The partisans had lit four large bonfires in the wooded hills around, in such a way that by linking them with imaginary lines from the air, their crossing point marked the exact situation of the dump. And I knew that Anna had stayed away that night. When I met her coming through the village in the morning, she stopped right in front of me, which she normally did not do. An expression of triumph was written all over her face, as if to say: 'Well, what have you got to say to that?' 'Anna' I said, 'the ammunition dump at Starii had been blown up in the night, pinpointed by four partisan fires.'

'So I have been told, Genry!' was all she said. She did not walk away, she kept looking straight into my eyes. Seeing her standing in front of me in that old torn coat of hers and the large unbecoming felt boots, a strange feeling of pride came over me. Yes, I was proud of Anna! She had shown tremendous courage, and I could see in her eyes that she had got the message of my feeling.

Several days later we received orders to move closer towards the battle line near Feodosia. The night before we left it started to rain, and never stopped. Storm clouds chased each other like wild horses in the low hanging sky, then to break against the hills around us. Sheets of rain were driven by the howling wind, to then lose themselves in the churning mists which covered the valley below. It was about midnight when I stood guard on the verandah listening to the clash of the elements and trying to pierce a glimpse across the river. The overhanging roof protected me from the worst, I had kept my helmet on and had pulled up the high collar of my greatcoat. And I wondered how it would be on the battlefield in weather like this — the thought alone made me shudder. I told my mate who relieved me that all was in good order and when he questioned how one could differentiate between that howling rain-storm and a partisan attack, I told him that the partisans would not be so daft to come for us when they knew that we would be waiting for them under cover. Besides, though I did not tell him that, Anna was at home!

At the crack of dawn, life began to stir in our cottage. The rainstorm had run itself out when we were getting ready for an uncertain day. Michael had lit a fire and had fetched the water. After we had tied up our few belongings into bundles and packs we sat down for the last time to have our breakfast around the table. Everyone was grumpy and no conversation got off the ground. Our Russians too were strangely quiet and I wondered what was going on in their minds, as they were now going to have their cottage again on their own. We all agreed that the family had caused us no trouble and I like to think that we too, under the circumstances, had behaved correctly towards them. When we were finally ready to go, they all came out. The father had one of his coughing attacks, and when I shook hands with the mother, she looked at me in such a way that I knew that she had known all along! Michael even managed to present a faint smile, I was not sure whether it was cynical or friendly. And then it came to Anna. She stood slightly back from them all and I could see that she had been crying. I put my rifle on to my pack, turned my back towards my mates and took her offered hand into both of mine. There was no time for more than holding it for those few extra seconds, and I breathed, only for her to hear, 'Anna!' and then 'peace!' She rather gently put her free hand on mine to release my grip, then turned abruptly and ran more than walked up the stairs, to disappear from view into the porch. That was the moment which everyone took as the one of departure. I muttered a general *'do swydania'*, picked up pack and rifle and walked down the steep path to the village, never to turn and look back once.

Led by our Panzers we drove out of Sally on to the main road which wound its perilous path into the hills to the east. When we came to the last cottages, something drew my eye towards the slope to the right. There I saw Anna standing amongst the trees just inside the *Partisanen* wood, as we had christened it. She must have hurried, for she had changed into her grey-green dress, the same she had worn on that Sunday by the river. But today was not Sunday! No one else seemed to have seen her as she stood quite still. From having seen us in the village, she knew exactly which my vehicle was, and I felt as if she had been willing me to look at her. There was not much time until the next bend when I would be out of her sight. I gently raised my hand, and then Anna raised hers in the same way before she put it across her eyes; and though I could not see because of the distance, I knew that she was crying, crying for me!

We drove on in marching column towards the front-line where we were to do battle with Anna's people. Someone in the back of the half-track started a song, one of those rousing and melodic soldier songs for which the German Army is said to be famous. But when it rose into the laden sky, almost drowning the heavy motors and echoing back from Anna's trees, I thought that the words of the melody were arrogant and implicit of a denial of human love and all the values humanity should be standing for. I wanted to have no track with it, and no sound came from my lips. All my feeling, all my senses were back in the wood where I knew Anna was now slowly walking back to the cottage. A German soldier, a Russian partisan! What more deadly enemies could there be! If Anna and I could love, was there not hope for the world? The curving road now demanded all my concentration for driving, and while my heart felt like bursting, I realized that the vehicle in front was becoming blurred. I hoped that my comrades would not notice my crying — a soldier crying for lost love!

Climbing most of the way, we had crossed the Jaila Mountains on rough tracks. It came as a surprise when suddenly the view opened up in front of us, and we looked down on to the wide expanse of the very blue Black Sea, which today clearly belied its name. It was late April 1942 and the sun shone warmly out of a cloudless sky. Down below was a gravel road stretching west to east along the narrow coastal strip into which we descended through a cutting. To the east we could see a beautiful bay which cut inland and was surrounded by green hills with white chalk patches on them. Behind them, like a protective screen against the north winds, rose the more rugged higher mountains. Right at the centre of the bay stood a large grey country house on a flat bit of grassland, and an attempt at a park, through which ran a narrow river. From our distance it all looked as though it had been plonked there like a toy. Being part of the 22nd Panzer Division we were under orders to assemble with other units in the vicinity of that house. It was early afternoon and our column was rolling at a leisurely speed. The beautiful scenery changed with every bend of the road, and getting closer, we could make out that a football match was in progress in front of the house; shortly later we heard the shouting and the laughter of the watching crowd. We had arrived.

A *Feldgendarm* (military policeman) with his half-moon metal gorget dangling in front of his chest directed us towards a group of cottages further back. By the look of them, they had probably been the estate cottages for the house in pre-Revolutionary days. We heard that the big house had once been owned by an aristocratic family, and was now a workers' sanatorium. A couple of half-finished annexe blocks of flats stood away from it, but seemed to be part of the sanatorium complex. There were heaps of sand and cement and materials lying all over the place, and it looked as if the whole project had been abruptly stopped by our invasion. All our units were camping out in the open while the house had been completely taken over by our Divisional Command. Amongst a number of the officers leaning out of a first-floor window and cheering the teams on was our Division's Commander, General von Appell.

Though generally in an optimistic mood, we were bothered by the severe food shortage. The Crimea had only one heavily over-used rail connection across the Isthmus of Perekop, and the partisans had been very successful in blowing up the line, so the transportation of ammunition was now being given over-all priority; our pangs of hunger was the direct result. Shortages all too often make thieves, and several thefts of food had taken place which threw ugly shadows of suspicion into our spartan lives. All our vehicles had been stabled on a flat piece of land close by the sea, where they were sheltered from the air by low hills. When my friend August and I were out together on guard duty sometime in the early hours, we were well aware that our food lorry was laden with loaves of bread. It was pitch dark, and while we walked around it we started playing with the thin ropes which were holding the tarpaulin down. When looking at each other in a questioning way, we knew that our intentions were not right — but the hunger was so great. After an uneasy nod I put my thieving hand through the opening in the tarpaulin to search for the loaves. But all that happened was that my hand was gripped from the inside, accompanied by the swearing voice of our Sergeant Major: 'Got you, you bastards!' What could we say? August's feeble attempt to claim that we heard noises in the lorry was laughed out of existence before he could develop it. And when we had to appear next morning in front of the CO, it was a foregone conclusion that we both received two weeks' clink. A worse punishment than that, however, was being paraded in front of the Company as thieves who had tried to steal bread from their comrades while being entrusted to guard it. Clink was an open chicken run against the back of a cottage. Its structure, covering an area of no more than two by three yards, was held together by bits of wire mesh and sticks; we were hardly able to sit in it, as it was only about two feet high.

A strict curfew was imposed on the cottagers during the hours of darkness. One night when we were still in the cage there was a shot. One of the guards had seen a suspicious figure sneaking about in one of the back-yards. There was a smothered shout and then much wailing from the women and children in the cottage. But the guards did not allow them to come out and get near the shot body. After all, what was the price of a dead Russian! Looking at the scene next day, it was clear that all that had happened was that an old man had tried to go to his lavatory at the back and was caught doing it. The lad who killed the old man was known to be religious, often receiving religious literature with his mail. He had seen a movement, had received no reply to his challenge and had done his duty and shot. He received a medal for his exemplary awareness, and when questioned privately about his action, for most of us had known the old man, he said that he was proud of what he had done for the Fatherland, and that he easily could square it up with his religious conscience, as Bolsheviks to him were the enemies of God.

It was on 9 May 1942 when our attack on the Russian positions all along the entrance to the Kertsch peninsula began. Throughout the night there had been much troop movement and air activity since early dawn. Even our old Ju 87 Stukas, with their sirens howling, had come out of retirement. Throughout the previous weeks, whole village populations had been active digging the 'Parpatsch Trench', an anti-tank ditch about four metres deep and wide, which stretched from the Sea of Azov to the Black Sea coast. Its construction had been a major engineering success, but it did the Russians no good. Special heavy artillery shells were used to blast breaches through which our Panzers successfully crossed and were now racing eastwards. They left behind them totally demoralized and disorganized Soviet troops.

It was approaching midday when our unit was ordered to race through and take over the forward advance. The carnage we passed was horrible. Dead Russian soldiers were lying everywhere, and it was difficult to miss them with our tracks. I thought about horses and elephants and other animals who would never have trodden on human beings. I passed a small group of wounded soldiers, sitting together, trying to help and comfort each other, the horror of what they had been through still showing in their faces. After the initial assault we now found little resistance, and racing on like that gave us all a great feeling. Long columns of prisoners were coming back, a large number of whom had asiatic faces. Many of our infantry had climbed onto our Panzers and half-tracks for a ride, but quickly jumped off when we approached one village and received concentrated infantry fire.

The name of the village was Arma Eli, and it consisted of long straight rows of peasant cottages which stood in their own gardens. The land around was flat, without much tree cover. In the centre of the village at the crossing point of two wide streets an earth fortress with walls of about three metres high, around a circle of slightly less than 100 metres, had been thrown up. Several anti-aircraft guns were positioned within the fortress, which made it too risky for the *Luftwaffe* to fly direct attacks, and anti-tank weapons and machine gun nests had been cleverly dug into the earth wall which controlled all the approaches towards it. Ivan had again shown us how well he was able to make good use of the earth, better than us Germans who on the whole had grown up in cities.

To keep things on the run, the order for a quick Panzer attack on the earth fortress was given, and as one of our Panzer drivers had developed eye trouble, I took over his Panzer. The narrowness of the village street meant that we were only able to operate in a much restricted narrow formation, and the street we were now rumbling along on was only about 300 metres from the fortress. I was in the second line following the first five Panzers. Riding high on our overwhelming successes since we had breached the Parpatsch Trench, our command had not bothered to play safe and wait for our heavy artillery to soften up the target. What a mistake they made! With my own Panzer firing wildly with its 7.62 cm Russian cannon, there was an all-dominating deafening noise, to which then was added a horrible smell of burning. Through my narrow slit I had no chance to form an overall picture about how things were going. But as it had turned out, Ivan waited patiently until we had come into his close shooting field and then, and only then, did he open up. All hell was then let loose — and before I really understood, three of the Panzers in front of me were throwing up flames and smoke like large burning torches. Our attack came to a disastrous halt. Hardly being able to hear it anyway, I needed no command and acted more from instinct than sense when I wildly reversed out of it all behind the protective cover of a cottage. There was nothing we could do now but wait for our artillery. Too many of my friends had paid with their lives and when I watched our command officers going into a conclave, I pondered about their right to send young men to their deaths so recklessly.

I had been asleep, rolled up in my blanket beside my Panzer, when shortly before dawn I heard the arrival of the big guns. From where I was lying I watched them setting up position. I went over to chat with them and give them a hand, and stared over to where I knew the fortress was behind the cottages, and I wondered whether the Russians inside it realized that they were now nothing more than helpless sitting ducks.

It took more than an hour of preparation before the first salvo roared into the fortress and then it went round after round with utmost ferocity. The earth wall was pounded to smithereens, and I saw parts of guns and what looked very much like corpses and flying limbs being thrown wildly into the air. It was horrible, and yet fascinating to watch. Had we not reached the extremes of human madness? The whole performance lasted not more than twenty minutes. And when we then approached our second Panzer attack in brilliant early sunshine, weaving in between our shot-up Panzers from yesterday, which were still smoking, I could still hear rifle bullets hitting my armour plate.

We drove right up to the earth wall while the infantry following us quickly took up positions amongst us from where they could lob mortars and hand-grenades into the centre. And when they had climbed up to the top and jumped inside with bayonets fixed, we knew that all was now over and that we could come out from our protection. Climbing over, a horrible scene opened up before my eyes. More than a hundred dead were strewn all over the restricted space. Many of the corpses were torn open or were without limbs. Only a very few were merely wounded, but hardly any were in any real condition to fight. Their situation, they must have known, had been totally hopeless, but they had not hoisted the white flag of surrender. Sure, they were our enemies, should I hate them — or could I admire them? And when I went down and offered a mortally wounded young woman soldier a drink of water and held her head, I could not prevent having a lump in my throat.

The road to the East, towards Kertsch, was now fully open. As I could make out, the Red Army was now in total disarray, for we were able to cover many miles without encountering any organized resistance. The columns of prisoners became a flood and were becoming a hindrance to our advance. Often, while waiting for other units at our flanks to pull up and establish a manageable line of advance, I had time to think. I wondered whether the woman I had given water to was still alive — and what was my own place, had Christianity any room for me in it, the human family?

Our route of advance ran parallel with the Black Sea. From time to time we could make out the expanse of water in the gaps between the low bare hills. Kertsch was still more than fifty kilometres away, when we felt the atmosphere becoming strangely sticky. It was on the third day after Parpatsch that heavy mist came rolling in from the sea. Its intensity was extraordinary. One minute we had a clear view of the barrier approaching us and the next we were completely swallowed up in it with a visibility of no more than five metres. At one point we even had the suspicion that it was an artificial haze invented by Ivan. It was now almost impossible to move, all sounds became dull, all judgements of distance had gone completely haywire, and we felt isolated and lost. The fog lasted for about half a day — and then came the rain. Slowly the soup around us began to thin slightly with a new and different sort of mist steaming out of the damp earth. There was no let-up: while visibility was now restored, a new punishment settled mercilessly down on to us. Within hours the heavy earth became a dark quagmire of porridge, holes and ditches filled with water and little lakes appeared all around us. Ordinary walking became very difficult as our jackboots were sucked into the mud. Very soon our wheeled vehicles were unable to move, and soon after my own Panzer gave its last gasp and sat tight with its hull firmly embedded in the earth. That was it, only horses plodded on somehow, and some of our very heavy half-tracks. Field Marshal Erich von Manstein's Army had come to a complete halt. We were on a flat expanse which was rising slightly away from us to the east, and beyond the rim, though we could not see them, were the Russians. 'At least', we thought, 'they are in the same boat and as unable to move as we!'

With the rain incessantly hammering on the outside and everything enveloped in a wet, miserable grey, most of us dropped off into a deep sleep. We did not even bother to place guards as there seemed no necessity. Then suddenly, as in a dream, I heard infantry fire and the close-by explosion of artillery shells, and then came frantic shouting, I don't know in which language. I watched our loader open the hatch and look out. 'The bastard Russians!' he shouted, 'they are here! Out! Quick!' How we all got to our uniforms and weapons in our cramped space, I do not know. And when I slid down the side of the Panzer, I knew instantly that now it was a question of personal survival, no more, no less. All that I could do was throw myself into the watery mud. Wet to the skin with slippery mud all over me I kept firing at everything that moved, until my weapon jammed and I was left with nothing but my bayonet in my hand. I saw a Russian crouching behind my Panzer with his machine pistol at the ready only a matter of yards away. Being the colour of the earth and lying quite still, I had not been seen by him; when I looked up towards the rim, I saw his comrades coming in droves, stalking awkwardly through the mud, but still coming. Their officers were amongst them, shouting commands, while ours seemed to have disappeared from the face of the earth. There were piercing cries from the wounded, Russian and German. All was in desperate chaos. With that blasted Russian still behind my Panzer I tried to appear dead, and found that I had to concentrate hard to keep my mouth and nostrils out of the water.

Although time had completely lost its meaning, their assault probably lasted no more than half an hour. In a true sense, they had beaten us into the ground, but it now became clear that they were running out of steam. Not having achieved total victory over us, they suddenly seemed unsure of themselves, and they could not simply walk back to their own lines. Into this confused situation German infantry from the rear took up position on a slight rise to my right from where they could overlook the entire battlefield. Not being able to differentiate between the mud-clad figures as German or Russian, they could not make use of their machine guns, but concentrated on sharpshooting and picked their targets at ease. Having forced everyone to lie down, an infantry officer called by loud-hailer on the Russians to get up and raise their hands. At first there was no response; only after a machine gun, firing over all our heads to underline the point, did the Russians begin to crack. One of their officers close by me got up without a weapon; he then shouted commands in all directions, and slowly, very slowly, all the other Russians raised themselves out of the mud and collected into a loose bunch of well over a hundred survivors. As all firing had now stopped, I too got up and slowly walked back to my Panzer where I met up with my mates. What a painting we would have made! We were hardly recognizable, but luckily no one had received a scratch. Troops of medical staff were now coming in from the rear to collect our wounded. A wounded Russian near by waved at me in a pleading manner, but being very close to physical exhaustion, I did not respond at all.

While our infantry was trying to form the prisoners into a marching column, I saw a group of our own officers stalking from the rear towards us. They all wore wide, flapping rain capes, and looked like ghosts from the Napoleonic war. Most of them were of high rank and there was one General amongst them. He came over to us, was very friendly, and thanked us, as he told us that he had watched us fighting (while I had done nothing but lie in the mud) and that he would see to is that we would all get the Iron Cross. A metal cross for those who had managed to stay alive and a wooden one for those who had not made it.

At their lowest ebb, the prisoner column was soon trudging back towards us. They were dragging and carrying some of their wounded comrades. They had caused us so much agony, but looking at them in their complete misery, I simply could not bring myself to hate them. Some of them were crying, and even our otherwise arrogant officers, standing with their backs to us, seemed somewhat subdued and respectful while watching.

Then suddenly, before anyone could do anything about it, there was a shot! A Russian Lieutenant had stepped out of the column with pistol in hand and had fired point blank from no more than two metres at the General, who sank like a wet sack into the mud. Everyone's first reaction was paralysis. But then there was fury and swift action. Some of the guards jumped at the Lieutenant, and making the point that he was not worth a bullet, heavy rifle butts knocked him into the mud. That was where he was left while everyone turned towards the General. I stepped over to look at the Lieutenant. Myself not yet twenty years old, he might have been a year or so older. Blood was gushing from a gaping wound all over his face, though he still seemed conscious and obviously in agony and I had the impression that through the blood he was looking at me. I could detect no fear in him, he was asking for nothing, doubtless he knew that his fate was sealed! And when he looked in the direction of where the General was lying, there seemed a whiff of satisfaction sweeping over his face. One of the guards came over and told me that the General was dead and then seeing that the Russian Lieutenant was still alive, another heavy rifle butt completed the grisly execution. Slain like a rat into the mud, he had neither the strength, nor probably the will, to raise his hand in final defence.

The rain still came down, and we climbed back into the protection of our Panzer to find some warmth to dry. I ran the engine, a water-bottle made the rounds, and soon the ammunition box in which we kept our food was open and we began to feel human again. Crumpling up in my driving seat on the soft cushion as best as I could, I was soon oblivious to what was going on around me.

When several hours later I woke up, the rain had stopped. I climbed over my sleeping mates and opened the hatch. Torn clouds were sweeping above with the sun trying to peep down on our mess between them. Over the battlefield was now total peace and I slid down the Panzer to feel the squelching earth. One of the big half-tracks with its engine whining passed me with an important staff car in tow. It had passed over the Russian Lieutenant, of whom now only part of a leg and a bit of shoulder was showing. Had he done right, had he done wrong? He certainly had been brave and had paid the final price. I took a short spade and plumped some mud on his exposed limbs, the last respect I could pay to a comrade soldier in a different uniform.

The steam was rising everywhere and it was becoming warm and pleasant. None of my mates had arisen from their slumber and I sat myself on the turret to bandage an injured finger which lice had infected. A sad group of prisoners near by were being made to work, digging out cars. One of them was watching me very closely, making me feel almost uncomfortable. Then he came over, pulled his jackboot way down and showed me a nasty wound on his leg. He asked for water from my water-bottle so that he too could clean his wound, and then for a bandage, which I gave him as we had many. I asked him, wanting to know, what the hell had got into them to fight like devils in such a hopeless situation? Having been told from early youth that Bolshevism was bad and criminal, I wanted to know what made these Bolsheviks tick. He looked at me closely, questioningly and then shook his head in a frustrated way as if to ask what good it would do to try to make me understand. That upset me and made me challenge him again. 'Do you really want to know?' he said, 'really?' And when I nodded, he straightened himself from holding his wound, came close to my Panzer, put both elbows on to the tracks and looked at me, sitting above him, with expressive eyes. 'Will you Germans ever understand?' he squeezed through his teeth, 'what happened through the Revolution in Russia? Since that event we Russian people know that now for the first time ever we are fighting for our own sake, our own existence, our own future and not for those anymore who before the Revolution kept us down and robbed us! That's why we are fighting so hard!' All this was too much for me to understand and I just looked at him without saying anything. But then he went on and asked whether he could put a question to me: 'And what do you, German soldier, who still has parasites like landowners, big-time financiers, mine and factory owners to keep you down, think you are fighting for?' Again I did not know how to reply, so he shook his head, thanked me for the water and the bandage and slowly walked back to his comrades, a lost and sad figure.

Our Division had initially been an Austrian one, and one of my mates was an Austrian from the city of Linz. Although Hitler too was an Austrian, Franz was known for not including the Führer among his favourite people. Whenever the conversation turned to the theme of the liberation of Austria, Franz often asked 'Liberated — from what?' I told him about the conversation I had had with the Russian. 'Well', he said, 'and what was your answer?' I just laughed, as if to suggest that no answer was required for such stupid propaganda slogans. But Franz surprised me. 'Yes,' he said, 'I knew it all along. That Russian was right. Will you Germans ever understand the meaning of the Russian Revolution and what you yourself and me in our straightjackets are fighting for?'

That evening it was Franz's turn to fetch our rations from the food lorry. With the sun setting, the Russian artillery was still firing blind salvoes over to us. A stray shell happened to fall close to Franz, who was carrying our rations in a blanket over his shoulder. By the time we got to him, there was nothing to do but to pick up our rations. I had thought a lot about what Franz had said, and had planned to ask him to explain to me more closely. Though I was part of a closely knit crew, I could not ask such questions of my other mates. Suddenly I felt very lonely.

A day or so later, after the earth was dry enough to take our heavy vehicles, our Army was on the move again. Altogether it was a hard nut to crack, but we had taken the Russians head on, broken through and were now racing towards the city of Kertsch at the eastern end of the peninsula. Masses of prisoners were now flooding back through our advancing lines, while the rest of the Red

Army was in headlong flight. Manstein was apparently aware of the importance to settle the issue quickly and decisively before Stavka, the Soviet High Command, had a chance to build up strong defences to the west of the city.

My own Panzer had developed mechanical trouble and had to be taken in hand by the Repair Troop. As I was therefore without a job, I was ordered to join our Division's Grenadiers, the 129 Grenadier Regiment, whose main task had been to follow in the wake of the Panzers and mop up behind. We reached a line just to the west of Kertsch and found its way blocked by a treeless hill called 'Hoehe 175'. Just above the top line beyond our range, the Red Army was dug in with strong infantry and anti-tank defences. From afar we had seen the freshly thrown-up mounds of earth, which had been cunningly arranged. Our infantry, however, successfully took the slope below the Russian line and established its own fortifications consisting of trenches and foxholes. When I joined my new mates, I had to take my place with two of them in one foxhole, and I reckoned that I would be in for a cushy time.

It was early evening, the weather was pleasantly warm and I quickly found my bearings in my new surroundings. We had put down blankets in the hole on which we were lying, and being so close to the enemy, no Sergeants or officers bothered us. After dark, one of us kept a look out while the other two slept. Peace seemed to reign supreme. I looked up to the stars and thought about the unfathomable distances and the enormity of space. All our vehicles were behind us in a valley protected by willows and thick shrubbery.

By dawn, a faint strip of light was tentatively showing itself over Kertsch, and things began to happen. Using the oldest of tricks, the Russians had been well aware that drowsy soldiers are at their most vulnerable in the very early hours of the morning. They managed to creep over the ridge undetected, silenced a few foxholes on the quiet with knives, and used only their firearms and hand-grenades when they were already well amongst us. My mates began firing the machine gun while I, having just woken up and still not quite with it, fed them with ammunition. There was utter chaos, with one Russian even jumping over our hole. I was nervous, fiddling about with the ammunition boxes and very frightened.

But then the Russians were no supermen either; they seemed to be losing each other in the gloom, and probably had no clear perception of the position of our foxholes, which without destroying they had no chance of subduing us. And once our lot had woken up further back and had brought the machine guns into full play, the enemy lost his chance and withdrew, leaving a large number of dead and wounded lying amongst us. Light now came quickly and I saw two dead Russians lying in front of our hole, so close in fact, that I could have reached out and touched one of them. His helmet had rolled away from his head and he seemed to be gripping into the earth with both his hands. In death his face had no enemy look about it. I could not keep my eyes off him, and wondered what kind of a man he had been, how he had earned his bread, had he a wife, parents or children?

Our Command had brought up an interpreter with a loud-hailer who called for a truce so that both sides could collect their wounded. All of them were unattended, and there was much moaning and groaning. Then one of the Russians waved something white which looked very much like his shirt and asked if he could walk back and make arrangements. Then a Russian loud-hailer arrived and half an hour's truce was agreed upon. Several from either side with Red Cross armbands then started to tend and collect their wounded, and it was decided to leave the dead for the time being where they had fallen. Everyone around, Russian and German, now raised their heads and looked around at the carnage. When I saw two Russian soldiers walk slowly and uncertainly towards us, I came out of my hole to meet them. We shook hands and they offered me a cigarette. It was horrible tobacco and not being a smoker anyway, I started to cough and one of them kept patting me on the back. We looked at each other, smiled rather wryly, and did not really know what to say. I then remembered a little bag of sweets in my pocket which had been doled out to us the night before as an extra battle ration, and gave it to them.

They then asked me whether they could walk over to their dead comrades next to my foxhole. So we three, me in the middle, hands in our pockets and none carrying a weapon, walked together in the warm sunshine towards the German line. They took the paybooks from their friends' bodies; in one of the paybooks they found photos, family pictures of parents, a girlfriend and a child. They asked me what time it was, and we grinned at each other sheepishly and agreed that it was time to get back to our positions. They called me *Tovarish* (comrade) and I did likewise. We shook hands again, warmly with a firm grip and looked into each other's eyes. Comrades indeed, that's what we were. When walking away from each other, one of them picked up a small stone, called and then threw it towards me in such a way that I should catch it. Before I settled back in my foxhole, I looked towards their line and saw them standing by their hole and looking at me; we waved a last greeting to each other.

Just before the truce was up, a white flag was shown again from our side and I was ordered to come back at once and report to the Command Post. Being prepared to get a telling off, I was surprised that the Captain was friendly and merely asked me whether I had found out something important. He also said that I had looked rather ridiculous, standing in no-man's land with the Russians and coughing my head off. A number of our wounded had been loaded on to a half truck and I was to take them to a *Fieldlazarett* (field hospital) which was in a *Sovkhoz* (state farm) several kilometres to the rear. When I asked for someone to accompany me, he said that he could spare no one and that I was being pulled out in this way because I was too valuable as a Panzer driver to die in a fox hole. The 'road' was no more than a rough farm-track full of potholes which were difficult to avoid.

Listening back, I could hear that the truce had ended and the shooting had started again. Then I heard shouting from the back of my truck, stopped and walked round to look in. Most of them were in a very bad way, bandaged only with field dressings. They were packed in like sardines, and all that they wanted to tell me was that one of them had died. But then another one said that part of his guts were hanging out from a stomach wound, and never having had any medical training, I tried to put them back and told him to press the shirt over his wound. Some wanted me to drive more slowly, others faster, so I did what I thought was right, but feeling very miserable and guilty.

Weaving around low hills, I finally emerged on to a small plateau from where I could see the *Kolchose* nestling below in a narrow valley. Its main buildings were arranged around a cobbled square, in the centre of which was a large, steaming dung-heap. I could see many wounded lying in a row beside the wall of a long stable, with medical orderlies rushing to and fro. The place was like a beehive and stretcher bearers, some of them Russian prisoners, were coming in and out of the buildings with their grisly human loads. Obviously, there was an operating theatre in the stable.

As I pulled up by one of the doors and asked one of the orderlies where he wanted me to put my load, a frightened figure stepped out of the building and came straight towards us. He was a little man with a large, almost bald head and a neatly cut reddish beard. His shirt sleeves were rolled up and he wore a leather apron which, like his boots, his hands and arms and even his face was smeared with blood. 'Count Dracula himself' was my first impression. Before even listening to what I had to say, he shouted at me that he was the surgeon here and that he was not going to take any more wounded. I thought he was joking and laughed at him, then realized that he was deadly serious. Although he wore no insignia, his lowest possible rank was probably Major, while mine was the lowest but one in the whole *Wehrmacht*. He ordered me to stand to attention while speaking to a superior officer, but when I still carried on using my hands so as to make my argument more convincing and told him that I had been ordered by my superior officers to take these badly wounded men to his *Lazarett* and that I was going to carry out this order whatever he said, he went red in the face and lurched forward as if to hit me and I had to run round the truck to get out of his reach. Someone then held him back, but he kept shouting at me that he had not slept for several days, that wounded men were already dying because they had been operated on by orderlies, and that his decision not to take any more was final. Several orderlies collected around us, expecting some cock fight perhaps, and when I asked them where the nearest hospital was, they had, as I had expected, no idea — and all the time there came moaning and weeping and shouting from the back of my truck, ignored by all. The surgeon was clearly at the end of his tether and it was no good arguing with him. I felt like crying in utter helplessness.

I climbed back into my motor and drove out of the yard to stop behind a high hedge where I could cool my feverish mind. I took a bucket and walked slowly back into the yard where I filled it with water from the well. There was no sign of the surgeon and no one took particular notice of me. Then I drove round the yard until I came to a ramshackle gate hidden behind shrubs, lowered the side flaps and with all my strength and possible care lifted and pulled and carried each of my wounded and laid them out side by side in the grass. Another one had died and I put the two dead amongst the living. I gave them water to drink, and when they realized what I was up to, they pleaded with me not to leave them on their own. I felt like a miserable cad and walked back to the pump where I told the most innocent looking orderly that there was a row of wounded as well as two dead by the fence on the grass. Then I started the engine, drove carefully back round the yard and then raced up the farm track to the plateau out of view. My hands and my uniform were covered in blood and I was physically and mentally exhausted.

Suspecting that the surgeon might send a fast jeep after me, I pulled in beside a brook which ran across the track, until I was completely out of sight. I arrived at a beautiful green patch, switched off the engine and threw myself into the fresh grass to bury my face into it. Feeling the warming sun on my back, I lay there for a long time oblivious of everything around me. When I woke out of the doze, I smelled the fresh grass and the sweet earth and slowly began to feel like a human being at peace with myself. After the rain the water had risen slightly over the bank and was playing its way, weaving and glistening, through the grass. I sat up; the bed of the brook was no more than a foot deep, the water was clear as crystal and was gurgling and rushing around the boulders. It was like paradise, an oasis in a mad world. I took off my jackboots, rolled up my trousers and waded into the cold water to wash the worst of the blood off me. Small fish darted to and fro and I tried unsuccessfully to catch some. Then I took off all my uniform and submerged myself completely in the water. It was so cold that it almost stopped me from breathing, but it was as if this dramatic act would cleanse me of the accumulated horror I had gone through in the last hours. I ran along the brook over the soft May grass, forward and backwards, the warm air dried my quickly and I felt my blood circulating with newly found strength. I laid down naked on the grass, and rolled over several times as playfully as a child. I felt alive.

Then I realized that it was time to get back, and I began to worry about how I was to account about my long absence. A low-flying Russian Yak made a circle right over me, and then gently spluttered away. I had had no food for hours, and felt hungry. After stealing a few more precious minutes, sitting in full uniform by the brook, I backed on to the farm track from where it did not take me long to come back to Hoehe 175. Coming to the last bend, I was surprised at not hearing any battle noise, no shooting, no nothing, and when I came into the open, I saw everyone walking about in the open. To cover my long absence I drove straight to the repair troop and told the sergeant that he would have to do something about the faulty brakes. Only then did I report to the Captain, said something about my brakes and trouble at the overloaded *Lazarett*. But he was very tired and did not really want to listen to what I had to report. Smoke came from the field kitchen and soon I was sitting with my mates, spooning lovely thick soup with slices of good hard bread. What had happened, I wanted to know, seeing Russian prisoners being led away further along. Manstein it seems had thrown in fresh Panzers from the flanks and had rolled up the entire enemy position like a carpet. The Ivans, as usual, had fought like devils; but it had done them no good. What had happened to the two Russians from the foxhole whom I had given a bag of sweets? 'Dead, all dead', they said; 'We shouted at them to surrender but they refused and kept shooting. So in the end one of the Panzers had to get right into their foxhole and twist and turn and roll over them, as otherwise we could not get out of our own holes!' 'My God!' I thought, and the dreadful image entered my mind that they might have suspected me in the Panzer when it was coming for them, and I wondered whether they had eaten my sweets before they died.

We had won the battle of Hoehe 175. With Hoehe 175 out of the way, the back of the Red Army at Kertsch was now broken. There was still tough resistance from isolated pockets, but once we had broken through and smashed into the city proper from several directions at once, the fighting was over. Our unit took up position on the bank of the shore north east of Kertsch, roughly at the dividing point between the Sea of Azov and the Black Sea, and looked across the Straights to Asia where we could clearly make out the Taman Peninsula where the River Kuban runs into the sea.

Remnants of the beaten army were trying to escape across the Straights in all sorts of boats, small ships and even hastily put together craft, like the British at their escape from Dunkirk two years earlier. We took potshots at them and managed to blow several of them to smithereens. After thus having achieved our objectives, Manstein wanted us back in action, and we hurriedly returned the 100-odd kilometres to Feodosia where we were loaded on to a train which took us back to the Ukrainian mainland at Slavyansk in Kharkov Region. One part of the war was over for us, and we wondered what the next would bring.

5
Storm into the Soviet heartland

*Wenn ich dumm bin
lassen sie mich gelten;
wenn ich recht hab'
wollen sie mich schelten!*

'When I am stupid
they don't mind me;
but when I am right
they want to scold me.'

Goethe, from a poem

Following a short beautiful spring, summer came late to the Ukraine in 1942. Altogether we had lost almost half of our number in the Crimean battles, but then reinforcements in men and weapons arrived at Kharkov railhead which met up with us in the forest of Chuguyev and restored our Division to its full strength. We joined up with the Sixth Army, which at that time had received a new Commander, General Paulus, who had a reputation of professional excellence. Judging by remarks by some officers, however, there was surprise, if not indignation, as Paulus was said to have been appointed in favour of more senior contenders for the post, and had had no real front-line battle experience.

Being newcomers to this theatre of war, we soon realized that it was common practice here for civilians who were merely suspected of partisan connections to be summarily hung from gallows in their towns and villages, so as to put fear into the population. It was rumoured that General Paulus, when being taken on an inspection tour, had unexpectedly come upon such a scene and that he had turned white with rage. As a result one of his first Headquarters directives expressively forbade this kind of hanging without proper judicial procedures, at the threat of court martial with a possible death sentence for the guilty.

After Marshal Timoshenko's attack against the German positions around Kharkov had failed in May before our arrival, Paulus gave orders for a massive counter-attack which developed early in June. Our Division was ready, and after having waited in the forest of Chuguyev for the earth to dry after heavy rains, we successfully smashed through Soviet resistance and were soon heading cautiously east, advancing seldom less than thirty kilometres a day. Things, we thought, were looking good for us and we were told that the Führer back in Germany had made an important speech in which he had promised to bring the war to a speedy, victorious end. But then, we remembered that the Führer had said many things in the past. We remembered that in the early days of Barbarossa the Red Army had been described as a 'heap of proletarian rubble' which we were to sort out. But nobody spoke in those terms any more.

What seemed strange after our breakthrough from Chuguyev was that, though we had skirmishes and minor battles almost every day, we seldom came to grips with the real power of the Red Army. At the last moment Ivan always managed somehow to successfully withdraw, and we were by no means sure whether he did this out of pure weakness, or whether he had something up his sleeve. What also surprised us when we entered the industrial region of the Donetz was that almost all valuable machinery had been stripped from the factories probably to be taken to the smithies in the Urals and beyond. Whatever our Führer said, we knew somehow in our bones that Joe Stalin had not run out of steam, and was alive and still very much kicking. And when we saw the so-called *Wirtschaftsführer* (economic officers), whom some vicious tongues called the vultures of Krupp, Siemens and Thiessen, looking long-faced into the empty factory halls, we could not quite suppress our sly smiles.

Most of the time the weather was beautiful, the earth was now hard and dry, ideal for pushing on with our heavy-tracked army. Using the 'thick arrow' formation with our Panzers providing the main thrust, our advance took shape in a general straight ahead direction. We did not bother much about what we left behind at the sides; the following infantry divisions could easily deal with that. At times though, we made quick wolf-pack reconnaisance darts to the sides with three or four Panzers. On one of these marauding runs we overran an earth-bunker which had been dug into the side of a ravine. Not having had any idea that the bunker was there, we took the Soviets by complete surprise, they reacted in total panic. Had they come out quietly with their hands above their heads, I am sure that nothing would have happened to them; but when they ran like mad hares, our machine guns did the rest. Amongst the dead were two young women, and we took three prisoners with us. Entering the dug-out, we realized that we had disturbed a propaganda unit. There were stacks of leaflets, posters and maps all over the place, most in striking colours and making strong, though to me, overplayed propaganda points. We burnt the lot on a huge bonfire, except for those which we took back to our units. Some of the leaflets showed carricatures of Hitler, Goering and Goebbels which we found very funny. When we showed them to our mates, there was much laughter, until an officer took them away.

Going forward, we were of course in a buoyant mood. We had great faith in Paulus, and thought that we were on a winning streak. But when we swarmed out in front of the industrial town of Izyum on the River Donetz we were met by unexpectedly heavy resistance. It was rumoured that Workers' Battalions from the local factories and miners from the pits had joined the battle, and we knew from some past experiences that this would sharpen the enemy's steel. Having lost my Panzer due to mechanical trouble, I now drove a half-track with a 5 cm PaK anti-tank gun in tow. While underway, the *Zugführer* usually sat beside me while the gun crew, consisting of the gunner, the loader and the ammo 'boy', lounged in the back.

We quickly took up position on a falling slope with the town sprawling in front and slightly below us in open countryside. From our position the setting of the battle was ideal, and I wondered why the Russians let us come so close. A fascinating scene unfolded in front of our eyes: winding their ponderous way around the small houses of the town's outlying districts, a large number of T-34 tanks were coming towards us, still about a kilometre or so away. With the sun high in the sky we were all clearly visible to each other. From time to time they stopped and fired wildly in our direction; we could sense the bright blasts from their guns as the air vibrated and the earth trembled from their shells falling around us. Closely following the tanks, sometimes taking shelter behind them or the cottages, came the infantry, and it looked as if some of them were in dark workers' clothes.

Only when they were within our range did we receive orders to open fire. Apart from the blasts there was a tremendous whining in the air from the heavier Panzers sited behind us as they let fly with their short cannon over our heads. The battle lasted about a couple of hours perhaps and the Soviets, as always, fought heroically; but as we not only had a material superiority in numbers and firepower, but also the psychological advantage of having been the successful attackers for weeks, as well as the tactical one of being placed above them in a wide half circle, they, in the end, had no chance.

Fiercely burning tanks and cottages sent curling columns of black smoke into the summer sky. We could see many of their dead and wounded in the dip and on the slope before us. Several of their tanks rumbled back, and though it was victory for us, it was also a sad and pathetic picture. One could almost feel their utter frustration and helplessness. They had tried to defend their town and had failed, and now they had no choice but to admit the enemy. Watching it all, I wondered how I would feel if the boot were on the other foot and I had failed to protect my own family. With the battle so obviously and completely decided, there was outrage and anger when some of our Panzers behind us still kept firing. Our gunner waved back at them to stop and grumbled something about 'not kicking an enemy when he is down'. Then we rumbled slowly into the town. Our infantry followed us at heel, and we were pleased when one of our officers quickly arranged for the wounded to be picked up.

After having cracked the nut of Izyum and crossed the Donetz, the Great Bend of the River Don now lay invitingly open in front of us, with the Soviets unable to do anything about it. Further on to the east, we knew, stretched the Volga, Europe's mightiest river, with the city of Stalingrad along its western bank. We had been told repeatedly by our officers that reaching and conquering that city would be tantamount to the end of our thrust and that we could then look forward to a period of well-deserved rest.

We left the town of Izyum on the same day and turned south-east towards the industrial centre around Rostov on Don. When we came towards a village which stretched right across our path of advance, we let our cannons fly, just to be on the safe side, as our gunner always said. We targeted a low cottage which was partly hidden behind a high scruffy hedge and when we came closer to it, we noticed a tree with early apples on, just showing above the hedge. To replenish our supply we decided that I should pull up behind the now shattered cottage out of our officers' view and that I should fill one of our ammunition boxes with fruit while the rest of the crew stayed in position. Approaching the hedge, I heard a sobbing sound and when I stepped through the opening, I saw a girl of about twelve lying in the grass under the tree. She wore a light summer dress and I noticed pretty, puffy sleeves. Her hair was blond and tied in pigtails. Her whole left side was torn open and around her the grass was in a bloody mess. She was still moving, still in convulsion, but I could see that there was nothing anyone could do. Her mother, I presume it was her, was bending over her with her back to me. She was pleading and sobbing and calling the girl's name. Having heard me coming, she turned her head, her face wet from tears and her expression bewildered and desperate. Next to them lay a wooden plate with broken pieces of bread. The mother then slowly raised herself and when she realized who I was, a complete transformation came over her. As if with a swipe she managed to wipe away all her outward signs of grief, her face screwed up and her eyes narrowed and out of the grief showed so much hatred, so much contempt for me. The words, of which I understood only a few, screamed out of her like a torrent and hit me as seldom anything had hit me before. Though trained to be arrogant and overbearing, I knew I was guilty, and though having experienced many tight situations, there had never been anything like this. All I could manage was to mumble '*Prostite!*' (I am sorry) but I instantly realized how hopelessly wrong it was. In the agony I dropped my wooden box. '*Prostite...?*' she said, 'Is that all you can say, you dare to say after what you have done? She came out to greet you, to offer you bread and salt and peace! It took some courage to do that; and you coward, you beast, what have you done to her...!'

I simply did not know how to react. Like a miserable coward, as she had said, I turned and ran to flee back to security amongst my mates. Falling back into my driving seat and driving off into the village where all the others had already assembled. I then told my mates what I had experienced, why I had come out without any apples, even without my box. They just looked at me quietly without saying a word, but then one of them said 'Yes, so what? One Russian girl killed by one of our shells. But why did you not bring any apples?'

We had a rest on the village green and something to eat when I saw three human bundles lying in the village street not far from us. I asked my mates how that had come about. 'Well, you know, a mother with two kids, they just ran out of the cottage at the wrong moment when we moved in, you know how it is? Yes, I knew all right. A mother and two small children and though apparently dead, no one had gone over to have at least a look — and neither did I. Then our Captain walked across the green, and talked about our well-executed attack, about another victory, another village taken and all for Führer and Fatherland.

Shortly after, we entered the small town of Komsomolsk where we pitched our tents in what the local people called their 'Park of Culture and Rest' Many of the towns we had come through on our drive east had such a park, mostly fairly newly laid out, and it was said that this had been the work of the Communists following the Revolution, which I found difficult to tie up in my mind, having all my conscious life been told that the Communists were oppressors of culture.

Komsomolsk was a pleasant town with an old centre and a suburban area, consisting mainly of pleasant wooden dachas standing in their own gardens along straight and wide tree-lined avenues. With their country such a very large one, everything about the town breathed space. In our park were many trees, grassland and flowerbeds and after we had made ourselves comfortable, it was of course declared 'out of bounds' for the townspeople. To protect our vehicles from possible air attacks, we dug deep sloping holes into the soft earth into which we drove them, making a mess of the park. At a secluded spot behind high shrubs we dug our latrine hole above which we placed long beams to sit on. This was the only place where all were equal and no saluting was necessary, and it was a place where, apart from other things, so many wild rumours found their source. Out of town was a beautiful lake surrounded by woodland. It had a diving board structure of several levels, and there were benches between the trees, and a children's play area with sand-pits, small roundabouts and swings. Almost every evening we paraded through the town, tramping our nailed jackboots on the old cobblestones and singing rousing soldier songs, to impress the natives. Lying in the grass one evening and looking at the peaceful scene, I was reminded of a similar lake near home where I had often gone swimming as a youth and I had a touch of sadness that this Russian lake, though as pleasant as the German one, did not give me that carefree feeling. The thought that I would have to go on to do battle was always present.

It was a warm Sunday morning when a small group of us were commanded to set up a pulpit at the edge of the grassland. We used ammunition boxes to lay out a small platform onto which we built the pulpit; Then we draped a Swastika flag in front of it, and were pleased when the Lieutenant who had given us the order congratulated us. Replacements in men and weapons had arrived and it was for this that a ceremony was arranged. The new weapons were placed in a large half circle and the battalion lined up in sections between them. A trumpet was blown from between the trees when the regimental padre with his assistant arrived. He wore a cassok over his uniform, and his jackboots stuck out from underneath, which made someone next to me say: 'Jesus, motorized'. While we presented arms and two pipers blew a march, the padre stepped on to the platform behind the pulpit. Our Sergeants stood amongst us while all the officers were lined up under the trees in their best uniforms, facing us. Then, 'Jesus' raised his arms towards heaven, wringing his hands as if to ask the Almighty for help, and brought down his arms rather heavily. The whole carefully erected edifice of the pulpit simply collapsed. 'Jesus' himself stumbled forward, but somehow managed to stay on his feet. A few of us dashed forward to quickly rebuild the structure while the Captain darted a threatening look towards the gigglers, and the whole embarrassing situation was saved with the padre carrying on as if nothing had happened. He gave us the usual sermon about God, Hitler and the Fatherland and denounced the godless Bolsheviks as the enemies of everything decent and human, and urged us to fight to our utmost to establish peace and freedom in our country and the world. He mentioned how fortunate and honoured we were to live in such a great time when our Führer was enabling us to break the chains of our slavery. The pipers then played *I had a comrade*, and while sinking on our knees and quietly singing with it, 'Jesus' with his assistant walked slowly from section to section to bless weapons and men by drawing little crosses in the air with their fingers. For the Finale the two padres knelt with us and we recited the Lord's Prayer. From where I was, I could see a group of Russian townpeople watching us from the fence. They must have wondered what those kneeling Christians were praying for, after having come a thousand miles to burn, destroy, and murder, and to steal their cattle and their land.

The petrol transport which had enforced our week's rest in Komsomolsk had now arrived and we left the town on a sunny afternoon. The Red Army, we had been told, had withdrawn towards the Don, but we had to be careful of rearguard action, planned to slow our advance. Towards evening, moving across a field stacked with bundles of hay or corn we came under sporadic fire. Someone shouted, 'Go for the bundles!' We drove straight over them; looking back, we could see a bloody mess. For the Russians being so 'treacherous', no prisoners were taken that day.

Just before it turned dark we approached a village which stretched along both sides of a narrow stream, and we were told that we were to stay there that night. Most peasant cottages have a dug-out in their back gardens, serving as a cool food storage. Approaching over a low brow, we rather suddenly came into view of the village, and I saw a woman running along with two soldiers whom she helped down into her storage; I made a mental note of this. We entered the village without a shot and after having sorted ourselves out, a mate and I went to that cottage, each carrying a pistol and hand-grenades. The woman must have seen us come from her window, for when we barged in, she stood under the icon, shaking with fear. Next to her was an old couple, and several children were huddled around her. I asked her sarcastically whether she had something to tell me but she trembled so much that she could not get a word between her lips, all that she was able to point out to me was that she had children and parents to look after. Waving my pistol I told her to come out with me and to open the flap door to the dug-out while we kept back and knelt amongst the vegetables. She begged into the hole for the two to come out. Next I saw two hands rising up over the top of a ladder and then a head with a very worried face. Then there was a crash, the head had disappeared and it was obvious that the soldier had fallen down the ladder, as there was much shouting down below. The woman assured us that everything was all right down below, and then the two came crawling out of the hole; when they saw us laughing, they put up a wry and rather unconvincing smile. We took them to our field kitchen where our cook employed them profitably. When it got dark we crawled into our tents; the air was soft and warm, there being no sign of winter yet. There was an earthy touch about that village, the dirty pond with the reeds, the unmade road and the low thatched cottages; it all looked so very natural and so peaceful. Lying on my blanket and thinking over the events of the day, I remembered our padre saying that we were building a new order in the world and that God was surely on our side. I wondered what the Russians had done that He was not on theirs.

Early next morning we dismantled our tents and tied the various bits of equipment to the turrets of our Panzers with the grass still heavy with dew. Before us was Steppe country, the Russian prairie, and as the golden, dusty sun was rising to make the last patches of mist disappear, we knew that it would be another hot, demanding day. Being in the mood of warlords, we never gave ourselves much rest, and being aware that the Russians were on the run, we knew that it would be to our advantage to go on while we could. When we were advancing and I was driving the Panzer, I envied my mates, who could sit outside and lean against the turret in the breeze, while I was locked inside in an oppressive heat. Our CO, *Oberleutnant* Steffan, led our column in a *Kübelwagen*, a large open jeep. From time to time he stopped by the wayside to watch us roll by, and then would overtake us again. Like Rommel, he wore dust goggles on the front of his field cap, and the field glasses with which he frequently scanned the horizon dangled in front of his chest. Whenever a marauding German aircraft appeared, at least one of our Panzers draped a large swastika flag over its turret; when a Russian appeared, however, we quickly tore it off and menacingly bared our teeth.

At one point a *Kradmelder* (motorbike messenger) arrived from Battalion HQ with an order for Steffan. Aerial reconaissance reported that an enemy unit had dug itself in at the approach of a large village about two kilometres away which we were to attack. It had no tanks, only one light cannon, and being in buoyant mood, not having come to real grips with Ivan for several days, we looked forward to a good scrap. When we spotted the first roofs on the horizon, we swarmed out into battle formation and waited for Steffan's further commands. He gave instructions to the Lieutenants, they synchronized their watches, and then came back to us. Even in a situation like this, they never missed giving each other a military salute before they parted. A preparation for an attack always arouses hidden emotions, as if from some deep animal instinct. We sat there like wolves, ready to pounce. And when *Oberleutnant* Steffan, standing high in the turret of his Command Panzer, raised his hand and then brought it down, we all started to roll forward, ready for anything. Sometimes someone started a song, but deep down we were tense, the atmosphere in our tight cabin was electric and all conversation stopped.

We could now see the freshly thrown up earth of the trenches and raced towards them on the flat ground. Our gunner let loose a couple of shots without having asked me first to stop, a sure sign of nerves. But there was no need for all that; the Russian Commander whom we had been chasing for weeks, had sold us a pup again, had read our mind and battle plan like a book and had left the trenches empty. In one of them however, was a damaged German helmet tied to a stick rammed into the earth. It had a hammer and sickle painted on in black paint; and while we were laughing about such a stupid joke, there was an explosion from a craftily dug-in mine in front of the helmet, badly damaging the track of one of our Panzers. Our Russian adversary had already moved up a hill on the other side of the village and we could see him occupying new positions from which to rake us with his '*Ratsch Bumm*', which name we had given his very effective 7.62 cm artillery cannon-cum-PaK.

We swerved out to the right and disappeared from his view in the lower part of the village. We had arrived at a pleasant, green place, the cottages were all thatched and whitewashed, the gardens full of fruit trees and everything looked well kept. A narrow brook, bridged by sturdy boards at several places, ran the length of the street under shady trees. While the steppe we had come from vibrated from the heat, here by the brook was the refreshing coolness of an oasis. Soon we made ourselves at home, wrung the necks of several wandering chickens and organized a search for eggs. As our pay was doled out to us in roubles which we never had an opportunity to spend, we sometimes showed our generosity to the peasants, whom we paid for what we would otherwise have stolen. Having so much money, we sometimes called ourselves 'rouble millionaires'.

Later, to our great annoyance, a Divisional Staff unit arrived and set up a command post where we had spread ourselves on the grass by the brook under the trees. We were ordered to move a hundred yards upstream out of the way, and sat there sulking. We watched them unload from a lorry and several staff cars. There were a couple of Colonels, three or four Majors as well as several Captains and Lieutenants. Most were in their late twenties and early thirties; one or two wore monocles and we were told that a Prince of Hanover was amongst them. To us the scene was like something from another world, their behaviour was loud and self-assured, and their attitude arrogant. White-coated batmen quickly put up tables by placing long boards on ammunition boxes, most of which were covered with maps and other staff papers over which some of them studied the situation. But there was one table which was reserved for pleasure. A snow white cloth was spread over it, and the sight of what was put on that cloth made our hungry mouths water: bottles of champagne, other wines and spirits, white bread, cheeses, butter, meat, fruits and other delicious things. They surely knew how to live — and perhaps what they were waging a war for. Knives and forks, glasses, plates and corkscrews were neatly laid out in proper order. Then benches and chairs were taken from the lorries and, when everything had been done for them, the gentlemen themselves sat down to what they, no doubt, were accustomed to. None of us, living out of mess tins from very meagre rations, had seen food of this quality for years. We were always being told that this was because of the difficult transport circumstances, and that it was only right that we should tighten our belts for the good of the Fatherland. But why were *their* transport circumstances not also 'difficult'?

The officers behaved as if giving a stage performance, and as if we were the gaping onlookers, necessary as an outside framework to it. Apart from an odd patronizing glance in our direction, they ignored us completely. They addressed each other as '*Herr*' with no reference to rank, and they made sure that the 'von', the hallmark of German aristocracy, was never left out when it applied.

Suddenly there was an unexpected arrival! All heads turned as a group of about fifty Russian prisoners was brought along by German guards. They had broken ranks on this hot day, and had swarmed out over the grass to drink the cool water from the brook; almost all of them were now kneeling along its edge with their heads almost disappearing into it. When slowly, amidst the shouting of the guards, they came back into formation, one of our Majors swivelled round from the table and noticed a Russian Colonel at the head of the prisoners. In a very arrogant manner he ordered him to come over. The Colonel, behaving as if he did not understand, did not respond, so the Major sent his batman to fetch him. By this time most of the officers were somewhat the worse for drink, and when the Russian, carrying his coat over his shoulder, planted himself powerfully in front of the table and observed the scene with astonishment and open disgust, all talk around us ceased. Even we ordinary Fritzes on the sidelines could sense that something important was happening, that a situation had arisen which no one had expected and for which no one was prepared. There was no doubt: the Russian Colonel was certainly making an impression. He stood the test of comparison against what suddenly appeared to be a degenerate lot; there was something culturally superior about him as a human being.

The Major who had called him over stayed in his seat, his tunic open, his eyes bleary, and asked him in Russian for his name and unit, which the Colonel gave him. Then the Major asked for more information and the Russian replied, mixing in some German, that he had given all the information legally required of him and that he would reveal nothing more. We all realized, of course, that he was right, but with grotesque insensitivity the Major then set out to insult both the Russian officer and us, the onlookers, his own German underlings. He proclaimed in a loud voice to his fellow officers: 'Look at this common rascal, a Colonel in the Red Army! Pfui! I would not even have promoted him to a position higher than that of a stable lad! Common rubbish!' The Russian understood the insult only too well, for he showed his decided contempt by simply saying in a deep, manly voice — as compared with the rather squeaky one of the Major: 'Let me remind you, Major, that I am nevertheless a Colonel, while you are only a Major!' That somehow hit home! To be cut down to size in front of us all must simply have been too much for him. And before anyone could do something about it, the Major, without saying another word pulled his pistol out of its holster and shot the Colonel through the heart. He fell backwards like an iron rod into the dust, without a sound. From underneath his body came a narrow trickle of red.

The shock was immense, for a moment there was complete silence. But it was the lull before the storm. The officers made the first move, some jumped up and grabbed the pistol from the Major, a very unusual indecisiveness marking their behaviour. Then from behind us came a growl which swelled into loud shouting. The Russian prisoners were aroused and our guards became nervous. And then the groundswell of fury rose amongst us ordinary *Landsers,* our reaction, because of the enormity of the crime, being totally instinctive. Ignoring all the rules of military discipline and obedience, we moved up to the table, shouting loud abuse at our officers, who looked at us in silence and bewilderment as if not believing their eyes. We called them names, cowards, and demanded action against the Major. Then some of us, who were unarmed, including myself, walked over to meet the Russians and let them know that we were with them. The guards were shouting, but unable to do anything as we stood with the Russians, holding them by the shoulders as a gesture of comradeship. No one interfered. It was us who then decided to loosen the situation, having probably prevented a bloodbath, who shook hands with our Russian comrades and stepped back. It was one of the strangest confrontations I experienced in the whole of the Russian Campaign.

While the prisoners were led away, they kept looking back towards the body of their Colonel and as soon as they were out of sight, some of us received orders to quickly bury the Colonel further down by the brook. Later on, very much the worse for alcohol, a quarrel developed among the officers. The little Major just sat there with a bottle near by and said nothing.

It emerged that the officers differed in their opinion about what to do with the Russian position on the hill behind the village, less than a mile away. There was a bet between two officers as to whether the hill could be taken by frontal attack or not. All of us having much battle experience knew for sure that a frontal attack on such a hill in daylight condition would be pure madness. But they were the Staff officers who made the decisions and gave the commands, and we were the rabble who carried them out. Whatever we thought, made no difference.

The order which went out to the unit officers, who had reported to Divisional Staff, was short and there was no discussion. When Steffan came back he called the Lieutenants to order battle readiness. We joined forces with other units, and took up our positions at the foot of the hill. There was grumbling amongst us, and even Steffan looked unhappy. To top it all, as if it were all a kind of hunting game, a traditional Prussian attack bugle was sounded from the Staff and the attack got under way. As it happened, we smashed our attack up the hill on a wide front and were successful. Many of the Russians were killed or taken prisoner. But we too had losses, amongst them two of my friends.

Maybe one of the officers won a bottle of champagne or a hundred mark note changed hands — and as the night set in, we heard the officers singing, probably to celebrate the 'victory on the hill.' They sang a student song about Heidelberg, the University where, I knew, the philosophy of humanism had once been taught.

We went on realizing that Stalingrad, our principal target, was still several hundred kilometres away, and the Caucasus even further. There was talk that from there we would advance into the oil-fields of Iraq, and then towards Egypt, to meet up with Rommel and collect the British in a large bag. But that was all in the stars, all rumours.

We were attacking a small town when I received a nastly blow on the arm.

I looked around to see who had struck me, but when I then felt a stinging pain and saw a tear on my sleeve with blood on it, I knew that I had been hit. At first I panicked, but when I was taken at first by jeep and then lorry together with others, and dumped on the stone floor of a disused church, and was told by a medical orderly that there was nothing to worry about, I was much relieved. A short train transport on straw in covered wagons took us back to a *Lazarett* in a town called Stalino. Though an infection set in, I had a great time there. A few weeks rest from the front was worth a pot of gold.

Most of the hospital staff, including senior surgeons, were Russian. The treatment was efficient under tough war conditions, and when I was ready to leave, the Russian doctor said to me with a sly grin: 'Go east again, young man, after all, that is what you have come here for!' I was not sure whether I liked his remark, or indeed, whether I had any great wish to go east. After all I was not yet twenty years old, I wanted to live, not die.

Though I was fit enough to leave the *Lazarett,* I was not yet in a condition to rejoin my Division, which was then battling its way towards Rostov. I was sent to join a unit which was guarding a prison camp somewhere between the Donetz and the Dniepr. In flat country the large camp had been set up in the open. Kitchen, stores etc. were under canvas, while the uncounted thousands of prisoners were left with nothing to cover themselves with but what they could lay their hands on. Their rations were very meagre, and so, though not quite as bad, were ours. However, the summer weather was fine and the Russians, used to living rough were able to withstand the conditions. The whole camp was bounded by a large c' ·ular trench, which the prisoners were not allowed to approach. Within the camp, at one side, was a *Kolchose* consisting of a number of buildings. The entire *Kolchose* was ringed by rolls of barbed wire and had only one entrance which was guarded. Together with about a dozen other semi-fit invalids, I was assigned to guard this inner compound.

Guard duty generally was considered by most active soldiers as a mind-killing exercise and a punishment. Above all it was boring, and the goings on in the *Kolchose* compoud were a decidedly strange affair. The clue, I suppose, was to be found in Hitler's infamous *'Kommissar Befehl'*, according to which all political prisoners, *Politruks* (Political Army officers) and other members of the Communist Party were to be shot. For the Communists, the *'Kommissar Befehl'* was what the 'Final Solution' was to the Jews. I suppose that at that time most of us accepted that Communism was a crime, that Communists were criminals, and that there was no legal necessity to prove any further individual guilt. It dawned on me that I was now guarding a camp which had been set up to erase the evil of Communism.

Of all the prisoners who walked into the *Kolchose* compound, none walked out again. Whether they knew this would be their fate, I am not sure. Quite a number of them had been given away by their fellow prisoners in the large outer camp, and even in doubtful cases, when they claimed that they had never belonged to the Party or were Communists at all — or even that they were anti-Communists — they still did not walk out again. We being only the guards, the compound was run by a small detachment of the *Sicherheits Dienst*, the

SD which was under the command of the SS equivalent of a Major. In each case there was a vague investigation, after which the execution was carried out, always at the same place against a wall of a burnt-out cottage, which could not be seen from anywhere outside. The burial place, consisting of a few large trenches, was further to the rear.

Having soaked up a full Nazi 'education' at school and in the Hitler Youth, this first experience of direct contact with Communists in the flesh was very baffling. The prisoners who were daily brought into our compound, either alone or in small groups, were very different types of person from what I had expected. Indeed, they were different from the masses of the prisoners outside who on the whole looked and behaved like typical East European peasants. What struck me most about these *Politruks* and Party members was their intelligence and pride. I never, or hardly ever, noticed any of them whining or complaining, and they never asked for anything for themselves. When their time for execution came, and I saw many go, they did so with their heads held high. Almost all of them impressed me as persons whom one could trust, and I was sure, had we been living under peaceful conditions, that I would have liked some of them to be my friends.

Our daily routine was monotonous. One either stood at the gate with someone else for a couple of hours, or walked about the compound alone, the heavy loaded rifle always hanging ready over one's shoulder. Usually there were about a dozen to twenty 'patients' under our care. Their 'home' was a cleaned-out pigsty, which was itself surrounded, within the compound, by barbed wire. It was a prison within a prison within a prison. Our system of guarding them gave them virtually no chance to escape and on the whole we had little trouble with them. Since we were amongst them during all hours of the day and the night, we came to know them all by sight and often by name, and of course, we were the ones who handed them over for 'investigation' and delivered them for their last walk to the firing squad.

One of the prisoners had a fair knowledge of German, which he had learnt at school. I have forgotten his family name but his first name was Boris. As I spoke Russian fairly well in a pidgin fashion we had no difficulty conversing on most subjects. Boris was a Lieutenant, a *Politruk*, and about two years older than me. We discovered that we had both learnt the trade of locksmith, he in Gorlovka-Artemovsk Region in a large engineering complex, and I at the Railway workshops in Hamburg. On our advance I had passed through his town. He was blond, about six feet tall and had laughing blue eyes which even in this desperate situation had not lost their friendly twinkle. Often, especially at nights, I felt drawn to chat with him. As I called him Boris anyway, he had asked me if he could call me by my first name and I think that it surprised us both to find how easily we could get on with each other. We mostly talked about our families, our homes, our school and apprentice days. I knew the names of his brothers and sisters, how old they were, what his parents did for a living, and even some of their personal habits. He naturally was very worried about how they were faring under German occupation, and I was in no position to console him. He even gave me their address and asked me, that if ever I was going their way, to look them up and tell them. 'But tell them what?', I thought, and we both knew that I would never go, and that therefore his family would never find out what had happened to their Boris. In turn he learned all about my family and all the things which were close to my heart. I told him how in a harmless way I had had a girlfriend for whom I had felt much love. He smiled understandingly and told me that he too had had a girlfriend who had been a student. We felt very close at moments like this — until we suddenly then both realized what a gulf there was between us, that I was standing there with a rifle on my shoulder and that he was my prisoner. I knew, of course, that he would never hold a girl in his arms again, but was not quite sure whether he was aware of that. I knew that his only crime had been that he was a soldier and a *Politruk*, and my instinct told me all right that there was something very wrong somewhere.

Surprisingly, we talked very little about life in the army, and as regards politics we found we had no bridge of common understanding, not even a common denominator from where together we could analyse. So close in so many human ways, we both realized that in that we were a world apart.

Then came Boris's last night. I had found out from the SD that it was his turn to be shot in the morning. He had been to 'investigation' in the afternoon, and I could see that he had been beaten and hit in the face. He had also been injured in his side, but he said nothing — and neither did I — for what was the point? I am not sure whether he was aware that he was to be shot at sunrise, and I certainly did not tell him. But being an intelligent man, he must have come to some conclusion on why his fellow prisoners were led away after investigation and never returned.

I was on night duty from two to four, and the night was beautifully warm and quiet. The air was full of the music of nature, with the frogs in the nearby pond croaking as if in concert. Boris was sitting on the straw outside in the pigsty, with his back leaning against the wall playing, very quietly on his small mouth-organ, which fitted unseen in his hands. It was his only possession left, everything else had been taken from him. The tune he played when I arrived was beautiful, a typical Russian melancholic one, something about the wide steppe and love. But then there were shouts from some of his fellow prisoners inside, telling him to shut up, and he looked at me, should he ignore it and go on playing? When I shrugged my shoulder, he knocked the mouth-organ in the palm of his hand and said: '*Nitchevo*, let's talk instead!' I rested my elbow on the wall and looked down on him. There was a deep tension in me, and I did not quite know what to talk about. I was sad, wanted to be friendly and perhaps help — and did not know how. Why it happened, I do not really know, but somehow he looked in a challenging way at me and for the first time our conversation turned to politics. Perhaps deep down I wanted an explanation from him at this late hour, wanted to know what it was he so fervently believed in — or at least admit to me that he had been wrong in his belief all along.

'And what about your World Revolution?' I said 'it is all over now, is it not, and it has been a criminal nonsense — a conspiracy against freedom and peace from the very beginning...?' At that time, let us remember, it looked very much as if Germany would triumph over Russia. He kept quiet for a while, just sitting there on his heap of straw, still fiddling with his mouth-organ. I would have been satisfied, had he shown me some anger. And when he raised himself very slowly and came to the wall to look me straight into my eyes, I could see that he was very agitated indeed. His voice was calm, though with a shade of sadness and disappointment, but not for himself — but for me.

'Genry!', he said: 'You told me all about your life, you come as I do from the poor, the working people. You are friendly enough and not stupid — but on the other hand you are very stupid because you have learnt nothing from your life. I can clearly see that your brainwashers have done a very successful job on you for you have swallowed so totally the propaganda fed into your mind. What is so very tragic is that you are supporting ideas which by their very nature are directed against your own fundamental interests and which have made you a willing, sad tool in their evil hands. The World Revolution is ongoing history. Even if you win the war, which I don't think you will, the World Revolution will not and cannot be stopped by military means. Your very powerful army can do much harm to us, can kill many of our people — but it cannot kill ideas! Its movement might seem dormant to you at the moment, but it is there and will come to the fore again out of the awakening of the poor, the downtrodden ordinary people the world over in Africa, the Americas, in Asia and Europe too. People in their masses will one day understand that it is the power of capital over them which not only oppresses and robs them, but stifles their human potential, which either uses or discards them as mere pawns to make monetary profits out of them. Once the people grasp that idea, it will mature into an almost material force in popular uprisings like spreading wild-fires and will do what has to be done in the name of humanity. It will not be Russia who will do it for them, although the Russian working people were the first who have broken the chains. The people of the world will do it for themselves in their own countries, against their own oppressors, in their own ways and in their own time!'

His outburst gave me no chance to interrupt and it allowed no argument. Even though he had spoken quietly, it shook me to the core. Nobody had ever touched a chord of understanding in me that way and I felt naked and defence-less. And to give me the final knock, he pointed to my rifle, saying that 'that thing' could do nothing against his ideas. 'And if you think that you have the intellectual capacity to respond to me meaningfully', he concluded, 'please don't use any of your silly slogans about country, freedom and God!'

Anger, almost suffocatingly, welled up in me. My natural reaction was to put him in his place. But then I thought better of it, I remembered that within a few hours he would be dead, and that perhaps this had been his way to take a last swipe at me. My guard duty was now up. And not wanting to make a final show of saying '*Do Swydanya*' or '*Auf Wiedersehen*' to him, I gave him one last look, perhaps with a mixture of anger and sadness in which he might have detected a glimmer of almost lost humanism, turned on my heel and slowly walked over to the stables which were our quarters. Boris did not move at all, not one sound came from him and I did not turn once in my stride. But I knew for sure, I felt it, that he was watching me intently as I trotted away from him with my ridiculous rifle. And in the horizon there rose the first light of the coming morning.

We guards also bedded down on straw, and I always loved my first sleep after coming in from duty. But this morning I could not sleep. I did not even undress, just lay there and watched dawn creeping up. I twisted and turned, felt sorry for Boris — and also for myself. There was so much I simply could not understand. And then, with the sun already up, I heard the shots, a short salvo, that was all.

I got up at once and walked over to the place where I knew the graves were ready. Morning had arrived in all its pristine beauty and the birds were singing as if nothing had happened. I met the firing squad coming back with their rifles, looking bored. They just nodded at me, obviously wondering why I was going in that direction. There were two or three prisoners already shovelling earth over the bodies. Beside Boris there were three others, already partially covered. I could still recognize him, his tunic looked crumpled and his boots had been taken off but he still wore his leather belt, and I could see blood on it. The diggers looked at me, obviously wondering what I was doing there. Their expression was sullen, but I could also see fear and hatred in their eyes. I wanted to ask them what had happened to Boris's mouth-organ, had they taken it or was it still in his pocket? But then I changed my mind, thinking that they might suspect me of wanting to steal from the dead, and I walked away from it all, back to my stable, and I tried to get some sleep.

I was much relieved when shortly afterwards I was certified 'fit for front-line service' again, and set off to rejoin my Division, which was hammering at so many gates. There, at least, things were straight-forward. Hard and tough as life was, there were no disturbing experiences to deceive one's mind and conscience.

The lads were glad to see me back. With the Volga now so close, the Russians were fighting fiercely and showing what their army was made of. Several in my company, all close friends, had fallen. Our CO, *Oberleutnant* Steffan, had been shot in the head. As much as it hurt me, I could understand all that. But the execution of Boris — why? It seemed like putting Jesus on the cross all over again.

The sun had been beating down for weeks and the steppe was parched, with the dust settling everywhere. Though still going forward, we had many a hard nut to crack. The early days of 'Barbarossa', when we had had them on the run and our military superiority was only questioned by fools, were over. Having had to swallow devastating catastrophes in the beginning, the Red Army had learnt much.

After having taken one small town and settled in its main square for a respite, we noticed a large concrete building with big red crosses daubed on its walls. We wondered whether it was genuine, and a few of us went in to find out. From a large reception hall we walked straight into a hospital ward and were surprised to find it still in operation. On each side along the walls was a long row of beds, most of which were occupied by elderly female patients who stared at us with a mixture of fear and helplessness. Everything was tidy and clean, the floor was highly polished and our nailed boots made a loud clicking noise. I walked up to a group of staff in white coats who were standing huddled together at the far end of the ward, and asked them who they were. They were doctors and nurses, all of them female. I wanted to know why they had not evacuated before our arrival, and they told me that it had all happened so quickly, and that amidst the general chaos their hospital transport arrangements had broken down. We left it at that and walked out, and though aware that all hospitals were taken over by German authorities, I do not know what happened to any of them.

Moving out of town, we were suddenly attacked by low-flying Soviet fighter bombers, while a small group of Russian prisoners were being led to the rear. One of the bombs fell right in the middle of their column. The result was horrible. A couple of our guards and many of the prisoners were killed outright. The rest, every single one of them, were badly injured. Bright red blood was all over the road and there was screaming and crying. Some had had limbs torn off; after a couple of our medical orderlies had rushed over and had established that the German guards were dead, they were called back from the carnage and left the Russians to their fate. Some women came out from cottages along the road and brought containers with water and linen to tear for bandages. Several begged us to help, and when one of our lads went over to help, he too was called back by an officer, who told him that all this had been caused by a Russian bomb and was no concern of ours.

Later we reached the banks of a river, which I think was the Mius. To our surprise we received orders to take up defence positions on its bank from where we could overlook its course and also approaches from both sides. Shortly after a Pionier unit (engineers) arrived with heavy gear and set up a pontoon bridge. Several anti-aircraft guns were assigned to our Battalion, and we were told to get ready for long-overdue Panzer repair and maintenance, and at the same time to guard the pontoon bridge. We all liked this, and quickly set up our tents amongst the willows beside the river. Before long, most of us were swimming in the cooling water.

No roads came anywhere near our bridge across the steppe and vehicles of all sorts which were looking for a crossing point came from all directions. Apart from a Cossack village a few kilometres up the river, there was no human habitation anywhere. *Reichsmarschall* Goering, who at that time was in charge of the occupied countries' economies, had issued orders that our armies should live off the land as far as possible. Therefore, though we were aware that the parched steppe soil had left its village populations poor, we organized a quick raid up the river to replenish our dwindling supplies. Realizing that we were going to stay here for a while, we spread out in leisurely comfort in this idyllic spot and settled down to a life of rest, tranquility and little work.

The Soviet Command soon found out about our bridge and sent over a couple of raiding Sturmoviks which, when faced by our onslaught of Flak, found the instinct of self-preservation preferable to brute courage. Of our our Messerschmitts, which were probably heavily engaged nearer the Stalingrad battlefront, we saw very little. What bothered us a great deal, was a type of slow-flying plane which appeared with sickening regularity almost every night. Every German soldier anywhere on the Eastern Front knew it by its nickname of 'sewing machine', because of the peculiar whining noise of its engine. Because it never appeared in daylight, none of us really knew what exactly it looked like. Because it flew so low, our anti-aircraft fire could never effectively aim at it and its main trick was to approach its target with its engine switched off. Sometimes one could see the pilot leaning out, throwing hand-grenades and small bombs over the side, and we could hear him shouting insults at us. Of course we opened fire with our rifles, but I cannot remember a single case of a 'sewing machine' having been shot down.

What was even more upsetting was a mysterious performance which evaded our discovery for some considerable time. Almost every day one of the vehicles for whose safe crossing we were responsible, was either blown up or received some damage from a cleverly dug in *Tellermine* (plate mine). Someone dug them in at night, but as there was no road leading to our bridge, the large funnel-shaped area by which the vehicles approached was very difficult to guard. We knew that our Commandant had received a severe dressing down from Division because of these losses — which he naturally passed on to us, and we considered it a personal challenge to catch the blasted culprit. Then one moonless night success came our way! We had put out two extra guards to watch the village who had followed a small lone figure carefully moving across the steppe. And when they finally pounced, there was no doubt that they had caught the right one all right. It was a shrunken peasant woman of over sixty who had a plate mine and a spade dangling from a rope tied around her waist.

With the sun rising beautifully, getting out of my tent to wash in the river, I was surprised to see the old woman sitting under the willow tree with her hands tied behind the trunk. When I offered her the morning greeting she did not respond. Everything about her was worn, her clothes, her hands and above all her face. She showed all the signs of the hard struggle required to make a living out of the poor steppe soil. Her hair once blond, was now grey and tied together on the top behind. She had a slight hunchback, and while extreme poverty was written all over her, she somehow did not appear unkempt.

Seeing me standing there, one of the guards who had been sitting on the pontoon came up and told me what she had been up to. She watched my reaction closely and though of course I could show no sympathy for her, there was something about her which fascinated me. When I remarked that I was glad that we had caught her, her only response was to screw up her face and spit in my direction. I asked her for her name and she said 'Galina.' 'Galina what?' 'Galina!' she said, 'and that is all what you will get out of me!' Then as an afterthought she added 'and I have three sons who are all soldiers in the army!' Together with pride, there was a threat in her voice, as if to say 'and they surely will get you for this!'

It was still early morning when she was taken to the log cabin which we used as a command and map room. Our then Commander, a Major Matzen, a landowner from Schleswig-Holstein and approaching fifty years of age, who was conducting the questioning, was a decent man. With the evidence so overwhelming, the entire procedure took no more than five minutes. When I saw her coming out I was sure that Galina had not been beaten, nor had she been tortured, but Matzen had been able to give only one sentence, under the circumstances.

It was a rather pathetic sight, and also disturbing, to watch her being led from the cabin, walking between two tall strapping guards almost double her size. Her shoes were made of straw, and one of the laces had become undone, and she found it difficult to keep it on her foot. With her hunchback it was not easy for her to throw her head back, but she somehow managed to present us with a show of pride which stopped our silly jokes. Taken to the field kitchen, she refused food but accepted a drink, and watching her all the time, I could not help but to recognize her great courage in maintaining her spirit, alone amongst enemy soldiers who, she knew, would show her no mercy. Then one of the guards called me over to translate. She asked whether as a last wish she could go down to the river beside which she had been born, and had lived all her life. We watched her go down to the water's edge and none of us said a word. She put her hands together as if in prayer, and while there was moistness in her eyes, I could hear something like '*do swydania, Mius, spasiba*' ('goodbye, Mius, thank you'). She took a last look up and down the flow of the water, then tied her scarf around her head as if to make herself look nice for an important occasion, turned firmly around to walk up the slope towards us and said that she was ready.

While all this was going on someone had nailed a beam to the side of the cabin and I could see that she watched when a rope was slung around it and a noose tied in its end; I could detect not the slightest sign of fear. A couple of ammunition boxes were placed under the rope as a platform. She was too small to climb easily on to them, but determinedly refused any help, fell off once and hurt her leg. In the end, a guard lifted her up and that was that. She looked around her towards the river, towards the horizon beyond which her village was — and then down on us. There was utter stillness. When the guard started to put the noose around her neck, she grabbed it and as a last proud gesture pulled it out of his hand which made him almost fall off the box and made him look ridiculous. And then, with all the contempt her face and voice could muster, she spat out to us and shouted in a high pitched voice: 'Swines, Nazi swines! You all are so stupid! Long live the Revolution! Lenin will live! Down with you! You are the pest of the earth!'

Having had to listen to all this, Major Matzen became impatient. I sat right behind where he was standing and noticed that he nodded to the guards to get on with the job. He paid her the respect, though, of raising his hand to his field cap in a military salute. The guard then stepped down and kicked the top box away. There was a soft thud, and no other sound.

Matzen turned round to some of us, including me and said in a toneless voice: 'Get her down and dig her in and do it quickly!' I untied the rope from the beam, and we carefully carried her down the slope to just above the level of the water, laid her down and dug her grave. Looking her over, she had no personal belongings on her, no ring, nothing. It was perhaps from sheer laziness and because the sun was shining so caressingly warmly that we did not dig deep. When we laid her in it, I put the rope beside her, I did not quite know why — as an indication, perhaps, of how she had died. When shovelling the earth back on her, it crossed my mind that surely someone in the village was anxiously waiting for her; and when I put a large stone on the soft earth to show where they could find her after we had gone, my mates nodded their silent agreement.

The call came that morning coffee was ready. It was nice to sit in the sun on the grass and on the pontoons to have our breakfast. Some were already swimming and shouted back to us how beautifully mild the water was. The water of Galina's River Mius! We then heard the motors and shortly afterwards saw the whirling dust out of which a couple of lorries and a jeep came tumbling down to us to cross on the pontoons. One of the drivers shouted something about the danger of being blown up by plate mines. We called back to him that there was no need to worry anymore, there would be no more mines because we had caught the culprit who had dug them in. It was all right now. Justice had been done...!

From the Mius we headed south east, and took the city of Rostov on the mouth of the River Don sometime in July 1942, when the summer was at its hottest. Many dead civilians lay in the streets where they had fallen. There was no one to pick them up, and the summer heat was turning their skin dark blue, bloating their bodies. There was a horrible smell in the air. Mail had come through and I received a letter from my mother. Though we were not allowed to mention place names in our letters, mother had a very fair idea where I was. I had written to her about the great feeling of pride it gave me when taking the enemy's cities, towns and villages; she reminded me in her letter that there were people living in those places, ordinary people, men, women and children, and asked whether I had ever given any thought to what my 'success' meant to their lives. Mother was a committed Christian and she sometimes managed to plant seeds of doubt in my young Nazi mind, which annoyed me.

Rostov looked a very modern, clean and airy city, much more so than the older industrial towns we had passed through in the Donetz Region. The main streets were wide and in some there were special tram-lines in tree-lined central lanes. There were many parks with seats and bandstands in, and one could see that people had cared. Even after we had taken the city as a whole, remnants of the Red Army, actively supported by workers' battalions and civilians, were still resisting from the parks, and we had considerable difficulty in dislodging them.

With our Panzers and other vehicles we pulled into a modern industrial estate with large empty machine halls. Away from it were new housing estates, and further on was a big sports complex with all sorts of halls and recreation facilities such as canteens, shower rooms, gymnasiums etc. We had been led not to expect facilities like these in Communist Russia, in some ways we found these arrangements superior to what we had been used to back home. Further on there was a large stadium with red ash running tracks. Much activity was going on around there, and special SS *Einsatztruppen* were herding male civilians on to the football pitch. At least a hundred of them had already been gathered, and new groups were arriving all the time. We had just taken the city and it struck me how quickly and efficiently the grip of iron rule was implemented. An SS guard told us that they were engineers, university people and others from the intelligentsia, who were to be investigated. Like at a football match, we were leaning over the heavy wooden crowd barriers, watching the goings on with much curiosity but little comprehension. We heard some remonstrating with the guards in an appealing manner, wanting to know why they had been taken there, and saying that they had committed no crimes. But the guards pushed them away and told them to shut up. An elderly man in a white shirt, who seemed to have given one of the guards no peace, had been hit in the face and was sitting now on the grass, nursing his bleeding nose while others gathered around to help him. For us young soldiers it was difficult not to feel some sympathy for the civilians on the pitch. Many of their womenfolk and children arrived to bring them food and clothes, which the guards accepted and handed over, though they did not allow them to meet or to talk to each other. A woman with her teenage daughter came to us and asked for information regarding her husband. Of course, we could not tell her anything. And when we told her that we were *Wehrmacht* and her husband was in the hands of the SS, I noticed how frightened she became. I saw them both walking away and crying. When we left Rostov a couple of days later, these people were still there and I do not know what happened to them.

We were soon advancing again, this time in a northerly direction. In front of us was the flat country, the steppe of the Great Bend of the River Don. Not having access to any maps, we ordinary soldiers did not really know where we were. Few of us could even pronounce most of the place names correctly, not to say anything about spelling. At this time of the year the mornings in the steppe were exceptionally beautiful, the first sunrays struggling through the dawn mists to then devour them. The dew settled the summer dusts, and everything smelled fresh and all the artificial noises were swallowed up by the soft sounds of nature. Breaking camp always had a special atmosphere. The cooks were woken up early by the guards, and when the rest of the company rose from their slumbers, the tents pulled down to be packed away, and the first engines revved up for a test, the call for early coffee was passed on all over the camp. And after that was breakfast, and then the real day began.

The general plan of campaign was to reach the River Don at all its points, to then cross it and move on to Stalingrad. And once there, we arrogantly assumed that we would have destroyed the Soviet fighting power in the south of Russia. We were a very young army, with an average age of just over 20, and the thought of possible defeat had never been allowed to enter our minds. After weeks of blazing sunshine with only the occasional thunderstorm in between, the earth was baked, and drought gaps were opening up. The sparse steppe grass was brown and the steppe itself was often on fire, sending columns of smoke into the pale blue summer sky which could be seen from miles around.

Moving steadily northwards to reach the northern bend of the river, we crossed the paths of the bulk of our army, mainly Panzer Divisions, which were moving due east on a general course towards the large town of Kalatsch on the most easterly point of the River Don. And from Kalatsch, we knew, it was only fifty kilometres as the crow flies to Stalingrad and the Volga. With all our confidence, however, we were under no illusions that these last fifty kilometres might be the hardest of all. On our way, we met Hungarian, Romanian and Italian Divisions, which apparently all wanted a bite at the Russian cake, and once got tangled up with a unit consisting entirely of Slovaks. We never quite knew how to behave towards our allies. Apart from the obvious barrier of language, there was also one of arrogance, which was entirely of our own making. As far as we were concerned, our racial superiority over them was a fact, and that our military efficiency was greater than theirs, was similarly obvious. We considered them to be unreliable, and always felt uneasy when they were operating on our flanks. It was noticeable that the Red Army must have had the same thoughts about them, because whenever they chose to mount a counter attack, they usually hammered into our weakest link, which was the section of our allies.

Many of us were suffering badly from diarrhoea, which was causing a serious manning problem along the entire front. Only the very worst cases were taken out of the front line, while the rest of us had to make do with swallowing a very dusty kind of coal powder, which seemed to make little difference at all. Especially when I was driving my Panzer, it was quite a harrowing experience when I had to empty my bowels. In battle it was simply out of the question, but otherwise I would stop. But sitting there with one's trousers down, trying to do one's best quickly is no laughing matter when being watched and urged on by the crew to get on with it. To prevent the disease from spreading, we were under strict instruction to always take a short spade with us, but through my vision slit I saw many hilarious sights of brave soldiers, hanging on for dear life to the turret of a moving Panzer with their trousers round their ankles and screwing up their faces in a desperate attempt to do the almost impossible.

Though the Soviet Air Force was an ever-present threat, our own Messerschmitts were at that time in command of the sky. When they came low towards us, twisting, we looked out for the short written messages which they dropped, informing us of the general situation and warning about possible dangers. We learned that the Red Army was in full though orderly retreat, that many of their units had crossed the Don, but that they also had taken up strong bridgehead positions on our own side. Almost daily we saw some T-34 tanks with which we had short fire exchanges, but mostly without any results. More than anything they were a nuisance, holding up our advance for short intervals, which was probably the purpose of their operation.

Rolling along like that we were on the whole in a cocky mood which sometimes led us to take risks to gain time. Bringing up a battalion with all its support units is a ponderous process at the best of times. Our timetable was tight, and all too often our non-combat support vehicles were far too close behind us. It was August by the time we were approaching our operational target in the northern section against the Don Bend. We were well aware that the relatively easy time we had of rolling across the steppe was almost over. For the river, we anticipated, was something like the 'rope of the ring' for the retreating Russians.

It was getting dark when the information was passed through that we would soon enter a village where we would stay the night. Aerial reconnaissance reported that, though they had spotted no enemy troops in the village itself, a defence line had been set up behind it not far from the river. The weather was sultry and a pitching summer wind at times disturbed the calm. A short angry thunderstorm had lashed down on us earlier in the afternoon. The heavens had suddenly opened up then, but the thirsty earth had quickly soaked up the moisture, which was now rising in layers of damp mist all around us. We had witnessed beautiful lightning flashes, but then the dark, tumbling clouds had rolled away again, it had stayed hot and there was little relief for our prickly nerves. When the first cottages came into sight, we stopped. Our officers were called together for planning and instruction. I watched how they listened into the still night and scanned the entrance to the village with their field glasses. I switched my engine off and everything looked serene and peaceful.

As a boy I had read Michael Sholokhov's book, *And quiet flows the Don* in which the description of the unrolling revolution in this very area had greatly impressed me. Sholokhov himself was said to be living in one of the Cossack villages around here, and for all I knew, it could well be this one. Sholokhov's figures had impressed me by their fascinating earthiness and given me perhaps a glimpse of the enormous human strength of the Russian people. Had we awakened a sleeping giant? Never in my life had I dreamed of coming into the land of the Don, and I pondered that perhaps I would have preferred to have come as a visiting friend than as a conquering soldier. But then the command came to move on, and soon we were passing the first white-washed cottages of this village which we did not even know the name of. We were strangely unsure about it all, there was an eerie atmosphere in the air somehow. But then I thought that maybe it was just my tingling nerves.

Our head of advance consisted of about eight Panzers, and three abreast we nosed our way cautiously into the unknown. Our Commander, *Hauptmann* Zet, obviously relying on our Panzer strength, had made no attempt at reconnaisance, and neither had he given orders for our *Tross* (supply unit) to stay behind. Our whole column therefore, Panzers, lorries and jeeps, were all together, everyone looking forward to a good night's sleep. Being the right of the three front Panzers and moving close to a cottage wall, I had pulled my periscope out of its slide in order to see better. Apart from ours, there was no movement anywhere, we could hear no sound, not even that of a barking dog. And yet, there was something undefinable in the air, a kind of weaving, which told us that the village was far from dead. Life was ticking away close by — but where? Had our *Luftwaffe* been right that the Red Army, on their way to the river, really had passed through the village? We had now moved far enough for our lorries to have reached the first cottages behind us. Everything still seemed all right! *Hauptmann* Zet was in the Panzer next to me, and my Commandant quietly called down to me to move a bit faster. And it was at that moment when it all began to happen, when all hell suddenly broke loose.

I could hear the metallic clicks of the bullets hitting the bodywork of my Panzer, and then there was a dull explosion of hand-grenades. Having foolishly made sitting ducks of ourselves, we now wondered whether the Russians had anything stronger to deal with us than infantry weapons for piercing our armour. The maddest thing about it all was that we were unable to use our heavy firing power, and were effectively cut off from what was going on behind us. Ivan had fooled us again. He had patiently waited until our Panzers were safely out of the way — and then had opened up on our lorries. There were a couple of powerful explosions, and I saw the reflection of fierce fire against the white cottages before me. Our lorries were burning, and our gunner looking back from the open hatch reported cries of agony, chaos and frustration. There was no shortage of swear words and *Hauptmann* Zet's name was on all our lips. Unable to move forward into the unknown, neither could we move back because of the lorries behind us. Our turret had turned back but our gunner said that he simply had nothing to aim at.

With a single light in our cabin, we began to quarrel amongst ourselves. As so often in tight situations, I felt like emptying my bowels, and when my Commandant ordered me to move forward and then turn, I shouted back at him and refused to move. When he reminded me that he 'was giving me an order', I still did nothing. I respected him afterwards for never mentioning our 'misunderstanding', which could otherwise have had serious consequences for me.

Quite suddenly, in the same way as it had started, the fusillade stopped. The whole thing had lasted no more than ten minutes. There were shouts in Russian from the sides behind the cottages, and our gunner thought that he could make out some moving shadows. After a longish while of waiting there was a knock from outside, a *Feldwebel* had come to tell us to pull up into the village and, probably to forestall any ironic remarks, he assured us that no enemy soldier was left amongst the cottages. The street widened out into an open green with a pond in the middle, around which we pulled up to form up a hedgehog defence. Behind us several or our lorries were still burning, with a couple of thatched cottages close by also on fire. There were a number of dead and more wounded, and an ugly atmosphere of suspicion and accusation. None of us was in any doubt that, had ordinary military procedures been carried out, this catastrophe would never had happened.

Even with the fires still burning fiercely, life quickly returned to 'normal'. Our officers always saw to that. Someone on the other side of the pond had taken out a mouth-organ, and I laid back in the grass and looked at the skies. Not far from us, we knew, was that Russian infantry troop which had given us such a dreadful drubbing, moving towards the river.

After the event, of course, everyone was wise, with all the jigsaw pieces coming together. When the lorries had reached the cottages, Arthur, our cook, had stepped out, and while attempting to kick one of the doors open, a shot had been fired from within with Arthur falling on his face and bedlam following.

Apart from the obvious catastrophe, there was a very disturbing side story to it all. When Arthur's body was picked up, his pockets were found to be full of bars of chocolate! We had had no chocolate for weeks, and had been told that no supplies had come through for us. And it was then that some of us remembered that some of our officers had eaten chocolate which had the same wrappings as Arthur's.

It had gone close to midnight when we laid out our dead in freshly-dug graves by the side of the green. A young Lieutenant said a few appropriate words about each of them, but when it came to Arthur, he only mentioned his name and rank — no more.

I noticed an old woman, beckoning me from the door of one of the cottages behind. I walked over to her, and found her to be of that very motherly type, with kind eyes and deep furrows criss-crossing her face. Terrified out of her life as she was, she asked me whether she was allowed to walk over to the burning cottages. I thought I had better walk with her. A deep sobbing shook her body as she tried to tell me about a young mother with children in the fiercely burning cottage in front of us. All its beams had fallen in and were sticking out of the glowing ashes like a grotesque monument to human madness. There was no chance of anyone being alive in there, and as she walked unsteadily around the heap she tried to reassure herself, pressing me for my positive opinion that no one had burnt to death in there. But neither did she have any idea where those people could be. Walking back, I asked her what had happened in the night. All she was able to tell me was that a Russian troop had arrived, and then us, and then all the shooting and killing had started and that she had been very frightened.

To get some sleep I joined two of my friends, who were on guard at the northern edge of the village. The terrain in front of us was flat, but rising slightly to the river; there were no trees, no bushes, nothing, just the wide expanse. With them I felt secure and when I woke up at early dawn with hardly a sound coming from anywhere, I found it hard to recall the dreadful happenings of only a few hours previously. A petrol lorry then arrived out of the steppe, and with it life began to pulse again, and especially for the drivers, there were so many things to do. After breakfast our Lieutenants came back with their situation reports and told us that we were going to attack at ten o'clock. The River Don was less than five kilometres to the north, and the general idea was to swarm out from the village, to storm up the rise to the Russian line just behind the rim, to break through, of course, and to race through and with the mighty momentum to reach the bank of the river in one go. One of our PaK drivers had been wounded in the mêlée last night, and as I was the only reserve man with the experience to drive an open truck in battle, I was told to take over while someone else was to drive my Panzer.

The preparations were quickly concluded but we were unhappy to have had no chance to properly reconnoitre the area between us and the Don. Though the *Luftwaffe* had given us some warning of heavy flak close by the river, everything else was rather vague. Knowing that the infantry troop last night had had no anti-tank weapons, we assumed that there would be none on the slope before us either; in any case, we did not want to allow them any breathing space, and felt that we had to settle a final score with them once and for all.

By ten o'clock, the sun was well up in the sky, and to our advantage, slightly behind us. Everything seemed perfect, there was no sign of the Russians. The Panzers had spread out at the village edge to form their battle formation, while our half-tracks had lined up slightly behind them. Some of our infantry was to move up with the Panzers, and the rest was to follow in our wake. When our Panzers started off with a mighty roar, I too put my foot on the pedal to add to that aggressive 'Stuka' noise, to irritate the enemy. Following in the wake of the Panzers, I thought how ugly they looked, prowling like wobbling toads and puffing out blue smoke. There was something inhuman about them which I had never really seen in that light before. With the five-centimetre PAK hooked up on my half-track, we all four sat tightly together, heads down, staring past the Panzers to the sky-line, still a few hundred metres away, behind which we knew the Russians were waiting for us. We had no illusions that the next few minutes would prove decisive, one way or another. The plan, all thought out by *Hauptmann* Zet, was that once the Panzers had taken up commanding firing positions on the crest, we should follow into the gaps with our PAKs to cover their next move ahead, and the infantry was to protect all round against small arm disturbances, However, as we were to learn, the Russians also had plans.

When most of the Panzers had reached the crest, and were in full view, there was a hellish boom, the origin of which we were in no doubt. The Russians had a 7.62cm PAK in a well-camouflaged position; the effect was immediate and disastrous. Standing against the sky in superb target position, our Panzers had no chance. Two of them went up in flames almost at once, with none of the crews able to bale out, two others were in trouble and had to be abandoned, while the rest hurriedly reversed, then turned and now came rumbling past us. With commanding Lieutenant shouting in near panic, our crews unhooked and positioned the PAKs to cover the rim, should the Russians follow, while we drivers raced off down the slopes behind the Panzers to the regrouping point on the edge of the village. The mood there was one of utter frustration and bitterness, and at that moment we could hear the dull thuds from exploding ammunition in the two burning Panzers, with seven of our friends in them.

For the second time in less than a day, *Hauptmann Zet* had led us to catastrophe. When he had come to our unit it was known that he was a personal protégée of General von Appell, the Division's Commander. That, and his upper-class accent and arrogant bearing, and his all-too-obvious desire to win the Iron Cross, had made him few friends, and certainly none in the ranks. Even in battle situations like this one, he insisted on being addressed in the third person, and if one spoke to him, it was always '*Herr Hauptmann*'.

By now it had gone midday, and *Hauptmann* Zet again called the officers together for situation report and to issue new orders. When the Lieutenants came back to pass these deliberations on to us, we didn't believe our ears. In essence there was nothing wrong with ordering our infantry to dig in and man machine-gun nests in between and around our PAK positions, but to send all our PaK drivers, myself included, with them as gun reserve and ammunition carriers, was unheard of in military practice. Any emergency situation in which the PaKs had to be pulled out at speed, and the drivers first called back from the gun nests several hundreds of metres away, would have developed into another catastrophe. But there it was.

With the temperature soaring, two foot soldiers and myself crawled towards the line between the PAKs, dragging our machine gun, machine pistols, rifles, short spades and two heavy ammunition boxes with us. We had to traverse an uneven field, which was awkward, and a great strain on the arms. When we reached our position, we found that the chalky earth was very hard, yet we dared not stand up or kneel. All the time we were digging, our guns from behind were raking the enemy positions beyond the crest, forcing Ivan to keep his head down. We were slightly in advance of our PAKs, and were not much more than a couple of hundred yards from the Russians.

Situations like this sometimes provoke a strange psychological response. Being well aware that our opponents were suffering the same hardships in their own foxholes, the personal feeling of hatred for them completely evaporated and was to a large extent transferred to our officers, especially *Hauptmann* Zet.

Once we had finished our shallow hole, having used the thrown-out earth as protection in front, and spread out blankets on which to stretch, we found it quite comfortable. Food was brought up to us, and when evening came and we felt a little bored, we put our hands to our mouths and shouted across: 'Ivan, Ivan', plus something rude. They never failed to shout back, sometimes calling us 'Fritz', sometimes 'Michel', and *'Voyna njet chorosho!'* (war is no good). We knew from previous experiences that our officers did not like us to take part in these verbal exchanges. They wanted us to fight the enemy, not to talk to him, but being at the rear, they could do nothing about it. On the whole, the Russians gave us peace. There was the occasional rifle shot from either side, and sometimes a flare, when we kept our heads down and did not move. Though we could not see the enemy positions, we knew from the small-arms fire exactly where they were. Amongst ourselves we had arranged for two of us to sleep and for one to keep an eye on the line on the crest. At dark it was boring, and once when I woke up, I realized that all three of us had been asleep. But then, with other foxholes around, as well as the PAK positions, it would have been highly unlikely for Ivan to have come close to us without being seen by someone. I looked to our two still-smoking Panzers not far away and though I was annoyed that, as a Panzer driver, I should find myself lying in a foxhole with the infantry, I mused that I could so easily have been in one of the tanks, and stoically accepted my *Soldaten Geschick* (soldier's fate). A Sergeant then came creeping up to gather our reports about enemy movements. He told us that *Hauptmann* Zet had been severely taken to task by Divisional Headquarters over the telephone about the fiascos, and that he seemed desperate to some-how retrieve his badly-dented reputation. Shaking his head, the Sergeant warned us to be prepared for anything.

And how right he was, for not long after, the *Hauptmann* himself came crawl-ing and crouching from hole to hole. He sat down and without much ado came straight to the point: At one a.m. we were to attack from our foxholes, with the aim of taking the Russian nests from both sides, to make it safe for our comrades in the burnt-out Panzers to be retrieved. All three of us were stunned — of course, there was no way that we could question his order, but each of us had had much more battle experience than the *Hauptmann*, and it was a sad fact that our two crews were dead, but to risk any further life to get their bodies out was sheer madness. When he left our foxhole to crawl to the next, we just looked at each other, first in stony silence and then with bitterly hissed frustration. We all three felt like men condemned to almost certain death by that incorrigible fool Zet! Had it been possible, at least one of us would have preferred to run over to the Russian lines.

Then one o'clock came. *Hauptmann* Zet, together with two young Lieutenants, had come up again to an especially-prepared position, from which he personally was to lead an assault. Whatever anyone may have said about him, he was no coward. The night was clear and there was hardly a sound. Earlier on we had heard the Russians talking loudly amongst themselves, and one of them with a mouth-organ had played appealing melancholic Russian melodies. We had shouted across to them to be quiet, as we wanted to sleep. They had laughed and then, unusually for them, had shouted something rude. Our mood was subdued and sullen, everything in us rebelling against Zet's crazy plan.

The agreed signals were given and we were off! I saw Zet leaving his cover and waving his arms as a command for all to follow. Slowly, very slowly we moved up the slope, realising that every step took us closer to the Russian lines. Swearing under our breaths, one carried the machine gun, the other the machine pistol in loose readiness, and I trooped behind with my rifle on my back and two heavy ammunition boxes in my hands. Though I could notice movements from the corners of my eyes on either side, I could hardly hear a sound. Being in hearing distance of the Russians, we carefully tried to avoid kicking against loose stones. Trying to concentrate my mind on what was in front of me, I kept thinking of *Hauptmann* Zet. The hatred, the frustration and the feeling of helplessness was intense. Did Ivan know that we were coming for him? Had he already seen our crouching shadows in the dark, and was only waiting for us to get a little closer? I thought of my father, of all that he had tried to tell me that I had not believed then, about the ruthlessness of the German officer class and how they had used him and millions of others as expendable cannon fodder to protect their own privileges — and now this man Zet was doing exactly the same to me.

And then, out of the still of the night, what we had all feared in our hearts happened. Before our flanks of infantry had a chance to move up far enough to come in from the sides, Ivan decided to put a devastating stop to our game. All, of a sudden, the sky was alight all around us, and then those feared white-blue flashes from the Russian machine guns relentlessly scythed into us. All I could do was to throw myself down like a heavy sack. The rest was hoping, swearing, and praying with my body pressed as tightly as possible against mother earth. With that instinctive, naïve belief that by not looking at a danger, one could escape it, I did not even dare to open my eyes to look. Had the Russians followed this first barrage and come over the crest, about fifty metres away, to stick their bayonets into our miserable backs, I would not even have seen them coming. My mates were a few yards in front of me and gave no sound. And while that crescendo of flying bullets kept whistling over me, I tried feverishly to arrange my two ammunition boxes in front of me to protect my head.

A young mind, I suppose, re-asserts itself very quickly, and I grew more aware of what was going on around me. There were piercing cries from either side, and a lot of shouting from further back. To crown in all, I heard *Hauptmann* Zet call from my right something like 'close the line!, and 'fire the machine guns!'. 'Close the line' I thought, 'what line?' Not a single burst came from any of our machine guns; then a bullet hit my ammunition box. Was it a stray shot, or had Ivan seen me lying there? A horrible scaring fear crept through me, followed by an uncontrollable shaking of my entire body. I was not yet twenty years old. I wanted to live — not die! In desperation, I pushed loose stones away with my hands and feet and tried to claw out protruding bits of earth so that I could sink, as I hoped, a few life-saving inches deeper into the earth. The only comfort coming my way, the only reassurance that I was still alive, came from touching the cool fronds of prairie grass. From behind, our Panzers and PaKs had opened up a fierce barrage, but they could only shoot wildly behind Russian lines, and could give us no help at all in our confrontation with the enemy infantry as we were lying much too close to them.

After about half an hour, although it had seemed an immeasurable eternity, the enemy fire seemed to be thinning, and *Hauptmann* Zet's order was passed through to retreat back to our foxholes. There that stupid fool was again, shouting 'Abandon attack!', as if we had ever made one! And there I was, lying flat like a trapped rat, yet still with robot-like Prussian military discipline in my bones, grabbed my rifle, left my boxes and started to crawl my way back. The first ten yards or so I did not even dare to turn on my belly, but awkwardly crawled backwards, and only when I thought myself a little more out of the direct firing line from the crest, did I dare to turn, to then belly-crawl back to my hole. At first I had a job to find it, but when I finally dropped in, what a haven that shallow little square, hardly more than a foot deep, seemed to me! Still choosing to lie on my belly, I put my face into my arm and became oblivious to everything around me. All I was aware of was the cool earth below the blanket, and I did not want to hear, to look, or even to think.

How long I lay there, in almost total mental and physical exhaustion, I do not know, but what first aroused me out of my trauma was the recognition that I was still on my own. Then I heard *Hauptmann* Zet shouting, and I thought that I heard my name. When I glanced over to him, I saw him looking out from his cover. He wanted reports from the nests about the strength of his remaining troops, and nobody was bothering to oblige him. With a more normal flow of blood and life coming back into me, I became very concerned about my mates. Having been with them in a troika, but having come back on my own, what was I going to report? Perhaps they had lost their way back and had managed to plunge into another hole; but then, I thought, someone would have shouted that message over to me. And then came the worry concerning myself;

28. and **29.** Our halftrack with everything on it was hit.

30. Manning the PAK. I am in front, Kitt is second from right, Lazar is peering through the telescope on the gun.

31. On the 'Napoleonic' retreat, crossing the River Donetz on ice. All 'German' winters in Russia were colder than Napoleon's in 1812.

32.. Prisoner in England. Working for a family as a gardner in Hampshire

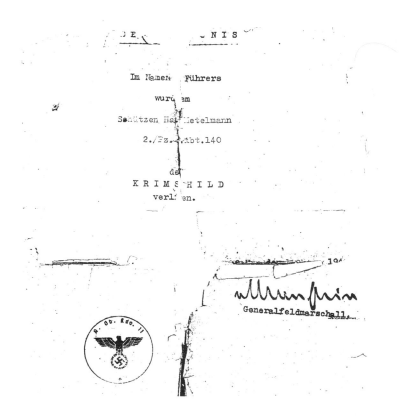

33. All that remains of the document awarding me the Crimean Shield 'in the name of the Führer'. It is stamped by General Feldmarschall Erich von Manstein.

Then an orderly came up from the village, apparently totally unsuspecting of anything, and moved straight for Zet's cover. I noticed his frantic activity. He looked out and round, and seeing me, gave a short wave with his hand. Next he came out of the cover and, slightly bending down, ran at high speed back to the village. Straight away, two Lieutenants came rushing up. It had become very much lighter now and I saw that all foxhole eyes were watching what was going on in Zet's cover. Then the Lieutenants went back to the village and a short time later the order came through '*Oberleutnant* so and so in command, Commander out of action!' Well, that was it, those three words 'out of action' said it all. *Hauptmann* Zet was dead. And looking around at all the other foxholes, I could see that the message had been understood. Later on, someone from the rear was sent up to join me but I did not say anything to him about what I had seen. We stayed in the foxholes throughout the day, and when darkness fell, infantry *Kampfgruppe* Sauer took over from us. As is now history, *Kampfgruppe* Sauer did not manage either to clear up this Russian bridgehead on the River Don. For Stavka, the Soviet Command, it was of utmost importance to hold on to it because it was from that bridgehead that Marshal Rokossovski had smashed through our defences later in November, then to close the trap on Paulus' Sixth Army in Stalingrad.

I was glad when I was back with the unit in the village. The following night, Sauer's unit managed to bring out the bodies from no man's land, laid them out in a shallow depression next to each other, and covered them with tarpaulin. Almost all had been personal friends of mine, and they were going to be laid in one grave. As was the custom, each of us 'walked the row'. Lifting the tarpaulin off each one, I took a very close look at *Hauptmann* Zet. The bullet had hit him fully on the left side of the face just below the cheekbone, had torn out at the other side and left a terrible mess. It was exactly as I had thought.

No question was ever asked, no official statement made. Everyone knew that Zet had a wild habit of looking with his field-glasses in all directions, and only a very few could have been sure which way he had been looking when the bullet hit him. And those who knew, did not say. After the prayers were over and the bodies covered with earth, we all walked back to whatever we had to do. I sidled up to a good friend who had been in a foxhole to my left and who, I knew, was a superb shot. 'Hello, Sepp,' I said, 'too bad, isn't it!'

'Yes,' he replied, 'too many have bitten the dust this time — and all so unnecessarily! All our friends! That damned bastard!' I nodded in agreement and patted his back — what could we say to each other, and what was there to say? We looked at each other for a few extra seconds, and the subject was never mentioned again.

6
Interruptions on the road to Stalingrad

Solang das Volk so übermässig dumm ist,
Der Teufel braucht nicht klug zu sein

'As long as people are so stupid,
there is no need for the devil to be clever.'

Goethe, from *Faust*

Our division then travelled south, where Marshal Timoshenko's skilful retreat was causing severe problems. One of the Panzer drivers was taken ill and I was ordered to replace him. A few weeks later we were told that he had died of typhoid. After a number of successful but minor battle engagements, my Panzer developed clutch trouble which could not be repaired under field conditions, and for which spare parts from the rear were needed. It was decided that while the Battalion moved on, I should stay with the Panzer in a near-by village called Mankovo, to await the arrival of the repair troop with the spare parts.

Mankovo stretched out generously on a flat, dusty plain. Most of its cottages were typically low, and thatched as if to duck close to the protecting earth from the raging east winds in winter. Its trees had only grown low, its streets were wide and straight, and on the whole unmade. While the Battalion had grouped itself at the edge of the village, I set up my tent close to a well near a peasant cottage. A young eighteen-year-old who had just arrived from Germany as a replacement was commanded to stay with me, and we were told that our stay would probably last two or at the most three days. We were given enough food and were looking forward to a restful period on our own when we watched the Battalion pulling out next morning. Having pitched our tent on the soft grass under an apple tree by the fence, we strolled into the village to explore. Everything was bathed in warm sunshine, the village had an earthy look about it, most of the cottages had large vegetable gardens, and some of the fencing as well as the outside window surrounds were prettily painted. Mankovo was much larger than we had thought at first, and we discovered that another German unit had taken up quarters at the other end.

During the first night my friend developed a high temperature. Luckily the other unit had a doctor and after he had examined him, he ordered him in his medical lorry to stay for observation. When I came next day to enquire how

he was, the unit had left and there was no one who could tell me what had happened to him. I realised then that I was the only German soldier in Mankovo and was not quite sure what to make of it. I observed normal village life from outside my tent. There was always someone walking past on the road, driving animals or pushing a cart. Sometimes I was given a cautious nod across the fence, which I always acknowledged. Though being in a rather precarious situation, I nevertheless considered myself safe, for I hoped that it was well known that the village would suffer terrible reprisal should any harm come to me. The fields all around were of huge size, so huge in fact that I could not see the end of them. Later I found that they were all part of a huge *kolchose*, a state farm. Down the road was a tractor station consisting of a large shed. The tractors were all gone, but there was a lot of farm machinery, the combine harvesters being far wider than those I had seen in Germany. Some mechanics, one a woman, were working at a work bench, and they watched me closely as I strolled around. When I finally spoke to them, they rather nervously assured me that there was nothing worth taking, obviously rating my thieving potential very high. When I asked them what had happened to the tractors, they told me that the Red Army had taken them with them. I found the village children quite a handful. However much I warned them off, they always came back and played around my Panzer and tent. After some had climbed on to it, I wrote in large cyrillic letters '*Njet*' (no) on the turret. In the setting sun a small Russian Yakovlev came flying low over the village. The pilot circled round my Panzer and I was glad for the first time that so many children were playing around and waving at the plane. I stood back under a tree with a rifle at hand, the pilot was looking out, but thinking of my glasshouse situation, I did not want to take a pot shot at him.

Four or five days went by, but no repair troop came back with the spare parts, nor did any German unit come through the village. Between my tent and the cottage was a well which served several families around, and there was always a busy nattering life going on. All the water carriers were obviously curious about me, but none ever came close to ask questions. Whenever I talked to them, there was the usual polite response, but the cautious conversation hardly ever went beyond the theme of the weather — which all the time was superb. I had a frying pan and sometimes used it on a small fire, and in the Panzer were several books which I read avidly. But then a week went by and I was beginning to run out of food. By now I was on nodding acquaintance with all the people in the next cottage, so one evening when I knew that they were all in, I walked in on them. They were all sitting around a large round table, having a meal; none got up but they all turned round to look at me. I came straight to the point and announced that as I had run out of food, I was going to share every meal with them from the next day onwards. The head of the family, a stockily-built peasant of about sixty, was almost bald but had a thick long black beard. His wife was small and shrivelled, but I could see that she was shrewd and had kind and intelligent eyes. There was the daughter-in-law, Sonia, about thirty with two boys of about eight and ten, a girl of four and a baby. Then there was daughter Katya, a couple of years older than me, who looked lovely

with her dark blonde plaits dangling down her side. Strangely none of them seemed surprised that I had turned up. There was a quick conversation, led by Magda (the mother), who simply said '*Chorosho!*' (all right). The atmosphere was cordial, if not welcome, and I left.

Later on in the evening when I sat by the well reading, Ivor, one of the boys, brought me a mug of brown tea, telling me that *barishna* (grandmother) had sent him. I took it as a sign of acceptance, and as he was eager to converse with me, I let him climb on to the Panzer. The family dog had taken a liking to me, and early in the mornings he came into my tent, it comforted me to cuddle him in my arms. It had been Army orders to keep Berlin time for all its troops in Russia, so according to my watch it got light at two or three in the morning and dark at six in the afternoon. My Russian friends had no clock, they did everything to a natural time sense, and I found that after a few days I totally disregarded my watch and accepted their routine.

At first light next morning I opened my tent, watched the entrance to the cottage and waited for things to happen. Smoke was puffing out of the chimney and soon Sonia came to the well. When I came out to wash and threw water over myself, she stood back, watched me and hummed a melodic tune, which bothered me. Though I was getting on for twenty, I had had no real experience with the female sex and I was suddenly very much aware of Sonia's eyes. She said 'Come in in ten minutes, breakfast will then be ready.'

There was only one room in the cottage, the kitchen area around the large mud stove was by the door. The floorboards were rough, and as there was no ceiling, one could see the thatch and the rafters, from which hung all sorts of utensils. In each of three corners was a wide bed, one for Adjetz and Magda, one for Sonia, the boys and the baby, and one for Katya and Sonia's daughter Tania. The walls were thick, rough and whitewashed, the windows small and unopenable, and the heavy door led to small porch. The table stood in the middle under the large hanging oil lamp, for which they had no oil. Against the walls were large home-made sideboards with cups, saucers and plates, there were a couple of benches, the odd box to sit on, and a few chairs. Living under these conditions, I would say that they were clean and tidy people.

The door, except at night, was always wide open, for most of the time there was a fire in the stove. When I walked in, I found the atmosphere very pleasant, they were all waiting for me around the table, except for Sonia who was getting things ready on the stove. Magda placed me next to her, and asked me whether they could call me 'Genry' (Russians do not have an 'H' in their vocabulary). Adjetz said a short prayer and they all bowed to the Icon in the corner, from a sitting position. A basket with delicious home-baked brown bread was handed around, after which Sonia put a large bowl of milky soup in the middle of the table. Everyone had a wooden spoon, and after Adjetz had started, we all dived into the bowl and ate the bread with it. There was a chuckling around the table when it was clear that I was the main dripper. Afterwards we were offered some cheese, then Adjetz said a prayer, lit his pipe which made a horrible smell, and then everyone was relaxed. It was a scene, I suppose, which had gone out of fashion in Western Europe two hundred years before,

and was therefore all the more charming.

Adjetz then left for the farm, and Katya walked to the village where she worked as a dispenser in the *Apoteka* (chemist shop). One afternoon I went in to see her; apart from various kinds of herbs there was nothing on the shelves. Of course I had no intention to buy anything and as everyone was staring at me and Katya did not help me at all, I made a hurried and embarrassed exit, never to repeat it again. The day was long and I wandered around in the village without my tunic. People on the whole, though reserved, were friendly in manner. It was clear that they all knew about me, but left me alone.

Adjetz stayed at the farm all day, and when Katya came home for her break, we had a midday meal consisting mainly of nourishing bortsch (vegetable soup) and bread. Each evening we had a lovely big meal consisting of potatoes, tomatoes, other vegetables, eggs and meat, mostly out of a large frying pan from which we all ate together, everyone dipping in with their forks. I learned that by eating out of one pot or pan a close relationship develops, with its own unspoken rules of behaviour and consideration for others. I quickly noticed that Adjetz always took the first dip and the last, and I made sure that I fell in with that custom. I tried to make myself helpful in many small ways; I saw to it that there was always enough water in the buckets by the door, and that the fuel-box in the porch was never empty. On some days the boys went to school. All the teachers, they told me, were women, and in the afternoons they did their homework, driven on by Sonia, and even I came in and did simple arithmetic with them.

The days went lazily by and the atmosphere was relaxed. My Russian was good enough for ordinary conversation, although at times I noticed around the table that my friends were saying funny things about me which I could not quite understand. They would look at me and laugh in a friendly understanding way, careful not to offend me. Once I pretended to be furious, got up from the table, fetched my rifle and threatened to shoot them all. They thought that was funny too, laughed even more and obviously loved me for it. After the evening meal Adjetz and I sat outside and played with the children. They had no toys, not even balls, but peasants are very inventive and we played many games. We played hide and seek, and throwing the horseshoe, and when I allowed them to beat me, they rushed in to tell someone. Sometimes in the night I thought that I heard the rumble of war but I developed a state of mind in which I did not want to know anymore.

One Sunday Sonia dropped a bucket into the bottom of the well. Buckets, like everything else at that time in a Russian village, were almost impossible to come by, and accusations about her clumsiness became rather emotional and in my view unfair. Adjetz flatly refused to climb down, cunningly complaining about some trouble with his leg, of which I had never heard him complain before. When I asked him whether he had a long pole, he all too quickly fetched one from the rafters and handed it to me. And then I suddenly realized, standing there with my pole, that all the eyes were on me and I did not quite know whether I should feel honoured or angry. Next thing, they somehow edged me towards the well and then decided that it was to be me who

was to climb down and get the bucket. The well was a bit more than a metre in diameter; large stones set into its side provided a foothold. Adjetz tied a rope to my belt, everyone was extremely helpful to get me over the wall, and before I knew it, I was descending those slimy steps into that deep, dark hole.

When I finally got to the bottom and stood very uncomfortably just above the water level, Adjez handed the pole down to me on a rope. All their heads were bending over the top, keeping the light out and shouting advice, and looking up at them, I realized how much I was at their mercy. Fishing around with the pole, I soon managed to hook the bucket on to it and when after several failures I lifted it to the surface, there came a loud 'hurrah', from above and it registered in my mind that it was the same 'hurrah' which I had heard so often before a Red Army attack. After a painful climb and with aching limbs I surfaced above the stone wall and was pulled over it like a returning gladiator. Sonia took me in her arms, with Madga putting a quick stop to it. Peasant joys, everyone was happy and I was totally caught up in it. That night there was reason for celebration and Sonia and Madga baked me very special pancakes.

Feeling increasingly like a fifth wheel on a wagon, being the only adult in the family who did not contribute to our living, I asked Adjetz whether he would take me with him to the farm. He obviously made enquiries first, and then told me in the evening to be ready the next morning. After breakfast we walked to the top of the road, where others were already waiting. Not long, and out of the swirling dust came two old-fashioned farm carts. We joined those already on it and went off at a lusty gallop across the steppe. Most of the others were women and girls of all ages, but also some boys, and men over 50. Amidst the bantering and joking, everyone was well aware of my presence. Soon they started singing those melancholic Russian peasant songs and they were pleased when I clapped. The steppe lay so beautifully silent, the corn had already been cut and was lying around in bundles. Our job was to pitch the bundles on to the carts and store them in small wooden barns which stood on low posts, to keep the mice and rats out. The atmosphere was lively and friendly, and I had the impression that it was genuinely understood that the war was not my personal fault. Everything was well organized by Mischa, the *kolchos* secretary. She was about forty, her word was law and when she told us to swop jobs, none protested, least of all I.

At mid morning we had a break, I had stripped down to the waist, and felt very happy in my surroundings. Chunks of bread and plenty of home-made cheese were handed round, everything in the communal way, and there was water to drink. At midday a churn of thick soup was brought out and ladled into all sorts of tins and wooden bowls. The bortsch was of a texture in which the spoon could stand up, and it tasted like heaven. Afterwards with our bellies full, we laid down on the grass in the shade behind the barns. However much I tried to lie next to one of the girls, it always came to nothing, the girl of my choice always got up at the last minute, and I found myself next to Adjetz or some other old man. When I was woken up, I felt little inclination to work; but I did my fair share and when sitting cleanly washed round Madga's table in the evening, I felt a sense of deep satisfaction, because this time I had worked

for my bread.

One evening there was thunder in the air and a threat of rain. Adjetz suggested that my tent might be blown away and that I should sleep in the cottage. Thinking very much of beautiful Katya, I agreed. I stretched my blanket on the floor along the wall by the door. When it turned dark, a candle was placed on the table. Everyone had quietly slipped into bed while I watched the flickering shadows being thrown against the walls and into the dark thatch. And with the thunder rumbling outside and the blue flashes from the lightning bursting through the small windows, I felt safe and protected amongst my friends.

From now on it was taken for granted that I went to the farm with Adjetz every day and that I slept in the cottage every night. And then, one Saturday evening, Adjetz nodded to me to come along with him. We walked to the other end of the village and into a peasant cottage. Many men were already sitting along the walls on rickety benches. It was noisy and smoky, and I was made welcome by nods and callings of my name. Leon was the man in charge, and Adjetz suggested that I should give him a few roubles. From then on Leon, almost automatically, kept filling the glasses. What he put into them, I don't know, but by Jove it was strong stuff and after an hour, though I kept pulling my cheek, I could not feel it anymore and the bench I was sitting on was becoming increasingly unsafe. How I got home with Adjetz, I don't know, but the village streets were wide and, luckily, there was no water in the ditches. According to Adjetz next day, I must have been singing something like *Lilly Marlene*, waking up the village. Once indoors we looked for food, crawling about under the table, and we could not stop laughing until Madga had had enough of us two and gave us a lashing of her tongue.

Life went on for a further two weeks or so, and nothing out of the ordinary happened. There was work and sun and sleep and Leon. All villagers called me now by name, but however much I tried, I did not achieve a friendly relationship with any of the girls or a younger women. For that love I yearned deep down. But it was out of bounds and the thought occurred to me several times that if Katya would have given me the word and the village its agreement I would possibly have kept out of German reach and could have stayed in the village for the rest of my life. And all the time my Panzer stood there, the weeds growing around its tracks; everyone in the village seemed to have got used to it.

It was at the weekend when Adjetz and I had just arrived at Leon's, when a breathless boy came running after us to tell me that a German Army car had arrived at my Panzer with three soldiers, who had been asking for me. 'My God, not that!', I thought and I must have turned pale because Leon asked me whether I was all right. Collecting my thoughts, I walked slowly back. My mind was in turmoil and when I came round the last corner, wearing only trousers and shirt and no boots, I saw that Army car! The mechanics were already working at my clutch and had almost finished repairing it, the Sergeant, who was in full uniform, looked me up and down. Suddenly I could understand why Russians hated that grey-green colour. Brown as a nut, I had probably already changed to a peasant's appearance. The Sergeant told me to collect my things and pack them into the Panzer. Madga, all of them, were

just standing there and looking at me wide-eyed, no one said a word, not to me nor to each other. Then Adjetz arrived. My German mates were laughing about them and one was trying to make a joke about them. I could have hit him.

It emerged that when our Division had left the village over a month earlier, it had been heavily engaged on its move towards Stalingrad, that the work for the repair troop was so overwhelming that I had just had to be abandoned for a while. And when I listened to all that, I found that my mind simply could not hook on to it any more, that I had lost all interest. All I could think of now was that I had to leave Mankovo and all my friends, and that I would not see them again for the rest of my life.

By now the repair was completed and the Sergeant wanted to drive it himself to test it; so at least I did not have to crawl into the Panzer just like that, out of sight of them all. All of them now, watching us attentively, stood huddled together by the door of the cottage. I went past them into the room which for so long had been my home, to have a last look round. No one followed me, but the Sergeant kept shouting. Coming out, I went over to Adjetz, he hugged me and we patted each other on our backs. He then held me at arm's length to look me up and down, and shook his head as if to say that he did not like me in that uniform. Madga then came into my arms and openly cried, and between her tears she was saying something about her two sons who were soldiers in the Army, who would have been my friends had we been here together in peace-time, and that the killing would now start all over again for me. 'You love our village, don't you, Genry', she said, but I could not answer because I had a lump in my throat which prevented me from speaking. I kissed the children, the boys clung to me and the girl was crying. And then I stepped to Katya and Sonia and just looked at them, they both opened their arms, pressed me against their bosoms and fully kissed me on the mouth, they then both ran quickly into the cottage and I think that I heard them crying. The Panzer was already disappearing in a cloud of dust when I got into the open car at the back. The roar of the engine and we shot forward through the dust and I waved until I could see them no more. Why had life to be like this? I felt as if I had lost my heart.

By the time I got back to the unit, things were on the move again. The Red Army had been forced to retreat again, but it was an orderly retreat and they had managed to disrupt Paulus's line of advance, especially in our allies' sections. We had severe communication problems, and there seemed to be a new spirit in the Soviet High Command. T-34 wolf packs had made daring forays into our rear areas, commanders had to act quickly on impulse, and many units were now lost all over the place, which was causing chaos in the map and planning sections. I could see telephonists sitting in the open outside their tents in front of their grey boxes, desperately winding the little handles, apparently without success. Frustrated planning officers could be seen leaning over them, urging them to try again. The wire pullers, as we called them, were out in strength with their small leather tool cases, but once they had connected two broken ends together there were ten others to mend. It was a never-ending problem and it was probably no coincidence that whenever prisoners passed

to the rear, our telephone wires somehow went.

We captured a Volga German. Hans had been born in Saratov Region, where many German people lived and mainly German was spoken. He had lived there all his life and told us that it was a lovely green area. We kept him with us because he was a good organizer and, of course, a perfect interpreter. He now wore a German uniform without the eagle and swastika, and he carried no weapon. His accent was quaintly old-fashioned, as if time had stood still since Tsarina Katharina had brought the German settlers out of Swabia. He was about thirty-five and had the most pleasant manners, and whenever I had the chance to converse with him, I did. When I once held forth to him about the political world scene and how bad Bolshevism was, he went unusually quiet, and when I asked him whether he did not agree with my judgement, he said: 'Well, Henry, you might be right about them having made many mistakes, crimes too; many careerists have probably joined them, but I think that you are wrong when you think that Bolshevism is bad — it is highly idealistic, very humanistic and perhaps still too much in the clouds regarding the rotten, greedy nature of so many of us.' Shortly after, he was asked to interpret an interrogation of a group of captured Soviet officers. I sat in on it and noticed that the whole procedure caused him much upset. The next morning he was found dead in a cottage, with our Sergeant Major's pistol lying next to him.

Then quite out of the blue I had a stroke of great luck. As all the married men in our Company — of whom there were not many — and all those with compassionate grounds had already been on *Heimat* leave during the months of our advance, it come now to us lower ranks and single men to go back to Germany on four weeks' front leave. When I was first told that my name had been mentioned, and being aware that my reputation with the commanding powers of Battalion were anything but high, I thought that it must all have been a mistake, but later the Sergeant Major announced it in front of the Company, together with the date of transport. I felt like sailing on the clouds of heaven.

About half a dozen of us were taken by lorry to the nearest railhead, from where we travelled in covered cattle wagons to Kharkov, to report to the Transport Officer at the station. Kharkov was the collecting centre for this purpose for all the armies around in that region. With hundreds of others we were billeted in a large hall across the station forecourt, where the higher ranks slept in camp beds while the rest of us made do on blankets on the floor. But we did not mind! We were used to sleeping rough, and we knew that we were going home on leave to Germany. The food was good, as far as Army food goes, and nearby there was a cinema unit which run old films all day long. There were loaded shelves with all sorts of books and we played endless games of cards and chess. We were also deloused, and each of us received a suitcase — to be given up again on return —, new underwear, and, where necessary, new items of uniform. We idled away several days in Kharkov, in the comforting knowledge that the four weeks' leave would count from the day we reported to the *Wehrmacht Kommandantur* nearest to our home town.

When well over a thousand of us, including lads from the *Luftwaffe* and the *Waffen SS*, had collected together, a long train with returners from Germany

arrived and we started our slow journey to the west. Though there were many rumours, to which we ourselves added generously, none of us had any idea which way we were going, but we were not bothered as long as the midday sun was on the left side of our direction of travel. Everything was reasonably organized. A transport officer, a Captain, was in charge of us all. He was already elderly, forty years or so, and because of his rosy cheeks, which had a distinct bluish alcoholic tinge everyone called him 'Cherry Blossom', though not to his face, of course. About once a day we were shunted into sidings, where Cherry Blossom started to run around like a blue-arsed fly, as a result of which we received a warm meal in our mess-tins, a canister of barley coffee for every wagon, and our daily rations.

Our mood was buoyant. Any hardship or delay was simply laughed away: we were going home — that was all that mattered, and any additional delay was time away from the grinding war. Most of us had not seen Germany for at least a year, and all our talking was about our loved ones and the many things we were going to do once we got home. All of us, I am sure, tried to brush away that hovering cloud in the distance, the certainty that in little more that four weeks' time we would again be rolling through this same countryside — in the wrong direction. Though each compartment was packed to capacity, no one complained about shortage of space, even at night. Our attitude was that today was today and tomorrow would look after itself. All officers travelled in soft second-class compartments, which were far less crowded, and from Major or Colonel upwards they were two to a compartment, or even alone, and their *Burschen* (batmen) all together.

When we crossed the Romanian border near Jassy, each of us received a large *Führer Paket* (Führer parcel) which contained hard sausages and other food produced in the occupied lands. We were all fully aware that the Soviet people were starving, but I doubt whether any of us felt the slightest pang of conscience about the fact that we were taking this food from their mouths. Such had been the hardening of our hearts.

It was a lovely sunny morning when we arrived in Bucharest; Cherry Blossom announced through his creaky loud-hailer that we had to change trains and that our next transport to Vienna would leave from another platform in twelve hours' time. As it so happened, we hung around Bucharest Station for a couple of days. In no time we had arranged a sleeping area amongst our luggage on the platform, and always having in mind an unforeseen early departure of our train, none of us dared to go far into the city.

The general impression from the station was that here was a nation under duress. It was strange, really, that we recognized this condition in Romania but not, later on, in our own country. Everything around us, as in Germany, was highly militarized. Uniforms were everywhere, and the Army and Police (sometimes in civilian clothes) were rude and arrogant when checking passports and other papers of ordinary people who, it was clear to see, were frightened of them. They had no right though, as otherwise there would have been a riot, to check on German soldiers.

Witnessing a commotion on the station forecourt, I was told that a German

26. Splendid transport!

27. A Russian peasant and a German soldier (right).

24. I am standing in the middle of this group: all but two of us were killed.

25. Holding the front line with a machine-gun. We could see the Russians who were in similar holes about 500m to 800m away.

22. A typical Russian peasant family. In the winter we always moved in with them.

23. Attacking a Russian village. I am in the forefront of this group with rifle in hand.

20. and **21.** Wide, flat countryside as it appeared in 1942-43.

18. Sleeping close together to keep warm in the front line. After about half an hour we were woken up so as not to freeze to death.

19. Our PAK in a defensive position on the front line.

16. Me in the driver's seat of the halftrack with the PAK behind.

17. Snowed and frozen in.

14. Me on the left before an improvised shelter.

15. Larking around - I am on the left.

12. Building an earth bunker. I am in the middle with the PAK visible behind us.

13. Our PAK in position. From here we saw one morning about 50 Soviet T-34 tanks approaching on the horizon. We took to our heels.

9. and **10.** The following photographs of me were taken during December '42/January '43 when our 22nd Panzer Division was trying to hold the line with our allies, the Rumanian Army, just to the north-west of Stalingrad. The coldest temperature at that time, we were told one morning, was -54°C.

11. In the first winter we had no special clothing for the cold conditions. By 1942-43 this had been addressed. This camouflage was worn over the ordinary uniform and could be turned inside out to show snow white. Some of us had these warm felt/leather boots. At that time I drove this vehicle, pulling a PAK.

Besitzeugnis

Dem Henry M e t e l m a n n, Gefr.
(Name, Dienstgrad)

2./ Pz. Jg. Abt. 140
(Truppenteil, Dienststelle)

ist auf Grund seiner am 5. 2. 43

erlittenen ein maligen Verwundung oder Beschädigung

das

Verwundetenabzeichen

in "S c h w a r z" verliehen worden

Gütersloh , den 7. 6. 194 3

(Dienstsiegel)

Merguet
(Unterschrift)

Oberstabsarzt u. Chefarzt.
(Dienstgrad und Dienststelle)

Nr. 21 /43
der Verleihungsdienststelle

8. My wound earned me the black 'Wounded Medal'. Subsequent wounds were rewarded by successively more prestigious medals in bronze, silver and so on.

5. Taken in Russia on the advance to Stalingrad, 1942

6. and **7.** On a special holiday in the Alps on the German-Austrian border, having been wounded on the Eastern Front in 1943.

1. In a flat in this tenement block (corner top) I lived with my parents from the age of one to eighteen when I was called up to the army. It was then in the Prussian town of Altona in Schleswig-Holstein and is now in Hamburg. The building was bombed flat in 1943.

2. In the village of Stapelfeld in Schleswig-Holstein at my Grandmother's where my mother was born. 1935 or '36.

3. At school in Altona when I was about 15 (third from the right, middle row). About half of this group were killed in the war

4. Back from Russia, 1944.

then come back and report that I had not found my mates, but in that case
I would not have put it past Zet to have sent me out on the search again. Strangely,
at a time like this, I remembered home, the loving care my parents had given
me and the sacrifices they had made to bring me up. I had always thought that
war was glorious but crawling in the mud now, alone and in a strange country,
I realized that I had never believed that it was like this.

I listened into the night and thought that I could hear the Russians talking
to each other: at least they were human voices, and I found them somehow
comforting. There was an indescribable urge in me to call over to them,
'Brothers, Comrades, don't shoot, I am looking for my wounded comrades,
let me come over and sit with you and let us be friends!' It gave me an awful
shock when suddenly out of the dark a small shadow appeared right in front
of me. Then I knew that I had found what I had been looking for. Another
shadow appeared, they were the boot-soles of one of my mates. And then I
saw the other, lying next to him, slightly in front. Realizing, of course, that
I was in the direct enemy firing line, I quietly hissed their names. One of them
was Erich Muth, but there was no reply, no breathing, no movement, nothing.
I crawled up to touch the boot to wriggle the foot, but it went back to its original position like a rubber doll. I managed to get in between them and touched
their faces which, lying on their cheeks, were both turned to me. One had blood
on it, the other had lost his helmet. They were both lying heavily on their bellies, and I found it impossible to get hold of their identity disks or their *Sold-
buch* (pay book) from their breast pockets. And all the time I was aware that
the Russians were only a stone's throw away. Seeing them lying there, it occurred
to me that they had probably saved my life, having soaked up the bullets which
otherwise would have hit me.

Hauptmann Zet had seen me finding my way back to the hole. He called
over from his cover, wanting to know: 'Dead, both dead, *Herr Hauptmann*!',
I called, putting as much accusation into my voice as I could. He did not ask
whether I had taken the disks and the books, but wanted to know whether I
had brought the machine gun, and I thought I heard him say something like
'damned' and 'stupid fool!', after my negative reply. Someone brought up a
mess-tin of hot food for me, which I wolfed down. I tried to sleep, but felt
so wet and uncomfortable that I only wallowed in cold misery. All the time,
Hauptmann Zet was calling for information and was giving instructions. It
became clear that our losses had been considerable again, and judging by the
tone of the answering voices I knew that the atmosphere was heavy with hatred.
I could see Zet in his hole, could just make out against the first uncertain glimmer
of approaching dawn how he was elbowing on the edge of his cover and scanning the Russian line with his field-glasses. His Lieutenants and others had
gone back and he was on his own. Then there was a single shot, which in itself
was not unusual. What seemed strange, though, was that it had come from
my left, and the Russians were in front. I clearly saw *Hauptmann* Zet slump
to his side away from me, and then roll out of sight. I was wide awake now,
and watched and waited. There was no further movement, no commotion, but
when looking around, I saw others watching from their foxholes too.

knowing Zet, he could choose to make it very difficult for me — 'abandoning my comrades in front of the enemy.'

I tried hard to recall exactly what had happened. When the Russians had opened up, they too had dropped like wet sacks — but I did not really know, had not actually seen it. And then, admitting it only to myself, I simply had not cared, all that I had really been concerned with was my own fate, my own skin. Judging by the calls which now slowly were going out from all around, I was not the only one who was missing his friends. By now the firing had almost completely stopped, and then I heard the Russian voices, copying our calls; they were mocking us, and the salt they were rubbing into our wounds was hard to bear. Clouds were now coming up and then, adding to the misery, it started to rain, at first finely as if spitting with mist, and then setting in, becoming thicker and thicker until we were lying in an all-penetrating summer rain.

Not long afterwards *Hauptmann* Zet, moving from hole to hole, came to mine and stretched himself next to me. Oh, how I hated him! Though still acting in his usual overbearing manner, I could sense that he was much subdued. Of course, as I could give him no definite information about my two mates, he wanted to know why.

'Because I just could not get near them, had I tried, none of us would have come back. They did not have a chance. No one had a chance, those of us who have come back were plain lucky. All that I can suggest to you is that my friends are dead, *Herr Hauptmann*!

He must have sensed the venom in my voice, for he just looked at me and said nothing, which was very unusual for him. And then, after just looking around, he synchronized my watch with his and quietly came out with another thunderbolt. He told me that at a given signal I was to crawl forward and find out what had happened to my mates, and the way he said it was as if giving me a punishment. Everything about him was cold, and all that was left for me to say was: *'Jawohl Herr Hauptmann.'* He then left, to crawl to the next foxhole. The thought of having to crawl forward on my own into that frightening hell from which I had just managed to extract myself, was horrifying. Of course I was sorry for my mates, and I realized that it could have been me out there in front, perhaps badly wounded and waiting for help. Possibly I was selfish in my resentment, or simply frightened, and being analytical, I could not really fault the *Hauptmann's* order, but I did not want to go, I wanted to stay in my hole where I knew I was safe.

When Zet had arrived back in the village and the signal was given, I pulled myself over the edge. The chalky earth was now wet and slimy and my clumsy uniform with its large awkward pockets clung to me like a dirty, wet sack. Not daring to raise my body, I kept my stomach as close to the earth as I could. Moving on my own, I lacked any meaningful bearing, and soon was not sure whether I was moving in the right direction. It was about three o'clock, and the night was still pitch dark. The thought came to me to just stay there and officer had been robbed of all his belongings except his weapons. He had been sitting on his suitcase to make sure that no one could pinch it, but had completely underestimated the ingenuity of the Romanian thieves. When he woke up from an uncomfortable doze, he instinctively realized that his suitcase had lost its substance to then find that a quick-fingered burglar with a sharp knife had cut out the end of the case and had completely emptied it with one raking swoop. '*Schadenfreude* is the greatest joy' is an old German proverb, and few of us managed to suppress a smile when told the story; after all there was not much love lost for our officers. He reported it to the Romanian 'Specials', who nodded in sympathy and had a quiet word with their station cleaners, who lazily mingled amongst us with their sacks and brooms, to no effect. When our train, puffing and belching clouds of smoke, pulled out of Bucharest station, there was exultant cheering.

The crawling journey via Budapest, Vienna and Prague took us through beautiful countryside for which few of us, all our thinking increasingly geared to the homecoming, had appreciative eyes. I suppose it showed our deeply ingrained, arrogant prejudices when we all agreed that this journey out of Russia through Romania, Hungary and former Czechoslovakia was tantamount to a trip back to civilization. The joy was tremendous when we crossed into Germany proper through the Ore Mountains south of Dresden. I don't really know why we had expected otherwise, but it struck us that most of the people, not so unlike those in the countries we had just traversed, showed a miserable if not war-weary expression in their faces. None seemed to bother about us, and when we tried to attract their attention by bellowing loud shouts, their whole demeanor seemed to suggest that they wanted us to shut up.

Then came Leipzig with its bustling life, our destination. Leaving our organized transport, we now continued our journey individually and had to find our own trains home. A fellow roughneck, with more travel experience than me, had made me wise to a useful trick. There was so much confusion all over the place that there was little danger of being found out. I tried it. After having arrived at home, I came back two days later to the station's transport office to report my arrival, purposefully unshaven and generally looking a bit wild and carrying my suitcase. I did not even need any of my well-prepared excuses, and gained by that two extra days' home leave.

As it so happened, my mother had not received my letter telling her that I was coming home, and when I arrived in our flat, she was not in. Everything was so homely, so *gemütlich*, so clean as she always had kept it. I quietly unpacked and waited, and when shortly afterwards she arrived with her shopping bag I called '*Juhu*' from the sitting room. She rushed in, threw herself into my arms, and cried and cried, until I too could not sustain it anymore and joined in. For a long time we were unable to speak. It was the most beautiful homecoming I have ever experienced in my whole life.

We decided there and then to be reasonable and to try to de-emotionalize everything around my stay for the next four weeks, so that we could enjoy every minute of it in a positive way, and mention my departure only during the last two days. At that time after father's death, mother worked as a kitchen help in the railway canteen. She immediately asked for four weeks' holiday and, of course, got it. Next we visited all our relatives, staying for a few days in the village of her birth, made a number of day trips to the places we loved, visited the Kozert Halle, the theatre, the cinema, and most of all, we did what we most loved — stayed in our homely home. Friends and relatives visited us. Some, in a suggestive way, mentioned my *Führer Paket* from Russia. But mother quickly became wise to the fact that too much sharing would lessen her aim to fatten me up a bit.

Almost every day I walked the town and visited all the places which had brought me joy in childhood and youth. I would have preferred not to have walked alone, but to have been with a girlfriend, but due to my natural shyness, as well as the rough life I had led for a long time in front-line conditions in Russia, I could not imagine that any girl would find pleasure in being with me. Almost all my friends were somewhere in the war on the many fronts, and the only one who hooked on to me was a chap from down the road who was on leave from his SS unit, with which he was lording it somewhere in Poland. Most of the time he kept talking about our great Christian civilization and the greatness of our Reich, but with Russia lying somewhat heavily on my subconscious mind, I could no longer digest all these high-flown words, at least not in Germany, and therefore kept out of his way whenever possible. Dancing was forbidden in the whole of the country throughout the war, and while very few places openly served alcoholic drinks over the counter, and cakes and such things were as good as unobtainable, there was not much point in hanging around in pubs or restaurants. And all the time, though we stuck to our agreement not to mention my departure date, it was like a suffocating cloud slowly creeping up on us.

Wherever I went, people were anxious to hear from me what was happening at the Eastern Front. Not because I had ever done any heroic deeds, but simply because I had been at a certain time at a certain place, I had received a number of medals, and on that strength alone my reporting of events was accepted as authentic. The last thing I wanted to give was the impression that Germany could possibly find itself on the losing side. Though I did not tell any lies, I did not tell the whole truth either, I kept the more negative aspects of my experiences to myself. It struck me that much of the questioning contained a measure of querying doubt as to the outcome of the whole war, especially amongst those who had experienced the 1914-18 war — and I always 'jumped' on the querying questioner and made it clear that, whatever the difficulties, for me the final victory for our Germany could be in no doubt. Then an uncle asked me what factual evidence I had for my total conviction, and trying to think of any, I sensed that I was talking myself into a corner and that I really had no evidence at all. It has to be borne in mind, of course, that my uncle and the many others who doubted on this matter could not afford to openly challenge me. Needless to say, I would never have reported anyone, but we were all aware that the Nazi Party had ears and eyes everywhere and that many strange things were happening in Germany.

The rationing of food and clothes, though severe, was such that no one, as far as I could see, was actually starving. And if things were getting a bit tight for us, there was always mother's village in Schleswig-Holstein, where undeclared food was available for use within the family.

I went to pay a visit to where I had worked as an apprentice in the railway workshops. There was an old chap, Max Weinreich, whom as a person I had liked but who, as long as I had known him, had never responded to anyone's greeting of '*Heil Hitler*'. Though that in itself was no criminal offence, it was certainly very unwise, and could easily have led to an 'educational' stint in a *KZ*, the popular name for concentration camps. Even more so, Max who came from 'Red Barmbeck', a working-class suburb of Hamburg, had the reputation of having been an active left-winger during the Weimar Republic. Some even said that he had been a member of the Communist Party. He greeted me very warmly, as personally he probably felt for me as I felt for him. But without saying so to him I did not like his close and informed questioning of me, and especially his unwillingness to express his doubts which, I felt, were there in heavy measure. I thought that he should not have distrusted me, and left him a bit dispirited, as I rated highly his intelligence and his ability to think independently.

There had been many changes in Germany during the years I had been away in France and Russia, which I did not like. I loved my Germany and felt that as well as a depressing war situation, there had been many other negative developments. There were many foreigners working in our factories, and some of them behaved as if the town was theirs. What bothered me too a great deal was the realization that those who so readily agreed with my estimation of the whole situation could seldom be counted amongst the more intelligent.

There were air-raid alarms at least three or four nights every week. Though everyone was urged to go into the cellars of the air-raid bunkers, I did not, and stayed in bed. Mother, who always went down when she was on her own, did not chide me for that, and stayed in bed too, saying that if fate would have it that way, then at least we would die together. During my stay, some bombs were dropped on our town and a number of houses were ripped to pieces, with people killed. But all that was as nothing compared with what was to come later.

One evening I witnessed a fight which had spilled out from a pub into the street. I was only passing and watched it all with a measure of amusement. Then the police arrived, and with them Gestapo in plain clothes, whom I had not noticed at first. When one of the 'plains' told me to stop laughing and move on, I objected to being given orders like that and demanded to know who he was and to show me his credentials which, of course, he refused. When consequently I still refused to move on, he nodded to one of the uniformed officers, told him to take me away and without much ceremony I was marched off to the police station. I kept protesting, and one of the officers, who had a body like a wardrobe and was almost a head taller than me, held his fist under my nose and pointedly asked whether I would like to smell that rose. Confronted so unequally, I shut up. And arriving at the police station, I realized that I was the only one taken into custody, and that not even the two fighting cocks who had started it all were brought in.

When I was told to produce my papers, I realized to my horror that I had forgotten to take them with me in the pockets of my civilian jacket. To carry no papers was in itself an offence. All my protesting that I was a soldier of a famous Panzer Division on leave from Russia was no help, and without much ado I was locked up in a cell which had only one chair and a bed with a smelly blanket on. A single bulb without a shade was hanging from the grubby ceiling, and when I banged the door and asked the guard outside to switch it off as I wanted to sleep, they switched on another one instead.

By now it was approaching midnight, and as we had no phone at home and no police car was available for an unimportant matter like my arrest, it took several hours before a beat policeman came back with my papers, which naturally must have worried my mother very much. Then the officer in charge let me out and read me the riot act, with the final insulting kick that, as a Panzer soldier and the bearer of the Iron Cross I ought to be ashamed at having contributed to a public disturbance. And when I walked away from the station on my long trek home at four o'clock in the morning I was in such a state of unmitigated fury that I wished I had a hand-grenade with which I could have blown up the whole stinking police station. As my leave was coming to an end now, this incident strangely helped me almost to wish to be back with my mates in Russia.

The last few days of leave were awful. The news from the Eastern Front was very disturbing, and mother became very quiet and I could see that at times she had been crying. Then on the last day but one she came out with what so obviously had lain on her heart: 'Henry,' she said, 'do you think that what you are doing in Russia is right?'

Knowing very well what she meant, I nevertheless asked her, 'What do you mean?'

'Well, you know very well what your father thought about it all and I now have come very much to agree with him. He called the invasion of Russia one of the biggest crimes against humanity in modern times. It came near to breaking his heart that you, his only son, whom he loved, could so willingly be involved in all this. And now you have to go again! I watch the newsreels about the burning of the villages and town and cities and it is very much in my mind that there are people in them, real living people, men and women, young and old and many children. And so many of them will have to die — and what for?'

'Yes, mother, but what do you expect me to do? Do you ask me to simply not go back to Russia? And then, what would happen to me? Then it will be me who will be sacrificed in front of the firing squad — and I have seen many a lad who went that way, most of them had committed no crime, it was only because their nerves could not stand this blasted war anymore!'

'Yes, I know, but you have got to be honest to yourself as I have to be to myself. Don't you really feel it in your heart that what you are doing in Russia, all of you, cannot be right. It must be wrong from whichever way you look at it. And when you keep saying that you do it all for your country, can you recall having read in the Bible that when Jesus said that you shall not kill, he made the exception that it would be all right provided it is done for your country?'

'Oh, mother, there you come with your religious stuff again! Why do you have to make it so hard for me? Whatever Jesus might have said two thousand years go, the reality at this moment of time for me is that I have no choice but to go back to Russia, as none of these Christian hand-wringers from the Pope and the Archbishops down would raise one finger to save me from the firing squad. Do you realize that if I thought the same as you do and as father did, my being a soldier would have destroyed me mentally already years ago?' And when I then added that I could not help being on this corrupt and hypocritical world where one has to lie to stay alive, that I had not asked to be born, I regretted it as soon as it had come out of my mouth. I could see that it had hurt her deeply, and that was the last thing I wanted to do.

'I suppose it is right what you say,' she voiced tonelessly. 'Maybe I am unfair to make it so hard for you at a time like this. But I am worried and I am your mother, I love you and want you to stay alive, but I also want you to be a good human being and do the right things to God and humanity which, to my way of thinking, is the same thing.'

After that we did not mention that subject again, though no doubt it was lying heavily on both of our minds, and the pangs of my conscience told me that mother was right, as father had been before her.

On the day I left for the station I was touched by the many neighbours who were waiting by the door of our tenement block to bid me farewell — farewell to Russia, what irony! They gave me small parcels of very rare and almost unobtainable luxuries like chocolates etc. I almost felt like crying. And none spoke of victory or the country or of other such windy and meaningless words — only of safe homecoming.

And when mother and a couple of close friends who like me had come on *Heimat* leave from the Navy and the *Luftwaffe* disappeared from my view from my train window, I felt mentally exhausted and was almost glad that it was all over — and wondered whether my homecoming from Russia had been such a good idea in the first place.

My first train journey took me to Berlin. From there I went to Warsaw, where I stayed a night or two to wait for a connection. The next stage to Kiev and from there, several hundred miles in all, it was on the backs of bone-shaking lorries. When I finally arrived at my destination I could see from afar our Panzers and other vehicles standing untidily on a field outside a large village. And when all my friends so sincerely welcomed me back, I felt more confused about everything than I ever had felt before.

A petrol train had been blown up somewhere in the rear and we were to be marooned in this village for a week or so. Our *Zugführer* (platoon commander) had been killed in battle, and when reinforcements arrived, we were told that a new *Zugführer* was amongst them. As all of us would have liked to have seen promotion through the ranks, *Unteroffizier* (Sergeant) Lazar, from the moment he jumped off the back of the lorry, started off with one enormous disadvantage: our resentment. My first impression when he was introduced by our Lieutenant was his pronounced unmilitary bearing. He was well built, perhaps slightly too stockily for this medium height. His hair was dark, his movements smooth, and nothing seemed to escape his grey, wandering eyes. His nose was prominent and fleshy, his neck short and strong, and his lips full. Unlike all of us, who came from the working class, he had a bourgeois accent, which grated on our nerves. But the biggest obstacle of all was his name. We all were convinced that if ever there was a Jewish name right out of the Old Testament, this one surely was it. What was a Jew doing here on the Eastern Front of all places, and more so as our *Zugführer*, our direct superior? Ours was a tightly-knit unit where survival depended very much on close comradeship. And now this! He was friendly enough and acted with caution all round so as not to upset anyone. He was precise in his military duties, and we had no grounds to object to being led by him, as apart from his name and appearance, we had no proof that he was a Jew. We called him 'Jewboy' behind his back though, but none dared say it openly to his face. Whenever a discussion veered towards that subject, he never reacted. Whenever we had to make a decision, even a military one — and all of us had much more battle experience than him — he always was open to advice. But as we saw it, a stranger had been put in our midst, all the usual easy bantering had ceased, and Lazar sensed it all right. He often looked up at us from whatever he was doing as if to say, 'Please, let me be your friend'. He said one day that he would like to be looked at as the first amongst equals, not realizing how disturbingly strange that sounded to our rigid military minds.

Our gunner's name was Kitt (putty), which had been given to him because he had been a glazier's apprentice. Without question Kitt, a typical Aryan type, was the most professional and efficient soldier amongst us. He had been a Hitler Youth Führer in his home city of Bremen, and more than any of us was a committed National Socialist. Though many of his pronouncements were no more than slogans, he was wholly sincere when he declared that he loved his Führer and was prepared to lay his life down for him. He hated the Jews; to him, they were the real roots of all evil, and he was sure that it had been the wisdom of our Führer which had saved Germany, us all, in the nick of time by having struck first against the Jewish-Bolshevik menace, and that it was therefore our right to be here in Russia.

Had it not been for Kitt, I am sure that we other three somehow would have accommodated Lazar in our circle. Life was hard enough without having to deal with a close enmity. But Kitt was adamant that there was no bridge reaching out across the gulf to Lazar, that man was a Jew which was the beginning and also the end of the story. When they were working together, and as *Zugführer* and gunner it was essential that they were, the air was always laden. Lazar was far more intelligent, quick-witted and knowledgeable than Kitt, but there was no possibility of overcoming their differences. When I was driving and Lazar sat next to me away from the others, I felt that he had weighty personal problems on his mind, at times I even felt sorry for him, and tried to get him to tell me about his troubles. Only once did he mention his family, saying that both his parents were dead. Even with all my prejudice, I did not dislike him personally, and found conversations with him always interesting and stimulating; but I considered it incredible that a Jew should be my immediate superior at the Eastern Front of all places. Lazar was no coward, but neither was he reckless. He expressed that a living coward was far more useful than a dead hero, and though we all could only agree with that sentiment, to Kitt it was further proof of decadent thinking. After a while, Lazar asked us to call him by his first name. Though first-name calling was frowned upon between Führer and man in our very disciplined Army, it was not forbidden. But Kitt kept calling him '*Herr Unteroffizier*', while we others made use of the offer in a quiet unobtrusive way.

At about this time autumn and the bad weather had arrived. While the main part of our Army was already battling in Stalingrad itself, our Division, the 22nd Panzers, was attached to a Romanian Army whose task was to protect the long northern flank which General Paulus's direct push to the east had created. Whenever a threat developed on this long line of operation, it was our job to clear it up. At that time, according to circumstances, I drove a half-track again, and there were many occasions when our crew was sent on individual, lonely missions to strengthen one sector or another.

Almost apologetically Lazar told us one evening that he had had the fortune of having studied economics at university. When one of us mentioned that we, working-class lads as we were, never had a chance to do that, Lazar pointedly asked whether it had never occurred to us that this was fundamentally wrong. And when I asked him how his father had had so much money to let him study, he speedily agreed that a place at the university should never depend on the size of a father's purse. We often had discussions about all sorts of subjects in which he seldom took part, except by asking 'don't you think —', and then leaving us alone to argue it out.

On one foray we had to guard the course of a narrow river along a valley, and had dug ourselves a comfortable cover in an earthbank, with our cannon close by in position. When it was Lazar's and my turn to be on guard at the cannon, he became rather pensive and then asked me outright what I really thought about Russia and its people; and when I told him that I had never really thought about it, he pointed out that this in itself surely was strange.

'You have fought and risked your life in this country for about a year, and you tell me that you have never thought about its people and what you are doing here?' I explained to him that Russia was simply the enemy and its people were Slavs, of a lower racial order. 'And why do you think they are your enemies and of a lower racial order?', he wanted to know. When I responded that we had been told that often enough at school, in the Hitler Youth, in newspapers and on the radio, he said something like 'Tell a lie often enough, and in the end even a liar believes that it is the truth! But I don't think that you really hate them, Henry, because I so often see you go out of your way to talk with them'. Having criss-crossed the Soviet Union in service with the Panzers for several thousands of miles, I naturally had seen a lot of it and had had contact with many of its people, and his question bothered me. And he dug into me even more by saying that he thought it much nicer to make friends than enemies, and that he really did not think that deep down I held any hatred for the Russian people.

'No' I retorted, 'not personally, but they are our enemies and I suppose it makes it much easier, to hate one's enemies than to love them.'

'So Christ's teaching to love one's enemies then does not mean anything to you, does it?'

'No it doesn't! In any case, Christian teaching and real life seems so often to me to stand in total contradiction to each other, and our regimental padre with whom we prayed for German victory, obviously does not think so either, and as our buckles have the inscription '*Gott mit uns*' does that not clearly imply, that God is *not* with the Russians? In any case, to fight them and love them at the same time does not make sense, does it?'

Exactly!, as you say, it doesn't make sense! So why do you fight them? I found it more and more difficult to follow this argument and I knew that it was driving me into a corner out of which there was no escape. And when I rather rudely told him to shut up as he was annoying me, he did so but handed me the binoculars through which I observed a small group of Russian soldiers carrying their mess tins to collect food, and the thought came to me: Yes, why should I hate and fight them, what have they ever done to me. What Lazar had said bothered me now very much, though I did not let him know.

As the battle in Stalingrad moved rapidly towards its critical outcome and all transport priority was given to it, autumn arrived with bad weather and much gloomy foreboding of what winter would have in store for us. To save our very scarce petrol resources, part of our division was ordered to quarter itself in the area around the large town of Millerovo and Panzers were only used for absolutely necessary forays. We dug sloping holes into the ground into which we drove our Panzers and covered them with straw against the frost. We even refrained from running the engines, being confident that everything would be all right once our petrol did arrive and we could take the straw off. But the enforced rest period lasted longer that we anticipated and when towards the end of October we finally took the straw off, there was catastrophe! However much the Panzer drivers pressed the starting buttons, no squeak came from the motors. And then we discovered the reason: mice, ordinary field mice, having nested in the straw, had found their way into the tanks and ripped the insulation covering off the electric cables.

No amount of shouting helped and attempts to blame anyone were academic. The delay before cables could be obtained from the rear was infuriating and probably very costly in operational terms as it gave the Red Army much additional breathing space which, no doubt, they used skilfully for their battle with Paulus in the Volga city.

The jokes we had to put up with from other units were not too hard to bear: we simply put up stony faces. But when we were told that *Stavka*, the Soviet High Command, had announced over the air waves that our Division of which we were so proud had been beaten by Russian mice, we felt hurt and not a little ridiculous.

It was early November when, after a tedious day of struggling about, we reached a large village, I think if was Perelasovski, to the south of the Russian-held Don bridgehead south of the town of Serafimovich. All day there had been a cold rain, and we were all very tired and fed up with it all when suddenly the long-simmering tension between Lazar and Kitt dramatically burst into the open. The Romanians, as so often before, had unnecessarily sent us on a wild goose chase and we were all angry with them and ourselves, and looking forward to a night of peace and rest. We had ordered the peasants in our cottage to keep in the back, had unpacked our food-boxes, and had put candles everywhere, while Balbo (we called him that because his black beard was like the Italian Air Marshal's of that name) was busying himself cooking a meal on the stove. Afterwards we cleared away when Kitt started it all right out of the blue.

'Well', he said, and as everything with him it was all either black or white, 'it won't be long now and we will have driven the Russkies into the Volga and all will be over!'

'And how do you make that out?' Lazar retorted, and I could see the danger signals flashing in their eyes.

'You surely would not doubt Paulus's ability to finish this little lot in Stalingrad with us here successfully holding the flanks, as we are doing every day, would you now, *Herr Unteroffizier?*'

'Ah,' said Lazar, 'I would not agree that this is a "little lot". Sure, Paulus has ability, but unfortunately he is not the only one. We have been close to the Volga now for many weeks, and you can bet your last hand-grenade that this delay was not Paulus's choice. Winter is now almost here and the "Red Rabble" has not been smashed to smithereens as so many had predicted!' He looked around the table at all of us, and sensing general agreement, glued his eyes back on Kitt and went on: 'Look here Kitt, why do we two always have to quarrel about things we have no power to alter, and let bitterness spoil the few hours we can snatch in rest? Sure, I want to get out of this never-ending hell the same as you, but it is no good if we fool ourselves by making statements which simply bear no relation to reality!'

With his elbows on the table and pushing his head forward from the neck, Kitt screwed up his eyes, which boded no good. His face had changed colour to deep red, and his eyes shot flashes of blue steel across the table to where Lazar sat.

'Are you suggesting that I am dishing up lies?' he asked almost tonelessly with his teeth closely together, hissing more than speaking. But Lazar was wise enough to have recognized the danger and withdrew some of the sharp edges of what he had said. 'No, I never said that, I would never level a personal accusation against you, you know that. With us five sitting around this table and the Russians only a kilometre or so away, the word "lie" would not come into it anyway, but I feel that we would be foolish to turn a blind eye to facts. As we all know only too well, the fact is that we have been here since the late summer, that it is now November and we still have not, apart from that short stretch to the north, reached the Volga. And that, the physical reaching of the Volga, is the rock of all the truth against which all mere words, yours or mine, will falter!'

Being put into his place like this, and by Lazar of all people, was too much for Kitt. What probably made him more furious was the smooth and convincing way in which Lazar had hammered his points home and he must have had the suspicion, though none of us said anything, that we were largely in agreement. But as it turned out, Kitt was not so easily beaten; as so often before when up against the ropes, he found what he thought was a sure way out. He used the trump card and brought the Führer into play, claiming that what he had just said had been said by the Führer only recently in his speech to the old Party Comrades.

'And now, *Herr Unteroffizier,*' and he looked around in a triumphant way, 'what have you got to say to that? Is Adolf Hitler a liar? Is he feeding us with lies and are we fools swallowing them?' And he sank his cold blue eyes into Lazar, who started to fiddle uncomfortably on the other side of the table. What could he say to that? Had he been wise and controlled enough, he would now have withdrawn and left the field and the satisfaction to Kitt. He was battling with himself all right, but then, in the end, he decided to go on.

'No Kitt, you are wrong! We all listened to that speech back in October and the Führer never referred to the outcome of the "Battle of Stalingrad", as history will surely name this horrendous clash when it is all done, he was talking about the war as a whole, about the unholy alliance, as he called it, of America, England and Russia, between plutocracy and Bolshevism, which had lined up as a convenience against our Germany, and the sacrifices we will have to make to overcome that evil. You remember when he said that battles might be won or lost, but that he will make sure that the last battalion will be German. This war is the biggest our world has ever seen, with economic, financial, social and industrial tentacles digging deep into the soil of Europe and the world. We might find that it is easier to start a war than stopping one.' At this, Balbo stroked his beard and looked around cheekily, saying that he hoped to be a member of that last battalion; a fleeting thought came to me about what good a German victory would be if all the other battalions had been sacrificed.

'Well, *Herr* Economist, clever words indeed!' said Kitt, and his voice was hard and sarcastic. 'But will you be so kind now and enlighten us on what these many different tentacles are?' Lazar leant back, tilting his chair and stared right in front of him under the table without saying a word for a long time. Did he realize that he was now on a slippery slope? Then we heard shots outside and Balbo went to investigate.

Coming back he said that the Romanians had been silly goats again, someone must have seen something. This interruption had given Lazar time to think and to come to a conclusion. He looked up at all of us, and when Kitt, addressing him as *Herr Unteroffizier*', goaded him with the promise not to interrupt again, Lazar pulled out all the stops. An uneasy feeling came over me, and I wondered what the outcome would be of all this. He lifted himself from his seat to extend his hand across the table, and said:

'No ill feeling, Kitt; whatever I say, I don't mean it personally against you, but I feel that we should talk about things sensibly'. Kitt took his hand somewhat grudgingly, and we all sat back in comfort, quietly, only the flickering candles on the table giving any sign of life.

Lazar began slowly in a quiet voice. After each sentence he asked us: 'Right?'

and Fritz said: 'No, not necessarily, but carry on with it and if at the end we disagree with what you have said, we will tear you to pieces!' From then on Lazar spoke fluently and with obvious conviction. The gist was that since the end of the last century the capitalist world system had been labouring in a deep crisis. In the so-called developed world there had been mass unemployment, with the masses becoming increasingly restless and revolution in the air. The 1914-18 War, he claimed, had been nothing more than the main robbers falling out amongst themselves over the loot from the rest of the as yet defenceless world in Africa and on other continents. Tsarist Russia, at that time socially and economically backward, had been as bad as any, but while its rich were making tremendous war profits, its poor had paid a terrible price in suffering. The outcome was that they had risen against the injustice. The first action of the new Revolutionary Government had been to declare peace, to call an end to the slaughter. But when the rulers in the West, in America, Germany, Britain and France woke up to the fact that the workers' government in Russia was deadly serious in its determination to abolish the capitalist system once and for all, and to replace it with a socialist society, a vicious civil war followed in which the old aristocracy, the big landowners, industrialists, and militarists tried to restore their former privileges. When that failed, the 'free' world invaded with their armies, American, French, British, Japanese and even the beaten German forces, and clamped their fangs into the bleeding flesh of Russia. But after enormous sacrifices, the Russians had flung them all out and had then set out to get their house in order.

All this was new to me. Apart from my father, who had hinted at this version of history, I had only ever heard that Bolshevism and Communism were criminally bad. I noticed that Kitt did not like at all what he had heard, but he said quietly: 'Carry on then, *Herr Unteroffizier*'.

'And that', Lazar continued, 'was still roughly the situation in 1939. The big capitalist powers, ours included, were still locked in deadly rivalry over the world markets, the minerals and above all the big profits, without which the capitalist system simply has no meaning. And if you tear the mask from all the faces who shout fine slogans about freedom, democracy, human rights and the new order, you will find nothing but greed, brutality and hypocrisy. The only change is that Russia has fallen out of that system, for in that country you will find no Rockefeller, Schneider Creusot, Krupp, Siemens or Vickers Armstrong for whom wars are extremely profitable. Our very fighting here at the Eastern Front is so relentless, so vicious, so brutal, because it is a head-on clash between two systems, one dying — and the other to be born. And there will be no give on that.'

At this point Balbo butted in, asking why in that case Russia was an ally of America and England, as after all, Germany was a National-Socialist country.

'Oh, don't be fooled,' said Lazar 'that alliance is nothing more than a marriage of convenience and will fall apart the moment they have us out of it. Believe me, there are many in the West who would simply love to see us and the Russians tear each other to pieces. And if Germany were socialist as you suggest, how can you explain that the land, the industries, the banks and everything else is controlled by a handful of super-rich families? Your trouble is, Balbo, that you believe everything you are fed with. Thomas Mann said that the world is suffering not so much from Communism as from anti-communism. And thinking about it, he might have a point.'

At this point Kitt could stay quiet no longer.

'Rubbish!', he said, 'all rubbish! Are you saying that National Socialism is nothing but a cover and our Führer no more than a tool for saving the capitalist system from socialism, and are you denying that Russia was not posed to fall on to our Germany, which only the Führer's foresight prevented by striking first?'

Up to now, Lazar had been clever enough to avoid mentioning the Führer and the Party. He could still pull out of the trap Kitt was setting, but he stubbornly went on.

'No, Kitt, in all honesty I cannot see that. I have not found one German soldier who entered Russia with Barbarossa who could say that this country was poised to attack Germany. The Russians' all-round problems were so enormous that they were not even ready to defend themselves properly.'

'So in other words you are saying that Hitler is a liar and that we are all merely here, paying with our lives, to keep the capitalists in power in Germany!' By asking that precise question Kitt had brought the whole discussion to a point of no return. Unless he withdrew everything he had said and thereby declaring himself a fool, Lazar could not get out of it. He was in a trap and Kitt, the young Nazi, kept him there mercilessly. 'Say it!', shouted Kitt, 'have the mental courage and answer my question!' But Lazar just sat there, his hands in his lap, and said nothing. He stared at Kitt in horror, he realized that he had let the cat out of the bag and looked around at all of us pleadingly. But whatever our inner-most thoughts and feelings, the argument had gone too far and we could not reach out to him. The name of the Führer had been drawn in to the argument, and Lazar had to stand or to fall on his own.

And then all Kitt's pent-up feelings, his hatred for Lazar, and the for Jews in general, came out:

'OK, have it your way. After what you have said this last hour there is no necessity for you to say any more. You have said, and we are all witness to it, that the Führer is a mere tool of the capitalist, a liar and that we are all victims of his lies. You Jewish swine, you skunk, you miserable Communist cheat, I have watched you for weeks, have listened to the many sly remarks by which you hoped to undermine our morale. But now you have gone too far. You have come up against me and I will wipe you out right here and now like a dirty louse crawling across my belly. If it's the last thing I do, I will do it right now!' Raging like a bull, he jumped up from his seat, and stalked back to the corner where our kit was hanging. With an unsteady hand he opened his holster to withdraw his pistol.

'I'll kill you, I'll kill you, you Jewish swine!', he shouted, and with that, having realized that Kitt had lost control, we jumped on him, wrestled the pistol out of his hand and pressed him into a seat in the corner. And while we held him down, suddenly everything changed in him, and he pointed to behind the stove where the Russian peasants were sitting petrified at this spectacle in their midst. 'Look, they have watched us all the time, they are our enemies, they must think we are mad.' And then again, turning towards Lazar, but this time in a very quiet voice: 'You swine, you Jewish swine!' By then he had burnt himself out. He bent forward, his body began to shake as if in convulsion, and when he lifted his head slightly I could see that his face was wet with tears. Kitt, who had never shown fear of anything, was crying like a child. We all knew that the danger had passed, and we released him.

While all this had been happening we had completely forgotten about Lazar. Since Kitt's outbreak he had uttered not a word, had made no movement, and his face was as white as a sheet. With a gesture of despair he said, 'What a mess, oh, what a mess!' There were tears in his eyes too, but when he raised his head shortly after, we could see that he had a firm grip on himself, and he said: 'Thank you, thank you all, I am sorry, Kitt!'

We carried on as if all was normal, we laid our blankets on the floor and had an uneasy sleep. Outside it was frosty, and we could hear the Romanian guards tramping up and down the village street past our cottage, quietly chatting to each other. We knew that the Russian positions were in sight.

It was an unspoken agreement that nothing was said of what had happened on that night, and from then on we were in action every day. Our Sixth Army was under great pressure inside Stalingrad, and had not yet reached the banks of the Volga. But we were successfully holding the flank. Kitt and Lazar hardly ever exchanged another word, and while the latter made some attempts at being friendly, Kitt totally ignored him. Kitt seemed much quieter, not so boisterous as of old; perhaps he had matured.

By the middle of November, I think it was the thirteenth, there came the first real snow of winter. Everything looked different now, not so hard, more serene, and sounds carried differently in the air. In a way it also calmed our nerves, it made us more fatalistic, deep in our bones we sensed that we would have to take what was coming to us.

Having been static for several days in a Romanian line of defence, we had dug ourselves a comfortable bunker, with our PAK only a short distance away pointing towards the Russian lines. Several times we had reported to our Command that during the night we had heard much activity on the other side. We knew what we were talking about when we insisted that the howling engines were those of T-34 tanks, but our officers knew better, they said the Russians were tied down in Stalingrad and on their last legs, and were probably driving the odd T-34 up and down to confuse us.

But then came the night of November the 18th. It was miserably damp and cold, snow flurries had covered most of the ground, and there was no echo in the air. It was about 2.00 a.m. when I crawled out of our bunker to take over guard duty. The night was unusually still and my mate told me that all the irritating Russian movements had stopped about an hour ago. My rifle over my shoulder, and well protected by my greatcoat, I walked over to the Romanian gun positions. One of their guards told me in a mixture of broken German and Russian that he did not like the silence over there, it was like a stillness before the storm. I was glad when my time was up at about 4.00 a.m. and

I crawled back into the cosy bunker, banked up the fire in our little cannon stove, undressed and stretched out to get some sleep.

The next thing I knew was that all hell had broken loose. The vibrating air blew out the candle and we were trying to sort ourselves out in utter darkness. The whole place trembled, bits of earth fell on to us and the noise was deafening. We were sleep drunk, and kept bumping into each other, mixing up our uniforms, our boots and other equipment, and shouting out loudly to relieve our tension. Somehow I managed to scramble into my things, realizing only much later when I felt the draught on my backside, that I had put my trousers on the wrong way round. We went out from one bedlam into a much worse one, an inferno of noise and explosions. We behaved like well-organized robots. Kitt and Balbo jumped forward to man the PaK, while I helped Fritz to supply the ammunition. The sky was lit up all around us, like day at times. Mortar bombs whined through the air, exploding with thuds which made the earth tremble. Everthing was in utter turmoil and I heard much shouting and crying from the Romanian forward line. And then, as suddenly as it had started, it stopped, with an eerie silence enveloping us all. We knew from experience that this had only been the first phase, the overture, and that the real conflict was yet to come.

By now dawn had crept faintly into the eastern sky, the fog had been completely blown away, and my truck further back was in flames. But the five of us were all right, no one was hurt and we signalled 'thumbs up' to each other. From now on we could only wait. Some flares were sent up from the Romanian positions, but our eyes were glued to the other side from where, we knew, the Russians would soon be coming. The overture was over.

And then we heard the revving up of the heavy engines. That lasted for a few minutes and still nothing moved. But that roar was of such a commanding nature. It was how I had always imagined the angry Gods of War to sound. Above us circled a lonely plane, but we bothered little about that.

Then we heard the heavy clanging of tracks. Someone further along quite unnecessarily shouted: 'They are coming!' And then we saw the first of them crawling out of the greyness, an ugly, frightening sight. They had their headlights full on, and from between them their guns were blazing. It was impossible to tell how many there were, but I fleetingly recalled our officers' statement that the Russians were 'fooling us with an odd tank'.

Right in front of us, parallel with our line, there ran a ravine with steep banks, perhaps three metres deep and twenty wide. Some of the tanks had already dipped down into it, disappearing from our sight, and I could hear them rummaging around at the bottom, right under our noses. Then the first of them came stumbling up reaching steeply into the sky, exposing its vulnerable belly for a few seconds, before coming down with a thud to move on towards us. When they were not much more than fifty metres away, I could see that they had infantry with them, saw their machine-pistols flashing, and knew instantly that the game was up, that there was nothing to do anymore but to dive for cover.

I flung myself into the small trench outside our bunker entrance, got somehow past the sack we had as a door, and huddled up in the protective darkness, away from it all. Then I heard Russian voices just outside — some were laughing — and I felt rather than heard their T-34s rolling through our positions, as if they had never existed. I crawled right into the corner by the stove, knowing that should a tank roll over the cover I might get away from its tracks in that blind spot. Never before had I felt like that, like a hunted, defenceless animal, not daring to move, with all the aggression, even the urge to fight and defend myself, knocked out of me. The air smelt like burning ashes, and holding my head between my knees, my only thought was 'Mother, why did you give birth to me?' And then suddenly — had it even lasted half an hour — it became quiet, apart from a faint roar dying away in the distance.

I could find neither matches nor candle in my nervousness, and the stove had gone out. I wondered why no one, German, Romanian or even Russian, had come in; anything, anyone would have been a relief. Carefully I crawled towards the entrance, to inch the sack aside. Morning had come and the sky was grey and heavy. For a long time I sat and listened, my mind confused, and did not dare move any further. And when I put my hand out into the trench I touched something soft — Fritz, who was lying behind the sack, face down. I shook him quietly and called out to him, but there was no response. I crawled over him and noticed that our machine-gun had gone, and that part of the trench had collapsed, crushed by the wide tracks of a tank. My senses were now alert, and when I lifted my head above ground level I could make out no movement; all around was eerie silence. Was I going mad, was it all a dream? Wherever I looked there was churned-up earth. Our PaK was rammed into the ground as if a tank had gone right over it. Kitt and Balbo lay behind the shield, squashed out of recognition. And further back lay Lazar, with his shoulder and half his head torn away. But what had happened to all the others, all the Romanians; had they managed to run away, had they been taken prisoner, or had they all been killed? When I climbed out of the trench and looked around I saw the many dead. My twenty-year old mind was in turmoil, but it quickly dawned on me that my only chance to stay alive was to get a grip on myself.

I decided to make a fire in our cannon stove. When on guard duty the night before, I had chopped some firewood, and I went over to the pile to pick up an armful of it. But just as I started walking back, I heard an engine down in the ravine. Next I saw a green Russian jeep scrambling over the edge and coming straight towards me. Its wheels were locked in tank ruts, and a soldier standing next to the driver was gesticulating wildly to show him a way out. They took no notice of me and I had to step back to avoid being run over. There were two officers in the back seats, and when they were passing me a yard or so away, one of them, while saluting me, pointed to his back side, making a grimace as if to say: 'bloody rough ride!' Not being able to salute properly with my arms full of wood, I just nodded, and he smiled back at me in a friendly manner. They must have thought that I was a Soviet soldier in a German greatcoat, and their jeep drove out of sight.

Soon I had a good fire crackling in the stove, and with warmth returning to the dug-out, life seemed to be returning in me. I had plenty of food now, and ammunition, much more than I could carry. I went out to the bodies of my mates to take their paybooks and break their identification discs. It was then that I heard some wailing and following the sound, pistol in hand, I came to a number of dead Romanians and Germans — but no Russians — lying all over the place in a hollow. Then I saw a Romanian officer with his arm almost torn off, looking at me with pleading eyes, and then I saw some more, including Germans, who were still alive, all of them badly hurt and beyond help. Having never had any medical training, and without bandages or cotton, I said nothing to any of them, gave none any comfort, not even a drink, and quickly turned and walked away from it all. Some of the Germans shouted after me: they might have been right that I was a bastard, but I knew that if I stayed, I would be drained of all my strength. Had there been only one, I would have given him the peace of the bullet.

Soon a good, rich meal of butter, meat and eggs was sizzling away on my cannon stove, and the dug-out had the smell of a restaurant. And after wolfing it down, I banked up the fire, made a soft bed with many blankets, and by the light of one flickering candle slept without dreams or any pangs of conscience.

7
Bitter retreat

Das ist der Weisheit letzter Schluss:
Nur der verdient sich Freiheit wie das Leben
der täglich sie erobern muss.

'That is wisdom's final recognition:
he alone deserves freedom as well as life
who daily has to struggle for it.'

Goethe, from *Faust*

On waking up I had difficulty in remembering where I was and what had happened. The temperature in the bunker was still cosy, though the fire and the candle had gone out and it was pitch dark. I felt thoroughly refreshed but dreading the thought of what lay ahead, it took an immense effort to crawl out of my blanket bed and get dressed. The comforting fire was quickly relit, and another big meal ready in the frying pan, the last hot one, I wondered, for how long.

I did not know it, but I had just participated in a great historic event, I had been caught right in the middle of the breakthrough of Marshal Rokossovski's Armies, which within two days trapped Paulus's Sixth Army and consequently led to its annihilation at Stalingrad.

This event was to be the watershed not only of the German invasion of the Soviet Union but possibly of the Second World War. My only concern for the time being, though, was to save my own skin. Where the German lines were after this morning's catastrophe, and how far I would have to walk to find them, I had not the faintest idea. Luckily the sky was clear, and keeping the North Star always to my right, I knew that I was heading westward, and that was where my instinct told me to go.

I took the best rifle and pistol, and packed up ammunition, food, some candles, and a small bottle of best French brandy, which I had found in the Romanian officers' dug-out. I also took a fur coat and hat from there, and later in the evening when I climbed out of my dug-out to start my walk dressed and booted in elegant furs, I would not have looked out of place in any fashionable winter resort. Only this was for real, not for show. I sneaked over to where I had found the wounded; there was no sound, and all was covered by a blanket of snow. Then I went to each of my four friends, stood next to their bodies and said their names, that was all. And when I walked away I felt like crying, not so much for the others, as for myself.

I walked all night, never daring to go close to a village, as I did not know whether it would be occupied by Russians or Germans. And when day approached I slept in barns, burnt-out cottages, on heaps of straw, or just under some protecting bush. Only occasionally did I manage to make a fire and to warm up some food. For drink, I sucked snow almost all the time while I was walking — and all around me was nothing but an endless white desert. What was perhaps strange under these conditions was that I felt bodily and mentally fit and very alert — in no way was I downcast. But oh, how great the distance from my home and childhood . . .

After I had walked for about four nights and daybreak was approaching, I came to a haystack, standing forlornly in the white nothingness. And then I noticed another figure also walking in the same direction towards the haystack. I crouched down on the snow, and realized that the figure had noticed me. He too knelt down, holding a rifle at the ready, and looked intently into my direction. Then, after we had stared at each other for a minute or so, he called across: 'Romanski?', judging probably by my Romanian fur hat.

'*Njet, Germanski!*' I shouted back in Russian, putting the emphasis on 'Ger'.

'*Ich auch Deutscher!*' (I too am German) rolled across the white steppe, and then we both advanced towards each other, swinging our rifles somehow in the air. What an extraordinary meeting it was. Fritz was a Lance Corporal of roughly my own age, and had gone through a very similar experience to mine. Two of them had set out together, but his mate had died, and he was glad now to have found a new one.

Standing there and talking, we suddenly realized that it was light, and decided to make our bed for the day in the haystack. We pulled out enough hay to make room for both of us to lie next to each other, and after we had crawled in and pulled in some of the hay to cover the hole, we felt warm and secure and quickly dropped off to sleep. It must have been in the later afternoon when Fritz woke me up, and when we listened, we heard much activity going on outside. As far as we could make out, a Russian platoon had arrived and had set up camp, and was feeding its horses from our haystack. We smelt tantalizing whiffs from a nearby field kitchen, and heard soldiers arriving all the time to have food ladled into their mess tins. Then they sat on the ground with their backs against our stack, and the nearest was hardly more than a metre from our feet. After dark we could make out the gleam of a big fire, and were worried that they might set us alight. There was beautiful singing and laughing going on, and also drinking. One of them was sick just outside our entrance.

The ordeal lasted for three nights and three days. Not having a torch, we were in pitch darkness all the time. Our conversations were held in whispers, and if one of us snored, the other had to wake him up. When they took fork fulls of hay from the top of our stack, the whole edifice shook, and we could sense the level of the roof coming down and down all the time. One of the horses seemed to be having fun throwing its weight against the stack, and there was one point when we feared that the entire haystack would topple over. When they were sitting near by it was dangerous to cough or even to clear one's throat and our lavatory business was becoming a very unpleasant problem. Having only one bottle of water, besides the brandy, our nerves were getting on edge and we began to hiss a quarrel about whether we should surrender or not.

On the fourth morning we suddenly realized that all was quiet. I crawled out first. The snow was blinding but there was not a soul to be seen. The whole place was in an awful mess with horse dung, tins, discarded equipment and other rubbish all over the place. The sun was brilliant white and there was a sharp, clear frost. When Fritz came out we hugged each other, unable to speak from excitement, or even to stand properly on our legs. But soon we jumped up and down and ran round the stack shouting to mentally relieve ourselves. We laughed and laughed, although we agreed that there really was nothing to laugh about, that our situation was still extremely serious. Fritz combed his hair as if to make himself look nice for the occasion, but I found that I could not get the comb through mine any more. We cleaned our teeth, faces and hands with snow, and then sucked the stuff avidly, realizing that thirst had been perhaps our gravest problem, and the reason for our quarrelling. There was an abnormal feeling about it all, we were euphoric and we called ourselves the 'gods of France'. But we knew that we were alive, and then we cooked ourselves a splendid meal over the embers of the Russian fire.

After that we walked for another three or four nights without any major incidents. The snow was covered with a coating of frost which crackled with every step we took. Then one night, after having spent a miserably cold day in a hedge, we found a large village in front of us like a barrier. We moved as close to the cottages as we dared, and then sat in a ditch and listened. There was much activity, with guards in white trotting up and down the village street, and we thought we heard German spoken. In the end we decided to risk it, as we were running out of food anyway. We shouted out that we were German and wanted to come in. As an answer a few bullets whistled over our heads, and when someone asked us for the daily password, of course we did not know it. The night was very clear and a few more shots came over our ditch. Then we were ordered to get out and hold our weapons over our heads. As we were walking we heard the whistling of more bullets. As our new *Kameraden* later explained, we had come right out of no man's land from the Russian lines and there had been many strange bands and individuals roaming around.

The unit was a *Kampfgruppe* thrown together from all sorts of remnants and stragglers, and we were ordered to report to a Colonel Heede, the CO. The moment I saw him sitting in his blanket, I knew that we were in trouble. He asked me whether I thought I was a figure out of Ruritania, and how I had come to look so elegant in furs. We had to undo our coats and he took a good look at our German uniforms. He questioned us closely about our units and the names of villages, and what we knew about the happenings in Stalingrad. But neither of us could tell him very much, only that it was chaos and hell out there. He mentioned the word 'deserter', and keeping an eye on us, and a possible court martial. But with Germany still more than a thousand miles away, many unforeseeable events were to occur and after a while with Field

Marshal Manstein, in command, trying to relieve Paulus in beleaguered Stalingrad, we were regrouped and separated from Heede.

Morale all round was at its lowest. All sorts of rumours circulated, and there was talk of betrayals by several high-ranking officers. General Seydlitz was mentioned, Field Marshal Paulus himself, and a Colonel Adams, who it was said had engineered the Stalingrad disaster. Of course, General Winter was still held to blame, but for those whose noses had really been rubbed in the snow at Stalingrad, that tale did not go down any more. There was the excuse of the 'long supply lines' from Germany to Stalingrad which, of course, was a fact, but it was never mentioned that there was nothing for hundreds of miles beyond Stalingrad and no free railway line leading to it, nor any bridges across the Volga, so the Russians had at least the same problem.

Luckily Fritz and I stayed together when we were attached to a rather hapless battlegroup of not quite a hundred men led by a Captain. Apart from the weapons we carried, our only other possession was one lorry of French make which was loaded to the top with drums of petrol, machine-guns, food, and equipment. In so many ways we realized how lucky we were that the Russians had still not digested their Stalingrad victory, and were still struggling with the problem of filling the vacuum which we had left behind. All in all, though, there seemed a great improvement in their leadership and in their confidence. They were generally shadowing every battlegroup of ours with a similar one of theirs. Had they had more tanks available at that time to the west of the Don, I am sure that they could have had sent all the remnants of our armies to hell. At times we met other small battlegroups, which, when small enough, joined up with ours. The gravest problem we often had to deal with was when Russian units managed to overtake us under cover of night, and to receive us somewhere with an unexpected 'welcome'.

One sunny, clear morning we approached a village. The cottages lay low in a fold and only came into view when we were almost upon them. As our food situation, as so often, was very serious, Fritz and I planned to make use of the surprise element and cash in on our own. While our group was still approaching, we slipped into the village for a quick private food search. Being in rather a hurry and without having checked on anything, we made for what looked like the nearest stable or chicken run. I had just managed to crawl into a hen house when I heard several shots and when I looked out through a hole in the wall, I saw Fritz cowering behind a fence while several Russian soldiers were rushing out of a cottage opposite, to disappear into a ditch, from where they fired in the direction from where our group was now entering the village. For a while chaos reigned, but then I noticed that whichever way I looked out of my cramped confinement, all the Russians and Germans had gone to ground. More from nerves than from expediency I fired some shots in the direction I had seen the Reds disappear. Later on I saw their footprints leading into a labyrinth of overgrown ditches, which I did not feel in any mood to investigate.

The wintry village had an eerie atmosphere — there was an almost perfect grave-yard stillness, and when we checked the cottages we found neither man nor beast. And when we entered the cottage out of which the Russians had rushed, we could see by the equipment they had left behind that they had been as surprised as we had.

Looking along a low ridge which extended from the village, we could see a small hamlet of about a dozen cottages about two kilometres away. Then one of us who had taken a closer look through his binoculars shouted out in surprise. And when I borrowed the glasses, I saw a group of Red soldiers, one of them looking through field-glasses straight at me. About four or five of us took possession of one cottage, and shortly afterwards comforting smoke was curling up from many of the chimneys in the village.

A large barn with a hay-stack in front stood opposite our cottage. We had hollowed out the top of the stack, which we used as an observation point from where the guards had a good view towards the Russian occupied hamlet. Information we were receiving seemed to suggest that our retreat was becoming more orderly, and we were pleased when the order came through that we were to stay put in the village for several days in a holding operation, to allow straggler units to fall back into line. Communications between the various battlegroups were often conducted by small groups of despatch riders on horseback.

It was during the second night, when I was on guard in the haystack, that the Russians from the hamlet attacked us. Luckily before darkness our guards had noticed unusual activity over there, which had suggested attack preparations, so we were at the ready, and our Captain had ordered an all-night alert for the entire unit. Our machine-guns had been placed in good positions and we were all waiting.

It was about midnight when we noticed movement right in front of us — white camouflage shadows were silently moving towards us through the undergrowth. We had strict orders not to shoot until the Captain fired first from a machine gun behind a low stone wall. Though none of us were unused to this kind of situation, a tension gripped us all. But then there was an accident — someone dropped a steel helmet from the stack, which fell with a loud clatter down the rungs of the ladder, and all the white shadows disappeared into the snow. As a result the first shots were fired far too early for our liking, as the Russkies were still too far away. Following a short bedlam, the Reds who had probably not been more than twenty as against our hundred, quickly recognized the hopelessness of their position and before we knew, they had retreated. However, we had chalked up one success: one of the raiders had been hit and was now lying in the snow not far from us. After we were sure that all his comrades had withdrawn, several of us approached him from several directions. He was a Sergeant, and though badly hit in the upper leg and in much pain, he was alive. He was carried into a cottage where a *Sani* (orderly) washed and bandaged his wound. He had been lying in the freezing snow for about half an hour, and after he had been given a warm drink he dropped into a deep sleep from pure exhaustion. I had a good look at him. He was well-built with a pleasant face, and cropped blond hair. Hardly a word, not even in response to our *Sani*'s questions, had come from his lips.

It was late in the morning when we heard shouts; and out of the snow came a white flag, steadily being waved from what looked like a ditch about three hundred metres away. A loudhailer voice asked in poor German if we were prepared to have a parley. There was some consternation when our Captain asked the guards how the voice with the flag had come as close as it had. As at that time I spoke the best Russian in our group, I was ordered to ask through a loudhailer what he wanted. 'Will you promise not to shoot if we come out?' the voice asked. After I had made sure with the Captain and the others, two Russians clambered out of the ditch and stood in full view. I then came from behind my own cover, without a weapon, and when I asked him what he wanted to talk about, he said 'Exchange.'

'What exchange?'

'You have a Sergeant of ours, can you tell me whether he is alive?' Assuring him that this was so, he told me that a while ago they had captured a German Sergeant, whom they were prepared to exchange. When I told the Captain, he instructed me to arrange a deal and to get on with it without referring every detail back to him. I told him that we would accept their offer, and asked how he thought the exchange should be arranged. By now our Captain and others had come from behind their cover, and were saying to me, 'Don't ask them, tell them.' I asked pointedly whether I should make the deal my own way. 'OK,' the Captain said, 'do it your way, but get on with it.'

'In that case,' said the Russian 'we will send an arranged signal back to our village and ten minutes after we start walking back, two of our guards will accompany your Sergeant and we expect two of you to do the same with ours.' As there was no sledge in the village, I asked my mates to look for a wheel-barrow. Then we put a long wide board into it, covered it with straw, laid the Russian Sergeant on to it and wrapped him up in blankets. When I asked him whether he was comfortable, he said 'No!', which made us all laugh and I realized the stupidity of my question. While watching the two Russians walking away, we could make out three figures leaving the hamlet, and started pushing our wheelbarrow through the snow. It was a very hard job and I regretted not having arranged for three of us to do it. Every few minutes we changed over, and in spite of the cold took our camouflage and gloves off.

The Russian was tough. One could see that the rough ride caused him additional pain, but he pressed his lips together and said nothing. When it was my turn to walk next to him I expressed my hope that his leg would soon be better and he responded that he would then quickly join his comrades again to fight us. 'Yes, but first you go to hospital and will have a nice long rest.'

'That's true, but I hope that it will not be for too long.'

'But why not? I was in hospital in Stalino last summer, and wished that I could have stayed there until the war was over.'

'Ah, but your situation is very different from mine. While you may look at this war as some sort of an adventure, as part of which you have invaded my land, for me there is a sacred duty involved to free my land, and I am prepared to back it up with my life.' And by the way he said it and looked at me, I could see that there was much anger and bitterness in him.

'But why should it be different? We are both soldiers even if your uniform is brown and mine is field grey, and at the moment we both look very much alike in our camouflage white.'

'But you have forgotten the main difference, you are in my country, I am not in yours, and as far as I am concerned, there cannot, there will be no peace until we have forced you out.'

'Are you saying that you would like to kill me, after I perhaps have helped to save your life?' Now I was angry and I think that he could read it in my face.'

'No, I did not say that, you are twisting my words, German. I have said that I will fight to the last to free my country from your occupation, which would lead to enslavery of myself and of my people.' At this moment we stopped for a rest and the three of us sat on the wheelbarrow, all close together. We could see the three figures coming from the hamlet, still about a kilometre away, and that all the Germans as well as the Russians were out in the open to watch our proceedings in no man's land. All around us was total peace. On the ridge to our right stood a number of firs, now heavily laden with snow, and the track we were taking, buried under snow, was indicated by bits of untidy hedgerow all along. I looked at our helpless Sergeant, who was obviously suffering, and my mind was disturbed. I was sure that he was a good human being, but we were enemies and I could not quite reason out why that should be so. When I picked up the handles to push on, he turned his head to me and said: 'Thank you German soldier, yes, personally, purely personally, I thank you. I will not forget this as long as I live.' I felt very strongly, though, that there was much between us as well as dividing us, and that mere words could not reach out over that barrier towards a better understanding.

Although I only realized how stupid it was after I had said it, I hoped that 'one day the war will be over and I might come into your country on a visit and then we could be friends.'

At this his face hardened, he looked firmly into my eyes and said: 'No, German, I don't think you want to understand. As things are I don't think that I would welcome you — and anyway, what makes you think that you will be coming into my country and I not in yours? Do you still believe that you belong to the master race and that you will win this war?' He said it with such a vicious undertone that I felt hurt and uncomfortable, and then trudged beside him without making the slightest effort to continue our conversation.

'Look', he said, 'I will try to explain, because you Germans simply don't seem to understand what you have done to us. I am a factory worker from Minsk and married my lovely Minka three years ago. She comes from the country, is very beautiful and we love each other very much. We lived with my parents in a small flat where we had one room which at night we had to share with two of my younger brothers. Then Minka had a healthy baby boy Sergei, and our plans were to work — not to fight — for a better life for all, which the Revolution had made possible for us. Then my mother died and a few days later you Germans fell into our country just like that. Did you ever think about what right you had to do that? I was called up to the Army and taken to beyond Moscow for training. But your Panzers moved fast. Minsk, my Minsk which I loved so much and was proud of fell in the first, very hot summer. And I heard nothing from home, what happened to Minka, Sergei, father, my brothers

and my sisters. Not so long ago I got a letter from my father by the under-
ground route, the first sign of life since I had left them. I was frightened to
read what was in there. He wrote that the conditions for all the Russian people
were dreadful, but that Minka and Sergei and the children had left the city
a few days before the savages arrived. He also warned me to be prepared for
the worst, for he had received no news from them. My heart is at breaking
point and I could cry all the time! And here you walk beside me after all this
as if nothing had happened and simply announce that afterwards you want to
come here on a holiday and be my friend. No, German, have a heart! I love
my people and my country and I always thought that I loved humanity as a
whole. But now I know that I don't love you and I hope to God that I never
set eyes on any of you Germans again. Now, do you understand?' He turned
his face to me, his whole expression open and sincere, though racked with
pain — and then I saw that he had tears in his eyes. And of the two of us,
it was me that was unable to hold the gaze.

I was surprised to suddenly hear voices. We had arrived. The three figures
were now only a couple of hundred yards away and had stopped. We put the
barrow down and I waved a greeting and an invitation to join us. Only one
of them came forward and I went to meet him. '*Stravdsvite, tovarish!*' (greetings comrade), and we shook hands. He opened his camouflage, and revealed
his rank as a Lieutenant. I opened mine and he seemed surprised that we had
only sent a low-ranking soldier on a mission like this. He was a few years older
than me, athletically built, with blond hair and friendly green eyes. We realized that my Russian was better than his German, and conducted our talk in
that language. Then he pulled a small green bottle of vodka from his pocket,
and offered me a good gulp, then waved the others to come and join us. Then
we all went to the barrow. There was much hugging between them, and handshaking amongst all of us. Then the Lieutenant held the bottle high, quietened
us by pushing his free hand in front of him, pointed to the Sergeant and said:
'To Vitaly's health!' And we all five joined heartily in that toast. Vitaly looked
sheepish when he took a little drop more than his share, but none of us begrudged
it. Then my mate took out a couple of packs of *Bahlsen* biscuits, which he
had brought especially for the occasion, and placed them in Vitaly's lap so
that everyone could help himself. It was the only time in my life that I had
had vodka with biscuits, and I liked it. Within a few minutes the stiffness of
the occasion had evaporated, there were smiles all round, pats on the backs
and even loud laughter. Everyone talked, and I was much in demand to translate.

The German Sergeant was in good health and assured me that he had been
treated correctly, and I heard Vitaly say to his Lieutenant that he had had all
the help and care he had needed. Each one of us saw the joke when our Sergeant asked me to translate that his captors owed him a receipt for the rifle
and pistol they had taken from him. To great amusement the Lieutenant pulled
out a bit of paper and scribbled a receipt on it, all correctly dated and signed.
To our disappointment the bottle was found to be empty, and had fallen into
the snow. Then the Lieutenant picked it up, demanded silence, held it high
again and said: '*Tovarichi, voyna nje chorosho!*' (Comrades, war is no good).

On that we shook hands. And only then did I notice that our friend in the barrow was sadly shaking his head. 'Yes' he said, 'all fine words, but what about
the reality? What about my wife and my son? What about all our dreadful suffer-
ings, does anyone think that words can put that right? And when our German
comrades go back to the village over there, will they stop the war against us?'

This outburst made us all embarrassed and serious again. We knew, of course,
that Vitaly was right, but none of us wanted to talk about it. The Lieutenant
patted me on the shoulder and said something like, 'I think we all understand.'
And we left it at that.

Suddenly there was a single shot from the hamlet, which seemed to roll across
the flat then echo back to us from the ridge. Someone was standing with his
rifle on an elevation, and waved impatiently in the air. 'Well', said the Lieutenant, 'they want us back; and as the bottle is empty and the biscuits gone
and Vitaly can do with some warmth, we just as well go.' There was more
handshaking, and a quiet '*Spassiba*' (thank you), and when I bent down to Vitaly
in the barrow, I felt apprehensive and wondered how he would react. There
was no smile on his face, only an expression of great sadness, but then to my
great relief he took my offered hand with a firm grip and said 'Thank you,
comrade.' No other word came from his lips and I wished him happy return
to his Minka and Sergei.

I turned on my heel and left without more ado — we all did. After we had
walked a hundred yards I heard a shout. The Lieutenant wanted to know whether
we wanted the blankets back. 'Keep them with the greatest of respect!', I shouted
through cupped hands. There was a final general wave from side to side, and
then we really walked away from each other.

Of course, our Captain wanted a word with me, wanted to know how we
had delivered our charge. 'He hated war', I said, 'was pining for his wife and
baby son.'

'Don't we all!', was his thoughtful response, and as if coming from an afterthought, he mumbled something like 'yes, what have we done to them? If ever
they come into our country and do half as bad to us. . .!' Unlike most other
officers, this one was generally liked as he flaunted none of the usual arrogance.

It was on the next day, with darkness an hour old, when we suddenly came
under heavy mortar fire. By the time we rushed out, our lorry, our only transport, was in flames like a torch. We had parked it out of sight behind the large
barn, but with mortars so close by and their shells falling almost vertically
out of the sky, a direct hit had put paid to almost all our belongings. Before
we knew, the ammunition boxes exploded like wild fireworks in all directions.
Then the haystack caught fire, and the sparks set our cottage alight. We were
now on a well-lit stage, while they were in total and protective darkness. Then
one of their machine-guns spread its deadly contents over us, making us dive
for cover in the snow and crawl and slither away into the dark.

With Fritz, I managed to get behind a cottage from where we could see the
flashes from their mortars. After having returned fire, we regretted it, as they
turned the machine-gun on us. Next I heard loud laughter, and a Russian voice
shouting something like '*Deutsche Schweine!*' They were now insulting us into

the bargain. And when I thought about the tone of the voice, it could have been that of the Lieutenant with whom I had drunk vodka from the same bottle only yesterday. What was the dividing line between one's feelings of respect, hatred and love? Having felt greatly drawn to him only hours ago, I now wanted to pump him full of bullets.

Then one of our machine-guns got into position and opened up from the side. That stopped them laughing. Between bursts, I heard the sound of heavy clanking, which told me that they were retreating to their hamlet, no doubt taking the same path along which we had pushed the wheelbarrow. Surprisingly only one of us was slightly wounded. We had lost our valuable transport, but had the Russians won? After all, the beautiful barn, our cottage, and the haystack, were their loss, not so much ours. What were we doing to each other?

While standing around the barn warming ourselves, the Captain told us that we were to stay for another day or so, until a horse-drawn unit had regrouped with us. He was easy to approach, a rarity amongst our officers, and I asked him what the general situation was. His family name was Back and he came from the Palatinate region of Germany.

'Your guess is as good as mine, what do you think?' When I still hesitated, suspecting a trap somewhere, he urged me to come out with it and have no fear. Speaking more to himself, he said that in a situation of this kind, all is levelled out and we should rid ourselves of all cumbersome illusions.

'Well, *Herr Hauptmann,* I think we have learnt very little from Napoleon's fate. There is a great strength in Russia of which we have taken little account. All that I suggest we should do, is to get the hell out of it now.' He nodded in agreement and reminded me that we would still have to walk about a thousand miles to the German border.

'You remember', he asked, 'when after Barbarossa the Soviets managed to shift much of their heavy industry to the Urals out of our reach? At first we thought that they would not be capable of doing it, and after they had done it we thought they would not be able to set it all up, and that anyway it was all too late for them. It's a fact that we have underrated them all along.'

'Do you think, *Herr Hauptmann,* that we still have a chance to win?'

'No, not unless America and Britain betray them and make a separate peace with Hitler. The British are wily foxes with plenty of sordid experience. Churchill, whatever he might rumble on about democracy and freedom and all that, fights this war for the exact opposite, for keeping a tight grip on his empire. He will understand all right that a victorious Soviet Union will in the long run present him with far more serious problems than Germany ever could. But I doubt that he can twist Roosevelt's tail, for there is much in the British sphere which the Yankees would not mind taking out of their troubled hands.'

'So what is going to happen to us, for if I understand you correctly, then we have as good as lost this war.'

'Well, when I talk about losing the war, I talk of the military situation, not of the economic one. Even if beaten on the battlefield, economically we will remain a very powerful nation, at the very least we will be in a very strong bargaining position. The demise of Hitler and the Nazis will not mean the end of Germany. If we get out of all this in one piece, we will see the West vie with the East to have us on their side, and if we are wise and far-sighted enough as a people, we will go with the Soviet Union,' He must have noticed how perplexed his conclusion left me, for he went on: 'Of course, you have not read Karl Marx, they kept that from you, for otherwise you would understand which way the wind is blowing. Capitalism, young soldier, is corrupt to the core and in an advanced state of dying. And to save it from its inevitable collapse you and I are here, killing, burning, destroying — and perhaps dying. When they try to tell you that you are fighting for your country, forget it, because you are fighting for something quite different. I appreciate your having listened to me attentively, thank you, young soldier.' And with that he turned on his heel to leave me standing by the burning barn, thoroughly confused.

I met Captain Back every day in one capacity or another, and now saw him in a quite different light. He too took more notice of me, but when a few days later I wanted to ask him another question, he said something about 'words not being good anymore and that we must concentrate all our energies to get ourselves out of this mess. Perhaps later!' But 'later' in that sense never really came. In the very hot summer of 1943, after he had taken up another command in what we called 'Operation *Zitadelle*' and which is known in history as the Battle of Kursk, someone told me that Captain Back had fallen in action.

A day or so after this, the stray horse-drawn unit arrived. They were a pitiful sight — just as I would have imagined Napoleon's remnants. They divided up into our already cramped cottages, and had frightening tales to tell. Often on skis, the Red Army had been cutting into them for days and nights. They had been forced to camp out in the open in bitter conditions, and their losses from sword and frost had brought them close to the end of their tether.

Surprisingly they had a doctor with them, and Captain Back had arranged that any of us in trouble could go and see him. As my old wound had become infected by lice, I joined the queue. None of us had washed properly for weeks, and when I unwrapped my leg the doctor said: 'You have not washed it, get out and come back clean'. So out I went and washed it in the snow. When I presented it again he said, 'Yes, it needs regular washing with warm water and a clean bandage to keep out the lice.'

'Can I have a clean bandage, please?'

'I haven't got one for you, can't you cut a bit off your shirt?'

'No, it's already too short as it is.' We looked at each other for a few seconds, and then I just burst out laughing.

'Yes, soldier, I know very well that you deserve better. Had I been a sorcerer as well as a doctor, I would get you a bandage. It's all ridiculous and hopeless, I know, the whole war is ridiculous — and now will you please get out and call the next one.'

When the horse-drawn unit left next morning in grey freezing fog, I noticed an old soldier opposite me in the corner, who was putting his things together. He was crying and I asked him what the trouble was. He pointed to his foot, which was stuck in a torn sock, and I asked: 'What about it?'

'Yesterday it felt very cold and I was tired, and then it began to feel comfortable and warm, and I fell asleep. And now it looks all blue and black and I have no feeling in it.'

I had a look at it. 'You'd better go and see the doctor, you know.'

'Yes, I know, but what can he do about it?'

Later I was standing outside, and I saw that old soldier, hobbling with great difficulty and holding on to a wagon. He answered my wave with sad resignation, and I wondered how many kilometres he would last, before collapsing into the snow for the last time.

Next morning we left our position, retreating on foot in a raging snow-storm. Suddenly Captain Back was walking beside me. With straw-filled steel helmets pulled low over our foreheads, and our collars up to our ears, we were bent forward against the wind, but he nevertheless gave me a friendly smile.

'We are going west, young man, towards Germany, *die Heimat*. Can you remember the rousing songs you learnt in the Hitler Youth about 'going east' to conquer new *Lebensraum*? Well, at least you can say that you tried.'

The war had entered a turbulent phase now, when fronts were beginning to tumble, when our Romanian, Italian and Hungarian allies — and to a lesser extent we ourselves — were being hacked to pieces. Fast Soviet wolfpacks had broken through in many sections, and we could never be sure any more about their presence. A few of our *Kampfgruppen* had been reorganized, and we lost Captain Back. To top it all I developed a nagging toothache with no chance, of course, of seeing a dentist, and our *Sani* told me that he was running short of painkiller tablets.

For more than a week we had dragged Egon, a wounded comrade, in the bottom of a flat-bottomed boat which we had used as a sledge. But then he had died on us, and out of the frozen earth we had had to knock out a grave for him. Though we were well aware that it was against a new regulation, we had wrapped him up in a canvas tarpaulin, then had covered him with icy earth lumps, finally smoothing it over with snow. When we looked at our handiwork, we had wondered how long it would take a hungry animal to sniff out the grave and do the rest. But then our nosy *Feldwebel* had discovered that a tarpaulin was missing, and we were in trouble. At first we tried to take the blame collectively, but then the last of us who had actually wrapped him up was singled out, shouted at in front of the whole group and punished with extra guard duty. We were ordered by our officer to return the tarpaulin, and had no choice but to reopen the grave and unwrap the body. We were all deeply upset, and considered this a sacrilege, an insult to Egon and to all of us. Thinking of our own probable fate, we considered that to be put into an icy grave with boots and all worthwhile bits of uniform removed was one thing, but not even to be wrapped in a bit of canvas was quite another. Was that the price the Fatherland had put on us?

The smell of open revolt was in the air, but putting our heads together, wiser counsel prevailed. Without really wanting to, I suddenly found that I was in the dangerous centre of it all. Someone called me the *Soldatenrat* (soldiers' representative), and I was not sure that I liked that kind of 'honour'. We were aware that we were many and the officers were few, and the depth of our sullen feeling was such that if one of us had been singled out by them for punishment, we would have turned on them, I was sure. All of us knew that there were many whose bodies were covered by snow and whose origin of death was no longer provable.

As long as we did not openly break regulations, our officers only shouted at us, but did no more. Where we previously had been very efficient, carrying out all that was necessary and much more without having to be told, we now did nothing without detailed instructions. And when an officer came close to blowing his top, we made a point of quickly gathering round in numbers. But they quickly got tired of it all, and with the Russians so menacingly close at our heels, they must have had second thoughts about the wisdom of making us resent them so much. From then on they treated us with more respect.

In many ways our tough training and even tougher experiences had probably made us into perfect soldiers. What had been neglected in our whole upbringing, though, and was now showing badly, was that we never had been prepared for defeat. In no way were we ready for this catastrophic retreat in the winter. Nevertheless, we discovered that we were able to adapt to this better and quicker than our largely unimaginative and dogmatic officers. On the whole we were closer to life, to mother earth than they, and our relations with the Russians as people were much easier than they could achieve in their arrogance.

Suddenly out of the blue one day there was an alarm. While keeping our customary daily eye on the shadowing Russians, we had grown rather bored of them and had probably let our attention slacken, when suddenly the situation changed dramatically. Not only had they come very much closer than usual, but they had acquired two armoured cars, one of which had detached itself and was now racing along our flank, with the obvious aim of overtaking us and probably cutting us off. As we had only a small Panje horse which pulled our sledge with a light PAK tied behind, we had little chance to do anything about our enemy's manoeuvre. Rather late, we discovered what this mad racing was all about: less that a kilometre ahead of us stood a bridge which spanned a narrow river.

Just as the car was about to mount the bridge, however, our PAK scored a direct hit on it, which sent it spinning to crash through the railings on to the ice two or three metres below. We rushed to the scene as fast as possible to find that the armoured car had crashed through the thick ice layer and was now half submerged in the swirling icy water. Several badly hurt and shocked Russians had managed to climb out of their sinking coffin, and now slithered and crawled about on the ice. Their soaked uniforms were almost visibly icing over in the freezing air. They had no weapons to hand to defend themselves with, and their platoon was still too far away to give them any help. They were completely at our mercy, and we did not give them any. Staring up at us on the bridge with begging eyes, probably hoping for some flash of human response, they looked instead straight into the barrels of our rifles. The ice was littered with them when we continued on our way only minutes later, in the doubtful hope that our miserable string of defeats had been broken by this 'victory'.

Dusk was already falling, when slightly to our right a hamlet appeared out of the snow. Its cottages looked huddled together, and one could almost sense the cosy warmth awaiting us in them. But our Commander, probably having the happenings by the river bridge in mind, gave the order to trudge on in search of the next village. But after having gone on through the loose snow for several kilometres, and the dark completely engulfing us, there was no other shelter for us, no hut, no stack, no bush, not even a ditch, and all around us was the white hell. After a short dicussion amongst the officers, the command came through to set up camp right here. It sounded like a death sentence, but we were experienced enough to accept that we had thrown our last card and had nothing left to bargain with.

The temperature was between minus twenty and minus thirty degrees, a bitter wind was blowing and we could find nothing to make a fire with. To keep warm we huddled ourselves around Esau, our Panje horse, which also helped him against the cold, and fed him with handfuls of hay which we carried in the sledge. Then he wanted to lie down and we stretched a piece of tarpaulin on the snow and then covered him as well as we could. When we wanted to get him up later in the morning, we found that he had died in his sleep. Having often talked to him and scratched between his ears while covering the dozens of kilometres together, I had come to like this friendly character. And a thought came to me that perhaps he was better off where he was now, and there was even a touch of hidden envy — just lying down and never to wake up again to the horrors of this world.

Without a tempering fire it was impossible to make the snow stick enough to build an igloo. Groups of four and five stood around in a human circle with arms over each other's shoulders and a blanket draped over their heads to keep the breathing warmth in. Some, being at the end of their tether, just lay down in the snow to sleep, but were forced to get up, often with kicks, as they surely would have slept into death. Most of our bread, except what had been carried against our bodies, was frozen, and we had to hack bits off to thaw them in our mouths. With it we ate lumps of honey, of which we had several blocks on our sledge. One joker said that at home he had a tiled stove, behind which he loved to sit and read while listening to soft music on the radio. Then, chewing his frozen chunks of bread, he told us about his visits to his aunt in Lübeck on Sunday afternoons, when he could have as many cream-cakes with chocolate coating as he liked, rinsed down with cups of really hot, sweet coffee. 'Cream cakes with chocolate and coffee', I thought, it was more than a year since I had last tasted them — would I ever taste them again? And then I remembered how only a few weeks ago, Egon's mother had sent him a parcel which contained brown cakes, which he had shared out amongst us. And now he was in that cold grave, not even wrapped in canvas.

The snow's reflection lit up the night to a fawn brilliancy, giving a visibility of several hundred metres, and the frozen crunchy top layer of the snow would have given away any would-be attacker making an approach. About midnight it was my turn to stand guard for an hour to protect our camp from the side whence we had come. Having relieved my mate, who looked thoroughly frozen, he said something about the advantages of fighting with Rommel's *Afrika Korps*.

All wrapped up in my camouflage, with only my eyes staring out over the desolate white nothingness, I could see no movement, nor hear any sound, apart from the occasional cracking of the frosty air. Silence was absolute and I tried to search out the planets between the shifting clouds, and thought of the vastness of the universe and what life was all about. What was I suffering for in this God-forsaken place? Tramping slowly through the snow, I shut my eyes and imagined that it was all a dream, that the misery was not real, not true. And the years rolled back like a magic carpet to my loving parents, our warm home, my soft bed, and friends I had played football with on those long, warm summer evenings, and Inge, a blonde girl for whom I had felt love but had been too shy to show her. I wanted to hold on to these thoughts with all my will, perhaps I was really in bed and this ghastly icy waste was all a dream.

When I opened my eyes and woke up to cold reality, I heard the crunching footsteps of my relief. My hour was up, and I told him that all was quiet on the Eastern Front. Hans was a jolly Rhinelander, but now he looked all crumpled up like a heap of bad luck, and I asked him what was the matter with him.

'You remember when in barracks we wanted to get away from the drill Sergeant and wanted to taste the action in the field, did you think then it would be anything like this?'

'No!'

'But you shouted like the rest of us, we all must have been stark raving idiots!'

'Yes, and do you remember how we were told that it was an honour to be sent to Russia, yet if someone committed a crime to be punished in the Punishment Battalions, he was sent to Russia too?' With that I left him, to huddle with my mates behind a snow wall. Apart from my toothache, I suffered from diarrhoea, as did so many of us, and it was always a major calamity to have to sit there with the wind blowing between one's exposed rear and the snow.

When morning showed its first light, we got ready and moved on. We were all in a bad mood, having had no sleep at all, our mental stress made all sorts of pointless quarrels break out. Over the horizon we saw smoke curling from the hamlet we had passed at dusk, and we were sure that our Russian shadowers had had a comfortable night in its warm protection. With Esau dead, we now had to pull the sledge ourselves, and we soon found that we were not strong enough to pull the PAK as well, as its big wheels kept getting stuck in the snow and it took all our strength to lift them out every few yards. It was a hard decision to blow the firing mechanism with a hand-grenade, and leave the PAK to the Russians as scrap.

It was a great relief late one morning several days later, when the large industrial town of Morozovskaya appeared out of the snow mist before us. Passing the outer gun positions, we were told that the town was to be held as a collecting point for the many units which were struggling to return west. We desperately needed a rest.

Passing a row of low cottages to our right, there was suddenly a commotion. Perhaps it was all due to our frayed nerves, which made us unable to react normally once there was the slightest provocation. A bunch of six or seven panic-stricken girls in their teens had come rushing out of one of the cottages, to run away to what looked like a quarry behind. It was their running which drew our attention; had they walked, none of us would have taken the slightest notice. At a distance of no more than three hundred metres our machine-gun opened up with its monotonous metallic stutter. There were screams, and one of the girls sank into the snow. The others came running back to help her, only to draw another slow rattle from our gun, and another girl fell into the snow beside the first. The rest went into a wild screaming flight and disappeared into the quarry. We walked on coldly as if nothing had happened.

The large, spacious town was packed with troops. Some were Italian, who seemed to have lost the last drop of will to resist anything. In one of the blocks was a *Luftwaffe* Field Battalion in their light blue uniforms, who had probably come from an abandoned airfield in the area. They made noises about being special troops whose training had cost a lot of money, and that they were too valuable to be used up in a grinding front section like this. They were sure that Goering, their Chief, would move heaven and earth to get them out of there. What they had probably not realized was that many of us had been members of the Sixth Army, which had been wiped out largely because Goering's *Luftwaffe* had failed catastrophically to keep its promise and supply it from the air, and that there was no love lost between us.

After having thrown out some disorganized Romanians, we took over a collection of five or six houses and cottages as our quarters. The one I moved into with about a dozen others was a pleasant two-storey family house, made entirely of wood with a large verandah all along the front. Its only occupant, a woman of about forty, told us that her house had been requisitioned by a German General with his staff, who was to come back shortly. When I asked her for a requisition form, she, had none. And all the time we were there, there was no sign of that 'returning General', and neither was he mentioned.

With my rather outspoken prejudice against Goering's *Luftwaffe*, I was nevertheless pleased that they had a dentist with them in the former Soviet hospital. When I got there the same afternoon, several stragglers were already hanging about in the large waiting room, looking miserable. When I enquired why, and not feeling over confident myself, they suggested that I should wait until I had seen that 'butcher's' stone-age drill. When I finally settled down in his chair, trying to give the impression that I was relaxed, he asked me whether I had been in the Sixth Army at Stalingrad. Luckily he did not ask for my thoughts about the *Luftwaffe*. He hit my nerve several times, and made me almost jump out of his chair, but afterwards, *Luftwaffe* or not, I loved him with all my heart as an angel. Getting back into the waiting room, I discovered that one of the other roughnecks had pinched my cap. But when I walked back in the freezing cold bareheaded, I did not mind and could have yodelled like a new-born man. No more toothache! The filling held for about three years.

On the whole, we left our 'landlady', Irena, in peace — her whole demeanour demanded respect from us. She withdrew into a small upstairs room while we took over the whole of the ground floor. There was no electricity, no gas, no toilet or other amenities. The sparse furniture was utilitarian but there was a fine woman's touch about it all. Rough and reckless as we generally were, we took reasonable care not to damage anything in her home. It was her job to continuously fire the large grey stove in the middle of the building with timber we scrounged for her from an army depot around the corner, and even with coal from the railway yard. As the water supply had completely frozen up, Irena fetched it from a well further down the road on a shoulder carrier. It was a pleasure to watch her walk so gracefully with those two heavy buckets on either side. She was of medium height, the blond in her hair was changing to grey, her eyes were large and greenish, and I imagined that she must once have been a very beautiful girl.

There were several occasions when I found her crying, and I asked her once if she was fed up with us unruly soldiers in her house. No, it was not that, she could cope with that, and it would not last forever. But she had lost several close members of her family through the war. There were other close relatives, including her children, of whose whereabouts she was unsure, and she feared that the fighting around town might start all over again.

The situation around Morozovskaya was fairly stable; we knew that the Red Army was on the prowl near by, but there was no actual fighting. While on the surface everyone's behaviour seemed normal, I knew that underneath our nerves were tense. To be in town at the moment was all right, but we were only too well aware that the white hell continued on the other side, and that we had to get through it.

Although it was bitterly cold at night, the sun shone almost every day, and I found the sunsets, spreading their falling mellow light through the rising snow mists, extremely beautiful. The railway yard was close by and we could hear the friendly puffing and whistling of the shunting engine. As long as they were doing their work, the road west, to home, was at least still open. And that, the 'road home to Germany', was the main thought occupying all our minds. As we were not integrated into the defence line guarding the town, and were only utilized for guard duty within town at night, I had plenty of time to stroll around and observe life. We were now in the coldest part of winter, and as far as I could make out there was no food distribution system for the local population — and neither were there any cats and dogs. A large part of the population were old, and the majority female. Some came begging for food, but we had little to spare ourselves, and some came to offer their bodies for it. Asking Irena about the food situation, she said that many had died from starvation, and that she herself relied on what relatives from the country could spare. Like many others, she grew potatoes and other hardy vegetables around the house and on a patch by the river which the local soviet had given her. But as she could not keep continuous guard on it, much of it had been stolen. Once people get really hungry, she said, laws and other decencies count for nothing. I had the suspicion, though, that the Soviets had organized some sort of food distribution from the partisan-controlled country around. The Communists, it was being said, controlled the partisans with an iron discipline, which was the main reason why we could not control the areas we had conquered. I gave Irena a very valuable bag of salt, and when I asked for some of it back afterwards, she told me blushingly that the partisans had taken it. And they must have taken it from right under our noses. I sometimes wondered about the great strength of the Russian people, and what made them tick. I tackled Irena about this, and straight away she talked about the Russian Revolution, which she had lived through as a teenage girl. When I voiced my Nazi opinion that the Revolution had been a criminal episode in Russian history, she violently shook her head and expressed the view that only since the Revolution had the Russian people had a personal stake in their own destiny.

Quite suddenly, enemy troops were reported to be on the point of breaking through to the north of the town. Several hundred of us were loaded on to lorries and dumped into a miserable village about thirty kilometres away. Before leaving, I gave Irena a requisition paper stating that her house had been taken by a Regimental Staff, and signed it as a Major.

We found it impossible to dig ourselves into the frozen earth, and instead set up machine gun nests in cottages and barns, and behind walls, from where we had an open field of view. Miserable to our bones, we then awaited the arrival of the enemy. Next morning we heard the roar of heavy motors from the east. All tensed up, we got ready for battle. But when they came into sight we recognized them as German tanks, which then came slowly rumbling into our village. They were as surprised to see us as we were to see them, and they told us that not many kilometres away they had had a successful skirmish with Russian infantry, and had brought about twenty prisoners with them in the back of a lorry. At that time I wore a Russian greatcoat over my uniform, and a fur cap with dangling ear flaps which I had picked up on some lost battlefield. I stood by when the prisoners jumped off, and noticed a staff officer amongst them. When he saw me, he must have thought that I was a captured Russian soldier who was on very friendly terms with the Germans. Possibly I had said something in Russian to my mates, as we sometimes did as a joke. He stepped right over to me, called me a miserable swine and a traitor, forsaking my own people and crawling on my belly to appear friendly to the enemy. It struck me as funny and I laughed into his face, which made him even more furious and it looked as if he was going to hit me. I myself got hold of some sort of cudgel, and the guards had to come rushing to restrain us, telling me not to hurt him as he was a valuable prisoner. Only then did I have a chance to unbutton my greatcoat and reveal my uniform. Noticing his complete surprise, I saw only the funny side of it, and laughed, while he almost visibly pulled himself together, bowed slightly in that gentle Russian fashion, and said '*Prostite, ja nje snal!*' ('Apologies, I did not know'). Together with the others he was then taken into a cottage, which I later entered to see him. He was sitting on the floor, leaning with his back against the stove and his eyes rivetted on me.

'*Stravsdite!*' (greetings) I said.

'Do me a favour and open your coat so that I can see your rank, will you.' When I did, he said that as I was no officer, he saw no reason to speak to me. I told him that I did not want to question him, only to talk with him as one human being to another.

'Did you say human being, is it from our dead you have taken the coat and the cap? No, German, I don't want to have anything to do with you and if you don't like it, you can go to one of your officers and report me.' With that he had managed to reduce me to a pitiful figure, and I went out as quickly as I had come in.

Next day we were taken back to Morozovskaya, and once off the lorry, I made a bee-line for Irena's house. My requisition papers had worked, twice she had been able to turn troops of soldiers away, and on the basis of 'the devil one knows', I think Irena was glad to have us back. We gave her food with a request to cook us all a homecoming meal, and needless to say, she took part fully in it.

Next day I went to the railway yard to watch the shunting and see whether there was something to scrounge. A German engine crew was doing the shunting, with the assistance of a couple of elderly Russian shunters. They invited me up to the footplate, where I enjoyed the warmth from the fire of the boiler. They told me that they were putting together the last train, to be taken out the next morning, before all installations were blown up. They wanted to know about the situation at the front and when I told them about being relentlessly driven back for weeks now, they openly doubted our ability to stop the Russian steamroller now it was in gear. I could only agree with them.

I got up especially early to see them off the next day. Climbing up to their footplate, I could smell the lovely breakfast they were preparing on the fireman's shovel over the open fire. Then the driver pulled bottles of beer from under his seat, and with tin plates on our laps we tucked into a hearty meal. When we raised the bottles, we could think of no better toast than 'stay alive!' We looked down to the two Russian shunters who were rummaging about between the wagons and wondered what was going on in their minds, undoubtedly knowing that we were on our way out. Behind the engine was an open wagon with an anti-aircraft gun, and on the end wagon a heavy machine-gun on a tripod. A train journey, they told me, on a cloudless day was now a precarious undertaking. We all knew that the Red Air Force was now in undisputed command of the skies. What a change this was from the beginning.

I stood by the crossing when they came, puffing and clanking over the points to wave my final greetings to my friends. How much I would have given to have gone with them. They both were leaning out over the cab doors, and bade me a loud farewell. I stared after the train until it was out of sight behind a curve. The engine whistle kept blowing, its shrill sound piercing the crisp air of the fine winter morning. I could hear it for a long time, and it gave me a feeling of happy pride to know that it was meant for me to hear.

Not being in the best of moods, I walked across the yard, making my way over the rails towards the old station buildings. Our *Pioniere* (sappers), who had laid many of their charges the day before, had already started to blow up the points. I watched them. The Russian signalman, after having pulled his levers for the train to depart in a safe manner, was now walking alongside the shunters, when there was a dull thud of an explosion which shattered the old wooden signal-box and blew some of the windows out of their frames. Flames crept out from between the boards, and climbed like leeches on the outside walls towards the gutter, after which only minutes later they formed into a roaring torch, sparking upwards. Though liking fires, this one made me sad. Since childhood, railways had been in my blood. My father, a railwayman, had taken me as a little boy with him to work in the old engine sheds. What would he have said if he could have seen this mindless destruction?

The three Russians stopped and watched the destruction of their workplace. I felt very much for them, shook my head in disapproval and said, '*Isvinite, ja snaju, eto plocho!*' (Sorry, I know this is bad). I don't know whether they believed me, because they said nothing in reply. But I saw something else in their eyes, which made me shudder.

When I got back to our quarters my mates were playing cards by the warm stove. They wanted to know why I had got up so early, and whether I had found something out about what was going to happen. One of them remarked that when in the summer everything had been going ahead beautifully, the Army padres were always around to offer us religious consolation for what we were doing; now, when some of our older ones were suffering from mental stress, and perhaps needed them more than ever, they were nowhere on the horizon.

On one of my escapades I had torn my trousers, and having only one pair, I had attempted to repair them with safety pins and thin wire, but this did not quite keep the draught out. Irena offered one morning to mend them for me. Sitting with a blanket around my legs, I watched her sitting in the sun by the window, doing my trousers expertly, and I pondered on why she gave comfort to an enemy soldier in this way.

We were sure that something was going to happen soon. The Red Army was becoming more confident again, and I had seen some of their heavy tanks prowling on the horizon, like wild and hungry lions ready to pounce. A couple of Shturmoviks had skimmed just over the rooftops, bombing and strafing, and had sent everyone, German and Russian, into a panic. A small house received a direct hit, and I later heard that several old people and some of our soldiers had been killed. I had shot at the low-flying planes, hoping to hit the fuel tank or the pilot, but without success. And when I went in to Irena who was in a state of fear, I said 'The bastards!' But she shook her head and said: '*Njet,* they are no bastards, they are our pilots and are heroes!' Then she sat by the window, put both her hands in front of her face and sobbed bitterly.

Not far from our quarters was a repair shop for Panzers, which I strolled over to every day. Being a Panzer driver myself, I was able to help, and was welcomed by the crews. Many had been on forays from the town, and it struck me how little confidence they had left in our own strength. All they were talking about was how to get out of this mess.

A few weeks earlier I had lost my own Panzer, in rather unusual circumstances, and I was now quite glad to be rid of that iron coffin which, almost like a magnet, drew enemy fire wherever I turned up in it. Now I was trudging with the infantry, able to quickly disappear into any old hole as soon as the shooting started.

It had all happened when we had moved into a small town. Partisans had pulled rolls of barbed wire across the roads, which they had taken from a near-by

German depot. Trying to be clever and driving right through the wire to make a pathway for our foot soldiers, I got hopelessly entangled in the wire and ended up dragging long rolls of it behind me, which badly affected my steering.

During a shooting lull my commander ordered me to get underneath the tank and cut the wire, while the now immobile crew kept an eye on the situation from the turret. Swearing underneath, and almost getting entangled myself, struggling with my blunt wire cutters, suddenly I heard the heavy diesel of an approaching Russian tank, though I could not see it.

Afterwards I could not remember the explosion as such; all that I was aware of many minutes later was that I was lying next to a wooden fence, my uniform badly torn, and bleeding from several wounds, luckily all superficial. I felt the heat and then made out through hazy double vision a huge burning torch about twenty yards away, which was my Panzer out of which none of my mates had had a hell's chance to escape. It was only after I had painfully stumbled back to meet up with others and I could not hear what they were saying that I realized that my hearing had gone. With no medical help in that area whatsoever, I was put on the back of a lorry from where I miserably emerged 'cured' several days later, ready to go into action again.

Then the order came through that we had to leave the town the following morning; we would have to give up the relative cosiness of Irena's home for the white hell we knew would be waiting for us. While staying in town we had been reorganized and built up to about two hundred men under a new Commander, and had also been given a couple of large jeeps which towed artillery to give us greater firepower and mobility. Still in darkness when we got ready, everyone was in a bad mood. There was a roar in the air from testing and starting motors all over town. And suddenly there was a formation of low-flying Messerschmitts, and in surprise we all shouted 'Hurrah!' Had they been sent to boost our morale? Afterwards we never saw them again. We were glad that the blokes from the *Luftwaffe* had not managed to wriggle out and had to stay with us.

All strategic points such as factories, bridges, telephone exchanges etc. had been prepared for blowing up, but nothing had been said to us about people's houses. Whether that was because our new Commander had a more humane attitude, or whether we were short of dynamite, I did not know. But anything could happen, especially after Stalingrad, and some of our number had revenge and hatred in their hearts, and could so easily take the law into their own hands, and burn anything at will.

After the sun had pierced the morning mists, the first columns pulled out. Our own job was to form the rearguard and I went back into the house and was soon asleep by the stove. When I was woken again, I said 'Do swydania' to Irena and thanked her for her personal kindness, and wished her luck. She was extremely nervous and was crying. When I stepped down from the verandah, I could already smell the drifting smoke from so much burning in the town.

We stood in a half circle around our officers, who issued general instructions. Few of us bothered to listen, and I stood at the end of the column concerning myself with my kit, when Irena came running round the corner, screaming and looking for me. She was in a terrible state; all I could gather was that some soldiers had set fire to the house. Without asking permission, a mate and I rushed back to the house with Irena, where I saw two soldiers coming down from the verandah. Behind them, smoke was curling out of the open door and a flame was sneaking behind an upstairs window. I shouted at them, asking why they had done it. When I went in I could smell that they had poured petrol on the floor, and that curtains and soft furniture were already well alight. We bashed around, threw some of the things out and tried to put the fire out. But then we had no water left and it became hopeless between the two of us and, coughing heavily, we were driven back by the smoke. When I saw one of the arsonists laughing at me, I got wild. The German asked me which side I was on, and when I threatened to thump him, he reached for his pistol and I thought better of it.

Then one of our Sergeants came round the corner and shouted at us to come back immediately. As an inferno was already raging, there was nothing we could do. I wanted to stay, I wanted to go, I did not know any more what I should do. I noticed some neighbours coming over to help, and when I touched Irena on her shoulder to make her understand that I had to go, she seemed to look through me as if I was not there. When I looked back from the corner for the last time, she was kneeling in the snow with her head going up and down; being so totally helpless, I was in a rage.

I was shouted at by our new Commander, but that made no impression on me any more. The smoke, the madness, the inhumanity of it all! As we trekked away in loose column, seeing so much smoke coming from Morozovskaja, my mind tumbled in hopeless uncertainty. When I felt like talking again, I turned to an older comrade who was trudging through the snow next to me. Without really expecting an answer, I told him about Irena's house and asked him what the Russian people had ever done to us that we had to come into their country and make them suffer so much.

'Nothing,' he said, 'they have done nothing to us — except, of course, that they have dared to have a Revolution, have challenged the rights of the rich and powerful of this earth by trying to enact the Christian ideal of civilization, according to the teachings of Marx. And to turn the clock back, to destroy their Revolution, that's why you and I are here, killing, and burning your Irena's house — and perhaps dying.' It was all too much, I could not understand any more. When I asked him a couple of days later to explain to me the meaning of his words, he cut me short rather abruptly, saying 'Oh no, sonny, no more of this, I don't want any more trouble than I already have by being in this mess, and for your own good, keep it in mind that the penalty for challenging the position of the rich, for asking meaningful questions about their very existence, is death! Think a bit about it; apart from a seemingly more democratic coating, the relationship between rich and poor has not really altered since Roman times.' Well, that did put me even more into a spin of confusion, how could I tie all that up with what I had learnt in the Hitler Youth?

A short time after this we were attacked by a large pack of Colonel Badanov's tanks, with ski troops in support, Badanov being something like a Russian

Rommel in the snow. With five others I had to run for my life. Being separated, we now had to try to regain contact with our *Kampfgruppe*. We walked for long hours in the dark, and it was almost midnight when we first smelled the smoke. Following our noses, we came to a low ridge from where we could see a hamlet below — hardly more than a dozen cottages, haphazardly placed against the slope on the other side of a narrow river. Chaos and confusion all around us, we had no idea who was in occupation over there, but we were exhausted and decided that we would try. We scanned the hamlet for a while and being uncomfortably aware of the noisy crunching from the frozen snow underneath our boots, we quietly slid down on the snow-covered ice to the river. All of us being well camouflaged in white, we could hardly make each other out. The temperature was far below freezing, and the sky was clear, with excellent visibility in the snow. We had spread out on the ice, our rifles were cocked and our senses alert. There was a candle light in one of the near cottage windows, which seemed to dance towards us across the rippled surface of the snow. Then, from behind the cottage we heard the unmistakable metallic click of the catch of a rifle. Knowing what was at stake, we froze in our tracks, ready for anything. A gruff and definitely German voice called: '*Halt, wer da?*', and '*Stoy!*' (stop, who goes there?) in both German and Russian, and we were quick to reply that we were Germans. The voice told us to drop our rifles on the ice and to come towards the cottage with hands above our helmets. There were two of them, both grumpy, and obviously annoyed that we had disturbed them. They told us that there was no chance in hell to find room in any of the cottages as they were crammed full with stragglers like ourselves. We went and tried a door and all what we got was heavy abuse by the one who was lying behind it. When we reached the top of the slope and looked back on to the icy waste whence we had come, we saw a tiny shed-like cottage, half hidden behind a hedge and standing away from the hamlet. There was no light from the window, nor smoke from its chimney, but judging by the footprints we were sure that someone was in it. The door was barred from the inside, and after vainly shouting in Russian and German we decided to ram it open with a wooden beam. We then heard the muffled cry of a small child followed by shuffling steps and the shifting of wood. The door opened only slightly and a young woman with some garment slung over her shoulder looked through the gap. We pushed the door open, went in and shut it behind us.

A warm, living, human smell met us head on. One of us lit a match and held it high so that we could see. The cottage consisted of one room and there was not even the usual porch. An iron bedstead stood in the far corner, taking more than a quarter of the space. The long mud stove on the other side took at least another quarter, and at the foot of the bed stood a small table with all sorts of utensils on it; apart from a chair that was about all. A frightened, wide-eyed little girl with a baby lying next to her sat on the bed. The woman, pretty in herself but looking rather dishevelled with her long hair dangling down was about twenty five. She stretched out her arms and pulled in her neck to indicate the impossibility of accommodating six of us in the already cramped space. But I told her that her protesting was no good as we were here to stay.

After ordering her to get back on to her bed, we unpacked and somehow managed to huddle together on the floor between bed and stove. After we had put a couple of candles on the table we sliced our bread, opened a tin of sausage meat and cut chunks from a block of hard honey. One of us gave the child some honey, which she licked and obviously liked, and held triumphantly to her mother. And when I patted her head and she laughed we all joined in and the ice had broken. Nine human beings, thrown together by fate into one tiny room. Who could be the enemy of whom?

Having asked her, the woman told me that a couple of days before Soviet soldiers had come through the village and two, she emphasized that it had only been two, had stayed in her cottage — just like us. They had then walked in the direction which we were going to take tomorrow, meaning, of course, that our enemy was already in front of us. She said her husband was a soldier and that she did not know where he was nor what had happened to him. The baby started to cry and it was obvious that she wanted to breast feed it, but naturally felt awkward to do so in our presence. When we told her to go ahead and not to bother about us, she responded with relief, unbuttoned her shirt and took out a beautiful breast. Though each of us dared to look at it only from the corner of our eyes, it was almost too much to bear, and threatened to choke our eating. The baby suckled away and the woman looked happy.

Lying like sardines and somehow stretching our legs under the bed, we had a fair, warm night. When morning showed its first light and I woke up, I watched the woman playing quietly with the children. Seeing me awake, she signalled that she wanted to go outside, picked up the girl and stalked carefully over us. Lying on the floor, I helped her and when I touched her in an awkward manner, my blood ran faster and when she looked down at me for that split second, I could see that she had understood. She returned with kindling wood and an armful of peat, and soon her experienced hands had a lusty fire crackling in the stove. When she stepped out again with a bucket, I took it from her and we walked together to the well down in the hamlet where soldiers and women were queuing and where we had to wait our turn. We were the only 'couple', which all the others seemed to notice, looking at us in silence. I was sure that she intentionally gave the impression that I was her escort, and I too felt like saying to them all: 'Yes, we two, she and I, are together.' By the time we came back, breakfast was about ready and we ate exactly the same as we had eaten the previous evening. This time, though, we shared our rations with the family and I tried to converse with the woman, asked her her name and told her mine. But she would not be drawn, and only kept repeating that '*voyna nje khorosho.*' (War is no good).

The time came to leave, and our few belongings were quickly put together. Though we were short ourselves, we gave the little girl a chunk of honey. The woman followed us to the door with the girl. There were polite bows and unconvincing smiles. When I tried to attract her gaze, I recognized the impenetrable barrier of sadness between us.

A bitter wind had blown the clouds away, and I was making up the rear of our party when we reached the ridge. Looking back I saw the woman still standing there, looking at us, and when I turned and waved at her, it was against all my expectations that she waved back.

The walking was hard as the snow was deep, and every quarter of an hour or so we changed the front man. Like yesterday, we were on a featureless plateau which stretched endlessly in every direction. The sun was slightly up and gave us the feeling of warming our backs. There were no bushes, no trees, no cottages to be seen anywhere.

After having struggled a couple of miles or so, we heard planes in the sky behind us. Then we saw them, flashing in the sunlight, Russian planes, and they were diving on to our hamlet, which we could not see anymore, and we heard the machine guns splutter and the explosion of light bombs. I thought about the woman with her two little children. How frightened they must be.

Then the planes turned and came towards us, having probably seen our tracks in the snow. They rose playfully into the sun to make a circle around us, and then dived low and aimed at us as if playing a game, one after the other. There was no ditch, no hole, no furrow to creep into, only the soft snow, more than a foot deep. The bullets went close, but they missed. Then they set out to fly another circle, mocking us again, dipping their wings and then coming right out of the sun. The bastards! How I hated them! Their engines screamed and their bullets whistled, hitting the snow all around us. When they finally left, there were cries of pain. All this had lasted no more than a matter of seconds.

One of us was dead, one side of his head was a gaping mess, another was badly wounded with his side torn open, and the white snow was turning red beside him. We looked at each other in silent agreement, what choice did we have? Being the eldest of us youngsters, I held his head with one hand and spoke to him with a reassuring voice. In the other hand I held a pistol. The ensuing sound with the body so near was muffled. And all around us was stillness and peace. No more pain. We shovelled the snow with our hands until both bodies were cov⁻red. Then we just walked away.

Later we stopped for a break. One of us pulled out a chunk of bread and tore it into four parts. As if there was nothing more important to talk about, we remarked that the bread was slightly frozen and that we should have carried it on the outside of the pack so that the sun could have got at it. When we packed away, we checked on what we had left and wondered how long it would take us until we would find our unit or any other which would supply us with food. We knew that only four of us would now share the food of six, which gave us a better chance of survival.

When we finally met up with our severely reduced unit, they had joined with another one which had a number of Panzers, and when one of the drivers was taken ill, I was ordered to take his place. My God, did I hate it! In our new-found strength we approached a small industrial town, situated on the west bank of a river, in which we had planned to stay the night. The town being in our rear, our command had taken no precaution when we crossed the river. But as we approached the middle, with no cover whatsoever, we unexpectedly came under massive fire from the town on the high bank opposite us, and had no choice but to turn back and regroup to mount an attack. Having been on the move all day, and with the temperature dropping dramatically, we were very tired and in dire need of a resting place for the night. The very last thing we wanted was to fight for it. The reason for our predicament, as we found out later, was that a Red Army unit had managed to slip past us unnoticed and had joined up with the local partisans to give us a welcoming party.

After a quick command meeting, our officers decided battle tactics and we were spread out and prepared to cross the river on a wide front to roll up the enemy positions from the sides, when a report came through that a formidable ·enemy tank pack with mounted infantry was approaching rapidly from behind us, only a few kilometres away. Too late, we realized that we were in a cleverly-set trap. Luckily for us, our side of the river, though flat, was well covered with low trees and bush which offered us good defensive cover against the oncoming tanks, and as soon as we had deployed into defensive battle formation, we saw them rumbling in from the horizon. All of us were experienced soldiers, and there was no need for our officers to tell us what was required and what was at stake, for we knew all too well that to lose an engagement of this kind would have catastrophic results.

My Panzer was standing amongst birch trees facing east, in an excellent firing position. To both sides of me, PaK and other Panzers were also in well hidden positions. The atmosphere was tense. We talked quietly to each other without really having the wish to talk, and standing low in the ground with the fading light behind us, we had the advantage of seeing them clearly without their having a clear view of us. They were like wolves, waiting for their prey to show the slightest sign of weakness. I watched them approaching slowly, moving a bit, stopping again, lifting their hatches slightly to scan the woods we were in. There were about a dozen of them. Some moved to the flanks, only to come back quickly. It was their showing of nervousness, exhibiting classic signs of not being sure what to do.

We had strict instructions not to fire until a Panzer to the right of us opened up, whatever happened. Then a Sergeant came creeping through the undergrowth to inform us that we had made radio contact with a brother battle-group about a dozen kilometres to the west of the town, which was now racing back through the snow to relieve us. In less than an hour's time they should be here, arriving in the town which then would be the signal for part of our unit to attack simultaneously across the ice. We relished the news, and as we silently watched the flashing guns of some of the nervous T-34s, who obviously wanted to draw our fire to make out our positions in the gathering dusk, we smiled grimly at each other in the dimly lit interior of our Panzer. We were sure that our luck was on the change, and that we would soon turn the tables on Ivan.

Though the white of the snow made good visibility, darkness by now covered the sky completely. We wondered why Ivan was holding back, why he was not attacking. And then we listened, at first there was only a faint rumble, but then we were sure, the Panzers from the other group had arrived at the outskirts of the town, and in a few minutes the first of them came into view high up on the opposing river bank. What a great sight that was! It was also the signal for our infantry and armoured cars to attack across the ice on a wide front.

When the Russian tank pack realized what was going on, they attacked immediately, racing towards us with their guns flashing, but were unable to hit anything. That was the moment we had been waiting for for more than an hour, what a relief for our nerves it was! As they came over the open terrain towards us, so clearly visible, they were like sitting ducks. Our fire was well co-ordinated and we gave them everything we had. Two of them received direct hits and blew up, while a third lost its tracks. And while they stood there like burning torches, the rest, realizing their impossible situation, turned and raced back as fast as possible. The entire battle had not lasted five minutes.

Now it was time for us to come out of the trees and race back to the river's edge, to get on to the ice and drive over it, while peppering the bank where we knew the enemy to be in position. But the job had largely been done by the others already. The scene in front of us was eerie, and at the same time fantastic. Several cottages above us at the waterfront were burning fiercely. Even down on the river, several hundred meters away, we could hear the crackling of fires. Probably having seen their own tanks across the river being beaten back, and finding that German Panzers had arrived in their rear, the Russians realized their situation was hopeless and threw in the towel without much further ado. We saw them coming out from behind all sorts of fortifications with their hands above their heads, presenting a pitiful sight. Most of them were soldiers, but there were also civilians, partisans, women and youths amongst them. They were collected and driven into a compound.

I drove up a ravine and along it to the top near a two-storey stone building, from where I could overlook part of the town and the river below. Across the road stood two Panzers from the other battle-group, whose crews had climbed out and stood warming themselves in front of a burning cottage. They invited us to join them. When I slid down the side and stepped into the snow, stiff and tired, but now happy, I realized how much of my energy the whole unexpected debâcle had taken up. There were handshakes all round, expressions of thanks and friendly pats on the backs. Our *Kameraden* told us that when they had entered the town, they had been fired on by partisans and one of their mates who had looked out of the hatch had been badly injured. From then on they had shot at everything that moved and had left many dead and wounded in the streets.

This had been a total victory for us and we wondered why the Soviet Command, knowing that we were on our way back, had taken an unnecessary risk.

The order was passed through for both battle-groups to assemble with all vehicles in a large factory hall. Our two field kitchens had already been set up and were exuding smoke and nice-smelling steam. Soon we were sitting around, sipping coffee and exchanging experiences. It was very reassuring for us after weeks of relentless retreat to have turned the tables after all, and to have shown that we could still kick. There were several coke ovens in the empty hall which we soon had going at full blast, and after we had had some warming soup, we felt warm and comfortable. After fuelling and repairs and maintenance had been done, we were ready for the night. Our blankets were spread out on the floor and we were soon asleep.

In the very early hours I was woken up by a disturbance. A guard had brought in a young woman, claiming that she was a partisan whom he had caught running away from some dead or wounded in the street. She was pretty, probably in her late twenties, and although she was very dishevelled and obviously frightened, there was a pride and defiance about her which commanded respect. The guards argued about what to do with her, and she was well aware that it was her fate which was being discussed. Tempers by now had calmed, the killings had stopped hours ago and no one was in the mood to start all over again, certainly not with a young woman.

The Commander of the other *Kampfgruppe* was a Colonel of about forty. Unlike most of us he was clean-shaven and properly dressed, and looked in every way an officer. He came over to find out what the trouble was, and dismissed the guards, who stepped over me sleeping near the stove, obviously relieved that the 'Old Man' had taken the woman off their hands. The Colonel asked her to sit beside him on some wood by the stove no more than a couple of yards away from me. He offered her a cigarette which she refused and then assured her that she need have no fear, that nothing would happen to her, and gave her his word of honour that she would be set free as soon as we left the town in the morning. All that he wanted was to have a word with her.

I could hear and understand every word being said, and as my knowledge of Russian was at least as good as that of the Colonel, I almost got up once to help him, but then thought better of it, as both of them probably thought that I was fast asleep. He called a guard to fetch her something to eat and drink. All the time they were talking quietly, and though it was dark, I could clearly see their faces from the glow of the fire, which the Colonel kept poking with a stick. He said that he was not even going to ask her whether she was a partisan, as he knew what she would answer. He told her that he had a daughter, not yet twenty, and a wife at home whom he loved and wanted to see again after all this was over, and he knew therefore exactly how she must feel. By the way she looked at him, I could see that she believed his sincerity.

She told him in a low voice about herself and her family. She had trained as an engineer and had worked in this very factory. Immediately after our invasion they had been ordered to retool from producing household goods to war production, but then the town had been occupied within weeks, the buildings and machinery had then been used by us for vehicle repairs and she, having to live somehow, had worked for the German *Kommandantur*. Her mother and one of her sisters had been killed in the first fighting. Most other relatives, including all the children, had got away to the rear, while her father and several brothers were in the army. Not having had any news from them for some years now, she was very worried. When she had been caught by the guards, she had been trying to drag a wounded woman to safety, who would very likely die now because of the cold. '*Eto voyna*' (that is war) said the Colonel, sadly shaking his head. '*Da, eto voyna*', she retorted, showing little inclination to hide her disgust.

There was a long pause, during which the Colonel became very thoughtful and said, 'Now that we Germans will leave your country very shortly, do you think that we had a case for coming in the first place? Tell me frankly and without fear, for you have my word and it is for my own sake that I want to know. Please tell me!' I was wide awake now, because I realized that the conversation had broken all set boundaries and I found that I too wanted to know, for that thought had bothered me a lot lately, too.

She looked at him pensively, said nothing for a while, shook her head and then forced a laugh: 'You Germans are strange people! You can sing the most beautiful songs and write the most beautiful music — and then you can be very, very brutal, both physically and mentally. There is the devil in you next to a little bit of an angel. You commit the most ghastly crimes against innocent people and then in a twitch you get all soft and sentimental and ask your victims to soothe your conscience. You came to conquer us, Colonel, to make us your slaves. And now you sit here with me and ask whether I think you had a case for coming here in the first place. You killed millions in our land including my mother and sister. You were brutal and reckless. But you have not achieved what you have come here for. You are right, you are on your way back, like Napoleon over a century ago. But you are not just going back, as you try to make it look like, you have been beaten and are being thrown out. If you don't know the answer yourself, Colonel, I cannot and I will not help you!'

He just sat there and looked at her, and then he simply said, 'Thank you, but now I want you to listen to me. You are right, every word you said, and also the ones you did not but which you flashed at me with your eyes. Yes, we are the damned, I totally agree with you. But what can I say now, *'kak zhal'*, or *'bedaure'* [sorry], which would only rub salt into your terrible wounds. So I will say no more than that I admire you personally and wish you and your people well for the future.'

'You admire us and wish us well, Colonel!' She shook her head as if in pain, just kept staring into the fire and I could see that she was crying silently. They then walked away to the other side of the hall, and though I looked for her next morning, I did not see her again.

I was restless and wide awake now. I was outraged; having been sent to Russia and being told that I was fighting something like a Holy War to save Christian Civilization, having made others suffer and suffered myself for a long time now, this Colonel should suddenly make it clear to an enemy that all that I have been doing in this country was wrong. Would he have agreed so readily with the woman, had we been successful in our campaign? Who could guarantee that these *Herren Offiziere* would not try to blame us ordinary soldiers for all that had happened in Russia, would not simply say, 'It was they who did the killing, the burning, the blowing up, not us!' I was furious, and at the same time sad, and fell into an uneasy sleep until the first morning light fell through the high windows.

The hall became alive, and the thought of the day in front made me forget what had happened during the night. The first Panzers pulled out into the open and after about an hour we were on our way again, heading west. A fleeting thought passed through my mind about all the fine songs I had learned at school and the Hitler Youth about marching to the east.

8
Mounting chaos, and growing doubts

*Wer immerdar nach Schatten greift
kann stets nur leere Luft erlangen.*

'Who keeps snatching at shadows
grasps nothing but empty air.'

Goethe

With their Air Force keeping an eye on us, the enemy was never far away, and throughout the day their T-34s followed us at a safe distance. Our main problem was fuel supply. Much of our artillery had to be used to accompany our petrol tankers, and if only one tanker did not arrive, the whole timing of our retreat was disrupted.

The frosts were often severe, and we had to be careful not to touch the metal with our bare hands since the skin would stick to it and tear off, causing very painful injuries. Especially during the retreat there had been suspicions about self-inflicted injuries, for which the penalty was death, and all injured going back to the *Lazaretts* had to have a special report by their commanding officers as to the genuineness of their injuries. The danger of the cold was repeatedly drummed into us; if we felt very cold and then for no apparent reason began to feel a cosy warmth, we would in fact be on the point of freezing to death, and should therefore move about energetically before it was too late.

One of us had already frozen to death. We had arrived at a place for the night and were very tired. While we were unrolling our blankets, Helmut had gone outside to do his business. When we found him the next morning, he was lying on his side, all rolled up, having apparently toppled over from his crouching position with his trousers still down, and with a very happy expression on his face, suggesting that he had ignored the creeping feeling of cosiness in the bitter cold weather.

The longer the retreat in the winter lasted, the more sullen and suspicious we became. Being sure that they had led us by our noses, we mistrusted almost everything which was passed down from our officers. We had many reasons to feel rebellious, but we also recognized that only absolute discipline and the cohesion of our army would give us a chance to get out of this unholy hell.

We arrived in a hamlet of huts grouped around a large pond. To receive straggler units, we had to stay there for several days, so we made ourselves comfortable. It had been snowing for some time, but now the wind had dropped, and though it remained well below freezing, the sun had come out. To the east, slightly less than a kilometre away, stretched a high treeless ridge which the Russian unit following us had quickly occupied. I was on guard duty at midday, and patrolled up and down the short village street and around and across the pond. The sun made it possible to unbutton my camouflage and for a short time to take my gloves off. Then I was sure that I heard a shout from the ridge. When I looked up, I saw a Russian guard standing there, like me with a rifle slung over his shoulder, the collar of his greatcoat up to his ears and his hands in his pockets. He looked straight towards me but there was nothing threatening about him. The distance between us was too great for rifle fire, and I just stood still and looked straight back at him, wondering whether it had been he who had shouted. He then raised his arm in an unmistakable gesture of greeting, so I responded in the same way. Visibility was very clear, and though I could not make out his features, I could see everything else about him distinctly, as he stood against the steely blue sky. He pointed to the sun and opened the flaps of his coat as if to say what a nice, pleasant day it was. Again, I responded in the same way, then I threw my helmet into the snow with a gesture of disgust and stretched my arms towards the warming sun. His movements, his whole behaviour suggested to me that he was laughing, and I laughed with him, putting both hands to my mouth, hoping that he would hear at least a faint sound from me. We then both waved our arms in the air, jumped up and down and about and behaved like two little children. He then took his rifle, held it up and fired one shot up into the crisp air. Not to be outdone, I again did the same. I waved and he waved, but then I heard trouble coming from behind. A Lieutenant, a Sergeant and some of my mates had come out of their warm cottages to find out what the trouble was. Seeing me standing there with my 'smoking' rifle, the Lieutenant asked me what I had been shooting at. I pointed to the Russian who had sat down in the snow, obviously watching with great interest our happenings by the pond. 'Idiot!', said the Lieutenant, 'can't you see that you have no chance in hell of hitting him from this distance?'

'But he shot at me first, *Herr Leutnant.*'

'That proves that he is a bigger idiot than you, which is no mean achievement, and no more shooting, understand!'

'*Zu Befehl, Herr Leutnant!*' They all trooped back to their cottages, leaving me alone with my Russian friend, who had probably found it too cold sitting down. He seemed to have read the situation correctly, pointed towards the cottages and raised his finger to his forehead to indicate that those who had told me off had a problem of mental deficiency. Again, we both threw our arms into the air and I am sure that he laughed as much as I did. One thing I was sure of: I would never have wanted to point my rifle at him in earnest. He then indicated that he had to go, and when I watched him slowly sink into the horizon I felt as if I had lost a friend.

I was glad when I saw my relief guard coming. All I wanted to do was to lie down by the stove on my blanket and shut my eyes. Why was life so contradictory? My mates had a cup of hot coffee waiting for me, and there was friendly banter about my being so silly, trying to hit a Russian from over eight hundred metres with an ordinary army rifle. I could not really explain to them how I felt. When I stood guard again later, complete darkness had fallen, a light moon had risen to the east, and I could clearly see the outline of the ridge against the sky. I looked for a sign, but there was no movement, no sound, only the all-surrounding white stillness.

Soon we were on the move again. Badanov's tanks caused us many serious problems, but we were still strong enough to deal with vicious kicks. One morning we ran along a river amongst some woods, and once the sun had risen we had come out of it and were now rolling along on the white plain again. Every day there had been heavy snowfalls, and we had camouflaged our Panzers and other vehicles with whitewash, as we had learned to do from the Russians. When we approached a large village, much to our surprise we caught an advance unit of two T-34s, whose crews had obviously been over-confident. When they saw us they came rushing out of a cottage, but before they could even turn their turrets they went up in flames from our massive firepower.

The village stretched along both sides of a narrow river, which was totally iced up. A frozen-in pontoon bridge took our Panzers, while most other vehicles crossed on the ice. A few hundred yards away from the river on the rising ground was a farm estate, obviously dating back to pre-Revolutionary days. Outbuildings of all types seemed to be scattered about in a large area. Set apart sheltered by high trees and unkempt hedges in a spacious and totally neglected park, stood a large, squat two-storey country house, which looked like a badly-decorated grey cube. Coming closer, we could see that much of its plaster had fallen off, revealing red brickwork underneath. There were bullet pock-marks all over the walls, most of the windows were broken and the shutters were torn off and hanging down. Part of the roof had fallen in as if hit by a large shell, with blackened beams reaching into the grey sky. We drove our Panzers round the front of the house to leave them under the trees, where they were hidden from the air and from where we had an unobstructed shooting range to the river and the plains beyond.

The mansion and the park were a reminder of bygone times, like a setting for one of Gogol's novels. In comparison, the village looked poor and miserable, and I could easily visualize how this vulgar clash of the extremes more than anything had brought the Revolution about. Our Commander, who was said to have served in the French Foreign Legion in Algiers, told us that only a few weeks earlier Field Marshal von Manstein himself had directed battles from this house. Rather obviously, his plans had not been fulfilled, for since then the Red Army had broken through our lines on a wide front, threatening to turn inwards in a pincer movement and forcing us to race back to avoid entrapment. Stavka, the Soviet High Command, had learned a lot since the early days of Barbarossa; now they had had great successes, which in turn had given them a degree of confidence which we could no longer match.

After we had organized our fuel and food, a few of us decided to investigate the house. We entered by a heavy side door and walked along a long corridor which ended in the main hall. Wide wooden stairs with a beautiful, though badly damaged, bannister ascended generously to a wide landing under a low ceiling. One could imagine the splendour which must have ruled here during Imperial times, when horse-drawn sledges were swishing up outside and guests in their furs arrived to be ushered in through the large double doors and into the ball room. Most of the rooms were empty, though there was ample evidence that soldiers had been in here not long before our surprise arrival.

On the first floor off the landing I entered a corner room via a passageway through a thick wall. The windows were tall with wide sills, and none of the glass panes were broken. In the corner, away from the windows, stood a heavy stove, reaching to the ceiling, with green and white tiles, showing a design of royal crowns and flowers. The paintwork looked rather grim, but the walls were still covered with dark wallpaper which showed lighter marks where large paintings had once hung. Huge old-fashioned sideboards stood along two of the walls, and a heavy writing desk with a large chair before it across the corner by the window. It was a forgotten oasis of culture surrounded by an unstable world.

From the side window I looked down into the overgrown park, its trees and bushes heavily laden with snow. The other window offered a view to the village and the iced-up river with its crashed bridge. I could see some of my mates arguing with village women whose help they wanted in the field kitchen, and there were many well wrapped-up children, jumping around like kangaroos and getting in the way of everyone. Turning back to the room, I found bits of paper, books, files and posters all over the place. On the sideboard stood a very old typewriter. Some of the papers had been pushed into the stove, in an unsuccessful attempt to burn them while others had been thrown out of the window.

Then there was a commotion on the landing. My mates were shouting, but I also heard quieter, protesting Russian voices. The door opened, with one of my friends appearing laughingly in the frame. He had made a very curious find, and was pushing an odd-looking pair towards me.

'You wouldn't believe it! We found them in a large empty drum in the wine cellar. It was their luck that we didn't test the drum with lead when we heard them rummaging about inside. At first we thought they were rats. Have a word with them, Henry, they might tell us something interesting.'

The *muzhik* (peasant), with a grey beard down almost to his chest, was about sixty. He was dressed in the usual padded peasant clothes, a dirty old fur coat hanging down to his knees and his legs stuck in heavy felt boots. To show respect — or was it fear? — he had taken off his flappy fur cap and was twiddling it nervously in his hands. His grandson Mischa, a boy of about twelve with a bright, rosy face, and clothes which were too large hanging heavily all around him, stood slightly behind, holding on to his granddad's coat. He was watching my every move suspiciously, and could not keep his eyes off the pistol on the desk. I told the old man to sit down, but he refused and kept calling me *'Herr Offizier'*. I told him that I was no officer but the son of a worker, and a worker, a locksmith, myself. All that I wanted from him was his story, and afterwards I would let him go free as a bird. 'Promise!', I said, but I could see in his face that he was not all that sure about the value of a German soldier's promise.

He told me that he lived in a cottage with his wife by the bank of the river, and that they had brought up a large family. All his life, except when he had been a soldier in the First World War, had he worked on the estate, which was now a *kolkhos* (collective farm). Having always been interested in the Revolution and what had happened in Russia during that turbulent time, I realized that he perhaps was one who could tell me about it. When I noticed him looking sheepishly about him and challenged him on that, he asked me whether I knew that *Generalfeldmarschall* von Manstein himself had occupied this very room, that it had been his study/bedroom and that large tables had been set up against the banisters on the landing, which had been covered with maps and at which his officers had been working round the clock. 'Is it then correct' I asked him, 'that I am sitting here in Manstein's chair?' He nodded and grinned, for we both noted my dirty jackboots on the desk, and were probably under no illusions about what 'the old Man' would have said to that. One of his daughters had worked in the house as a cleaner, and he himself had done some loading in the yard while Manstein was in residence. I wanted to know what impression the Marshal had made on him, but he did not want to commit himself and only mumbled something about the great 'Gods of War'.

After Manstein's Court had departed, the Red Army had suddenly come back, and had stayed there until just before our arrival. He recounted how he had seen us crossing the river, had panicked and had hidden himself with his grandson in the winevat. Young Mischa had now lost his fear, and laughed loudly when I asked him whether he had not got drunk from the fumes.

The Red Army, so the old man went on, had also used the mansion as a Headquarters, and this room had been occupied by a *Politruk* (Political Officer), a Colonel with the German name of Stahlmann. While listening to him, I could make out the cyrillic signature of Stahlmann on some of the papers. What a strange coincidence, I thought, that this room in this mansion should be connected with three German names; von Manstein, the Field Marshal, then Stahlmann, the Colonel, and now Metelmann, the ordinary soldier.

When Stahlmann had first arrived, he had called all the villagers together in the stables and told them that he was in command and that everyone without exception was to support the Army. Though he had conducted some close questioning as to who had helped the Germans, he was human enough to understand the reality of the situation under German occupation, and punished no one. He arranged for medical and other help and it was striking that all the other officers had had a healthy respect for him. He had handed out information leaflets, though some of the older ones had to remind him that they could not read.

I then questioned the old man about life in Tsarist days, and he told me that the estate had belonged to a very rich princely family. In 1917 there had been much confusion, hardship and hatred. There were rumours that the tsar had been deposed, that Russia was now a republic and that there was unrest in Petrograd, Moscow and other big cities. But as there were neither telephones nor newspapers in the village, all was vague and confused. A rising nervousness in the big house had been apparent; members of the family no longer came down to the village, the servants were saying that they were being questioned about the mood of the people and were better treated than before.

'It was somehow in the air that something big, something important, was going on, but the summer went by and the harvest came and work went on as usual. Our family supplies of essentials were running short, though, and when we told the estate bailiff, he said that the big house had not got anything either. But we knew that he was lying because some of us had ourselves carried supplies into the cellars. There was much grumbling, but none dared speak to the family directly, as we had been brought up never to speak to them unless first spoken to. There was talk about real revolution, but most of us thought that it was little more than wishful thinking by the firebrands. But when winter came, things all the time were getting worse and then one day out of the blue a group of workers and soldiers arrived on horseback. They looked tired and dishevelled, and said that they were Communist revolutionaries from Kharkov. They called all the villagers together in the large barn by the gate, it was as cold as now', and he beckoned me to the window to point out the barn. 'One of the Communists', he went on, 'made a speech, a very rough and unrefined one and we could sense that they were our kind of people, poor people as we were, and we took to them. He told us that revolution had broken out all over Russia, that the old days of servitude were gone forever, that the Tsar and all the other parasites had lost their power and privileges and that it was now up to us, the working people, to run our own affairs and to organize our own lives under the guidance of the Communist Party.

As he told me all this, I noticed that he grew quite excited, and I encouraged him to go on, as what he had said interested me tremendously. I had been in Russia now for quite a long time, and I could not help being aware of their great fortitude amidst horrible suffering, and of the sacrifices they were making. I was puzzled, and curious to know what gave them that strength, what made them tick. This old man, I sensed, could perhaps help me to open a window of understanding.

'Right down in that barn they told us to vote on who was for the Revolution and who was against it. Well, it was difficult for me to make a decision, but they pressed us and I think, while some fiddled about at the back, most of us put our hands up. Before we knew, we had voted that we were now going up to the big house to make revolution real — whatever that meant. While walking up the drive, some cheered, but most of us felt rather uneasy about it all. To vote to do something was one thing, but to actually do it, was quite another. After all, the Prince was a very rich man, he owned all the land and everything else around here, and many of the womenfolk looked up to him as "our father". All of us in one way or another were working for him, every single cottage in the village was his. No one dared to get married without his consent, and no sons were allowed to leave the village without asking him first, and if they were strong and healthy, they definitely had to stay. He owned the church and paid the priest, yes, he had it all sewn up, and together with all the other land-owning Princes in the *Gubernyn* [district], they controlled all life in the towns as well.'

One of my mates came in and we all had a share of a pot of coffee, but I wanted to know more, and asked Ivan, as I called him, to get on with his story.

'When we arrived at the house, all the doors were locked and the windows shuttered. They probably had seen us coming. Standing by the front stairs, we started to argue amongst ourselves; some had had enough of the Revolution and wanted to go back. There were women amongst us and children, and in any case, we had never been allowed to walk through the front door. The Communists, watching us, just laughed and then they got angry with us, saying that we had souls of slaves. A couple of them climbed up, forced a shutter, smashed a window and climbed in and then opened both double doors to let us all into the hall. And while we trooped in, some of them stood behind us to make sure that no one walked back.

'Most of us had taken our caps off, and while we were standing about, not knowing what to do now, the Communists told us to sit down on the nice chairs and sofas. We heard a noise and when we looked up, we saw the Prince and his family come out of a room towards the landing. Two of the Communist soldiers with rifles were with them. The Prince's eldest son was in Army uniform, and his wife and younger children looked very disturbed. The Prince and his soldier son then shouted at us to get out of their house and back to our work, but one of the young Communists went quickly up to his son, struck him into the face and told him to mind his arrogant tongue and only speak when spoken to. To all of us, it was like watching an old world, the only one we had ever known, falling to pieces.

'An old, dirty farmcart, which had always been used to take us to town, was made ready and the whole princely family was taken to Kharkov under escort where, it was said, the Prince had to work in one of his own factories, for wages which he had always considered to be good enough for his workers. Some women thought that this was a cruel thing to do. That might have been so, but many poor people had been sent to Siberia, and no one in the big house had ever raised the slightest objection to that — on the contrary, they believed that it was justified. After they had left, a meeting was held in the house which voted the whole estate to become a co-operative, and the Communists said that a majority law in Petrograd's Duma (Parliament) had made that act legal. That was our Revolution.'

I was interested how the Revolution had subsequently affected village life. He thought that at first there had not been much change, and that generally work had carried on as before. 'We elected a village soviet in which women were involved, a thing unheard of in our entire history. The soviet then elected an Estate Secretary for managing the farm and the house. It was like a new life, we never had thought that such things were possible, and some of us wondered where it would ever end. From then on there were many meetings. As every one was allowed to say what was on their minds, there was much disorder and shouting. Tempers often rose and sometimes fists went flying; the Communists called all this "budding democracy". Of course, we were all still very poor, few of us could read and write, and much went wrong with the organization. One Communist had remained behind to guide us — and probably to keep an eye on us as well. He gave strict instructions not to take anything out of the house or the estate.

'Then a couple of young teachers arrived. The old school behind the church, in which the priest as the only teacher had taught all the village children, was closed and a new, better one opened, in one of the estate buildings. During the day the children went, and in the evenings the older people were urged to come to learn to read and write. The priest stayed, but he was not an important person any more, and few males or young people went to his services.

'We learnt many a lesson the hard way, and one of them was that it was fairly easy to make a Revolution, but much more difficult to make it work afterwards. Soon there were shortages of almost everything. Spring 1918 came and we had hardly any seed left, and neither did we have the faintest idea of how to obtain some. When harvest came we had to send part of it to Kharkov, and we came very close to starvation. There was much grumbling and dissatisfaction, and some believed that it was a punishment for having interfered with the holy order of things. Wild rumours chased each other; one of them was that the Tsar and his family had been killed in Ekatarinburg.

'But despite all the difficulties, life went on and there were also great improvements. A number of the older children were sent to college in Kharkov, and several went on from there to university in Moscow. Never before had we had a doctor in our village. A young girl doctor and a nurse arrived and set up clinic in what were formerly the Princess's rooms. Because of a lifetime of neglect and ignorance, so many things were wrong with us, and now for the first time in our lives we could go to a proper dentist in Kharkov — and all these things were free. Several years later we received our first tractor and other farm machinery, and some of our boys and girls were trained as mechanics.

'Life was still very hard for us, but it had always been like that. Sometimes we ran out of money; nobody received wages, only bits of paper, and the village soviet sat all night and did not know what to do. But despite all the problems, there were very few who would have wanted the old times back with the Prince and all that. There was hope for our children's future and we knew all right that it had been the Communists who had opened up the new road for us and that we had no real choice but to walk it.'

He was talking very freely now and had obviously forgotten the reason for his being there. Mischa too was walking about the room; he looked out of the window, fed the fire and showed interest in all sorts of things. Suddenly the old man became very thoughtful and then asked me: 'Tell me, please, is it true that you Germans had intended to bring back the old times when our masters ruled over us?' He asked the question with such intensity that I realized it was an important point to him. I did not really know the answer, and as we were on the retreat anyway, I did not want to bother my mind with it.

As Mischa said that he was hungry, I gave the grandfather a note for the kitchen Sergeant. Watching him walk down the drive with Mischa, I thought what a rich man he was, having all these historic events in his memory.

I slept that night in von Manstein's room, right next to the green-tiled stove. Early next morning we could hear the sound of the Russian tanks coming on the east wind. The wheel of fate had turned 180 degrees, they were the hunters now, and we the hunted. Driving away through the snow, one of our heavy half-tracks towing an 8.8 cm cannon broke down. We had no chance to repair it, and had to blow up both of them. It was a terrible loss.

Communications became steadily worse. At times we got hold of the *Wehrmachtsbericht* (a daily military situation report), and when we looked up what was written about our section, all we learnt was that we were 'straightening' our front line. That, we were sure, was some way from the truth. Rumour had it that the Führer, from his Headquarters in East Prussia, obviously believing in his own military genius, was personally directing the movements of small units like ours — he was making a hell of a mess of it.

As had happened a few times before, I lost my Panzer, this time by pure accident. Over the months of battle, both sides had captured numbers of the other's tanks, and used them in their own formations. (In fact, one of the main reasons for the Russians' success in closing the ring around Paulus's Sixth Army at Stalingrad was that they had been able to approach and capture the undamaged bridge across the River Don at Kalatsch with Panzers from my own 22nd Panzer Division, proper markings and all.) All of us had learned to drive Russian T-34s which, while relatively simple to operate, were far more effective and deadly in almost every way than our own in the same class. Though we had difficulties getting the right fuel and ammunition for it, we had one operating in our *Kampfgruppe* for quite some time.

Driving in the dark one night, I got rammed by our T-34 from behind, when it almost mounted my tank. Its 27 tons did so much damage that we had to blow mine up. The T-34, which we had christened 'Molotov', was hardly scratched.

I became a grenadier in a two-hundred-strong *Kampfgruppe*. Most of us were in our early twenties, and though we were sullen, suspicious, and frustrated, we were not mentally beaten, not yet. Though all the idealism pumped into us about what we were fighting for here in Russia had completely evaporated, and we had no hope left for victory, we were still determined to get back to Germany in one piece, and we knew that our only chance for that was in fighting together. We knew now how the Russians must have felt during the early part of Barbarossa, when all they could effectively do was run away from our pincer movements. The boot was now on the other foot. And the Russians were now proving to be extremely capable and courageous soldiers, giving the lie to our earlier preconceptions based on our supposed racial superiority.

While we were on the march, our artillery moved in a leapfrog fashion, driving a kilometre or so in front of us, then waiting for us to pass. We had only two light Panzers, which operated mainly at the flanks.

It was getting dark when a long village, stretching north to south, appeared on the horizon before us. Its length was such that we could not see the northern end of it, but we decided to move into the southern part in front of us, to have a good night's rest. We set up defensive positions amongst the cottages, facing east, and did not bother about the northern part at all. We knew that the Russian unit shadowing us was weaker than ours and we had got used to the fact that whenever we stopped, they kept to a respectful distance.

Like all of us, I hated guard duty. Whenever we came to a strange village like this there were always two of us together. When my mate August and I were called out at one in the morning, we were told that an enemy armoured car was making strange moves to the north of us, but had not come close enough to appear in shooting range. So we decided to let it be and not worry. Everything was quiet, and when three o'clock came and we woke up our relief to then settle down on their blankets in a comfortably warm cottage, we were glad for the chance to sleep. Not long afterwards I was faintly aware of a commotion, but decided to pay no attention to it, as a soldier's sleep is often disturbed by all sorts of things which are best ignored.

To be woken up by a soft kick in the backside is sometimes necessary and mostly makes the point. But this time it was very different! The kick was very real, and my first reaction was one of unrestrained fury; I turned round and up like an angry snake. But to my horror, I saw a Soviet soldier with a machine pistol at the ready standing over me, and another in the door frame. The candle we had put on the table was still flickering, and the old peasant sitting up in his bed in the opposite corner seemed as frightened as I was.

There was no sign of my mate August, who earlier had bedded down next to me. Only later was the jigsaw pieced together — he had probably got up either to relieve himself, or to investigate a noise, when a knife had been plunged into his chest outside the door, and he had been dragged around the corner and dumped. Why they killed him but not me was a riddle.

The motioning with the machine pistol was such that I felt in no position to argue. Surprisingly they let me slip into my jackboots, and then marched me off between them. There were three more Russians behind the cottages, and together we went quietly to the northern part of the village. One of my captors made a sign with an upright finger to his mouth and his hand swishing across his throat, which I understood perfectly.

We came to a deep ravine with a reedy pond or streamlet at the bottom, which I had had no idea existed. Amongst the trees it was very dark, and I stumbled more than walked, feeling at times the cold steel of the machine pistol knocking against my back. I knew that my two mates guarding the village must have been somewhere around, but we saw no sign of them. At the deepest point of the ravine I sank up to my knees into the foul smelling mud, and my captors had to pull me out. Crawling up on the other bank, they hissed their password, which sounded to me like a birdcall and when we arrived at the top, we were met by a number of others. I could make out several machine-gun nests along the ravine, and seeing so much activity but hearing hardly a sound, I found it all very eerie. Coming amongst the first cottages, I was searched for weapons, and my paybook was taken out of my breast pocket. When I looked back through an opening among the trees, I thought I could see the cottage in which I had been sleeping just less than a quarter of an hour ago.

In a strange way I had completely lost the feeling of fear, and though I had been pushed about at first, I had not been roughly handled in any way. Standing with a group of six or seven, who quietly laughed and seemed very pleased with themselves, it struck me that none of them showed any sign of hostility to me. I somehow had become a part of their group, a very important one at that.

Walking further into the village, I was taken past the armoured car which had bothered the other guards, and I now found it difficult to understand why none of us had the slightest suspicion of its purpose.

It still being dark, I was taken into a cottage where soldiers were sleeping on the floor, and was told to lie next to them on a blanket. The room was lit by a candle or two and everything was peaceful. Outside I saw the guards looking curiously at me through the small window. Tired as I was, I could not sleep, and just lay back and stared at the ceiling. My thoughts were going round and round in my head, and I could not quite adjust to what had happened to me. So very often before I had been lying on the floor of a cottage like this; the only real difference was that now, those lying beside me wore Russian uniforms instead of German.

I must have been lying there for a couple of hours when daylight broke, and I realized that I was in a guards' cottage. Those around me started to get up and as I was lying across they had to step over me — though no one kicked me, as I probably would have done had the situation been reversed — I thought it better to sit up and lean with my back against the stove before someone told me to.

In essence, the Russian soldiers did not really behave differently from us. A couple said a few words to me which were not unfriendly, and to which I responded as politely as I could. They shifted the table to the middle of the room so that they could all sit round it — just as we would have done — unpacked their food and started to eat. The one who made the tea and looked after the fire at the same time, left the oven door open next to my head. I did not want to interfere and shut it, and when I choked on the smoke, everyone laughed at me. There was much banter and leg-pulling. Some of their jokes were at my expense, but when they all laughed I thought it wise to smile back at them in a friendly way. Seeing them eating made me feel hungry, and when one offered me a lump of dark brown bread and dripping, I gratefully accepted. He also poured tea for me into the top of his mess-tin. After they had finished their breakfast, they dressed up and went out on guard duty, and those who were relieved came in, had a bite and then bedded down on the floor.

A sergeant came in and told me to get up and follow him. A cold mist had settled, and I felt chilly. When I told him so, he said that I should not behave like a baby but like a soldier — I felt ashamed and said no more. When I wanted to walk in the middle of the road, he called me back, told me to walk in front of him and not muck about. He knocked at the door of a cottage, said something to someone inside, and unceremoniously pushed me in. I stood in front of two officers, a Captain and a Second Lieutenant, and there were a couple of soldiers at the back. The Captain was sitting on a bench behind the table and the Lieutenant leant against the stove behind him, with one foot on the bench. They both looked at me with a questioning air and said no word. I clicked my heels in the German way, saluted and gave my rank and name. None of them spoke German and the Captain asked me whether I could speak Russian.

They had my paybook on the table, and I could see that they were unable to read Latin lettering. They asked me my unit and I told them that it was not a real one any more, but a *Kampfgruppe*, and they then wanted to know what had happened to my original Division. I mentioned the 22nd Panzer Division, and they knew straight away that it had been wound up months ago, right after the battle of Stalingrad, because it had been so badly mauled, and they even knew the name of its Commanders. The Lieutenant took some pride in telling me that he himself had taken part in smashing it, I thought it wise not to respond to this.

They behaved totally correctly, never threatening me once, and when they asked me about the strength and weaponry of our *Kampfgruppe,* I told them, for I was sure that having shadowed us for a long time they must know anyway. When they asked me for the name of my Commander, it was probably to test me, because I had the distinct impression that they knew it already. What I could not tell them, because I simply did not know, was where our *Kampfgruppe* was heading. After having asked me questions on our food, ammunition and petrol situation, the Captain wanted to know whether we had had any idea when we moved in the previous night that they had been in occupation of this part. I pointed out to them that had we known, I most certainly would not be standing in front of them right now and they both laughed loudly; but when I joined in with their laughter, they suddenly gave me the impression that in their view I was getting too big for my boots, and I stopped rather abruptly. They called one of their soldiers, ordered him to take me away, I saluted, turned on my heel and found myself out in the cold again.

This soldier seemed very young, barely 18 years old and I became rather concerned about the very unprofessional, careless way he carried his machine pistol, nudging its mouth several times into my back and calling me Genghis Khan. We arrived at the unit's very old-fashioned kitchen, which was set up next to a cottage under a lean-to. A couple of supply lorries and horse wagons stood at the back, and three cooks, one a woman, were busy. It seemed as if the woman was in charge, and that the three of them had known about my coming, for they made no fuss at all.

While they were not exactly friendly, they were in no way unfriendly. They told me to keep a good fire going under a big bowl and then to clean pots and other utensils in its water. As everything was very fatty and smeary, I asked them for soap, but they just retorted by asking whether I thought I was in the kitchen of Moscow's Hotel Metropol, and told me not to be silly and to get on with the job. None of them carried a weapon and I didn't have the impression that they were guarding me. A couple of young soldiers came in from the village street, thought that I was a soft touch and tried to scrounge some food from me. When the woman cook realized what was going on, she let fly and the scroungers quickly scrambled.

My judgement was that the detachment was no more than a hundred strong.

Many seemed nervous, more so than me, and kept looking towards the German-occupied area. When a couple of the passers-by laughed rather loudly, our woman rushed out and shushed them.

While cluttering about with my pots and pans, I wondered what my mates were making of my disappearance, and what had happened to August. By now morning was giving way to midday, and I had no way of knowing whether my *Kampfgruppe* had departed. No sound came from over there. Altogether, it was strange. The cooks settled down for bread and tea, and the woman came over and asked me whether I wanted some. She did so with a friendly smile, and when I told her that I had some food in the guard's cottage in the morning, she said '*Nichevo* [never mind], take it, you need it as we all do'. The woman then told me to get a bag of cabbages from the lorry, which I was to wash and slice, ready for boiling. For that I had to fetch water from a nearby well, where I met other soldiers and villagers. Having to wait my turn in a short queue, none took any notice of me until an elderly woman who stood behind me started talking to me and remarked on my uniform. When I made it plain to her that I was not a Russian in German uniform but a real German, she quickly put her buckets down and crossed herself.

After I had finished with the cabbages, I had to peel a sack of potatoes. I moved to the side and sat in the sun; everything was so very peaceful, and I almost forgot that there was a war going on and that I was very much at the centre of it.

All of a sudden I heard rifle and machine-gun fire from the side where our *Kampfgruppe* was. And when shortly later I heard heavy cannon fire, I knew that it was from our Panzers. Then I heard the roar of their engines. All this happened in a matter of minutes and all around me was like a disturbed bee-hive. There was running and shouting, and my three cooks disappeared at the first sign of trouble. Then soldiers came running from the direction of the gorge. They looked troubled and out of breath, and I knew that they were running away. For the first time since I had been abducted from my cottage, I felt fear and I realized that my fate was now hanging in the balance. What were the Russians going to do — take me with them, or what? And all the time while I was watching the commotion in the street, I sat there with my little knife in front of a large bucket half full of peeled potatoes. I did not dare move, or do anything which might draw attention to my presence, and I knew that the next few minutes were to be critical to me in one way or another, whether I should live or die. Then I saw two Russians with a machine-gun rushing back. Commands were being shouted in Russian still, and there was more chaos and noise all round.

At the back of the lean-to was a stack of timber and boards, untidily arranged against the wall. I slunk back to it, pulled out a couple of boards and crept behind the stack, and hid. It struck me how quiet it suddenly became, the Russians seemed to have gone, but there were no Germans either. I had a feeling of total confusion, as if I did not belong to anything or anyone any more. Above all, I was very frightened. Next I heard the roar of the Panzers. Judging by the noise they were making, they were climbing up this side of the gorge. Had the Russians had anti-tank guns of any sort in positions, they would not be able to do that, I thought. There was no more shooting, no further resistance, and looking through a chink, I saw the first of them, the black cross on the white background standing out clearly. It was nosing awkwardly around a corner and slowly rumbling up the street towards me. I heard German words and German commands being shouted, and knew instantly that they had infantry with them. Then I saw the first grey-green figures crossing the street. Knowing their trigger-happiness, I decided to lie low for a while. After all, how could they know that I was still alive? I let the first Panzer go by, and then started shouting from behind my boards as loudly and clearly as I could: *'nicht schiessen, ich bin's, nicht schiessen!'* ('Don't shoot, it's me'). The nearest soldiers were no more than thirty or forty metres away, but only after I heard my name being called, did I dare to throw some boards down and then slowly step out from behind my stack and into the light where I could be clearly seen. To be on the safe side I even raised my hands over my head.

'You can take your hands down, Henry!', someone called — and then there was a roar of laughter from both sides of the street; I did not quite see the joke. The second Panzer had arrived, and one of our Lieutenants clambered out, shook my hand and asked me if I was all right. 'Well, well', he said, 'to be honest, that is more than we had expected, and there is not a scratch on you!'

Some of my mates wanted to go on and punish the Russians; I felt much relieved when the Lieutenant decided that it had all been enough for the day. We went into the officers' cottage but found nothing worthwhile, not even my paybook. From the field kitchen we took potatoes, cabbages, sugar and flour — it was not quite to my liking. When we were ready to go, I saw the old man who had been looking after the fire in the guards' cottage. He was carrying firewood now, and I said to him laughingly 'On the high horse today, Ivan, and in the ditch tomorrow, who knows!' He sadly nodded his head in agreement.

On the trip back I sat with the Lieutenant on the turret, rather like a trophy. Crossing the gorge, I pointed to the spot where I had sunk into the mud the night before, and the Lieutenant told me that they had taken a close look through their field-glasses at the Russian positions to make sure that they had no anti-tank weapons.

When we got back, there was much surprise, and then laughter. I was handed a brandy bottle, took a long sip and everyone raised their arm, saying, 'That is to Henry, *prosit!*' I was then shown my friend August's grave, and had a good look at the cottage from where I had been taken less than twelve hours before. There was an undertone of reproach when someone mentioned that I had suffered not a scratch, while August had died. He could not understand this, and neither could I. I asked him in return whether he could explain how I, asleep in a cottage, could have been taken out of it alive under the noses of the guards. That shut him up.

By chance they had stumbled on August's body, with no sign either of me or of blood in the cottage, in the early hours of the morning. They had called the Commander and only then had they discovered the gorge, and taken note of the other part of the village.

I had to report to our Commander, and I did not relish the prospect. 'Welcome back to the fold!', he said and laughed — and I was much relieved. He said he could not quite understand how it had all happened. 'Did you give information to them voluntarily?', he wanted to know, 'and what actually did you tell them?' When I hesitated, suspecting some sort of a trap, he said, 'Come on, don't be shy, I really do appreciate the situation you must have found yourself in.' When I told him that I had given the Russians more or less correct information, he wanted to know 'Why did you do that?' I explained that I had assumed that they would have known if I had lied as, having shadowed us for so long, they must have known everything about our *Kampfgruppe*. To my great relief he said 'Correct!', and added that under the circumstances he would have done the same. 'Well done!', he said, patted me on the shoulder and told me to get something to eat and then find myself a soft place on a lorry to get some sleep, as soon we would be on the move again. When I told him as an afterthought that the Russians even had known his name, he seemed quite pleased.

It was still dark when I woke up in the back of the shaking lorry, and at first I did not know where I was. My mates said that they had been involved in a skirmish, there had been some shooting, and I had not even woken up. The general situation was getting tougher all round. They had come through a village where they had seen a German Colonel still hanging from a beam. A bit of cardboard had been attached to his jacket with the inscription '*Ein Feigling vor dem Feind*' (a coward in the face of the enemy). His medals had been torn from his tunic, his jackboots had been taken, and his cap lay in the snow underneath him.

By now we were all very disillusioned, as well as suffering from physical and mental exhaustion. All we were interested in was sticking together and heading west towards Poland and then the German border, which was still hundreds of miles away. Through some enforced reorganization I now belonged to *Kampfgruppe* Lindemann, named after Captain Lindemann, its Commander. We had no vehicles left, no weapons of any weight apart from those we could carry. All our heavier equipment was packed into flat-bottomed boats, *Wehrmacht* issue, which could easily be pulled through the snow by two men. Our food situation was serious and we were on continuous look-out for abandoned food depots.

With the disappearance of a proper command structure, the military cohesion and formal discipline had become very lax. Only the lowest in rank, together in cliques, could totally rely on each other. When Lindemann once 'suggested' — and he did no more — that we should enter a village which we suspected was already occupied by a Red Army unit — we just looked at him with blank eyes and trudged on through the snow — and that was it. Democracy was making its first inroads into the Army. The temperature at that time was about minus thirty degrees centigrade. There were no roads we could follow, only snow as far as the eye could see. The only features were small copses of birch, huddled together as if to protect each other from the biting winds.

We received orders to stay in a certain village for a few days, to give other units a chance to get back into line. The first night, the Red Army unit following us came all too close for our liking, creeping up unobserved in their white camouflage, and dug themselves into positions no more than three hundred metres away.

When morning came, we discovered that they had erected loudspeakers, which kept blaring their propaganda over to us. Their speaker was obviously a Volga German, speaking in that quaint way Germans had spoken two hundred years ago, when Empress Catharine had taken them as settlers from Germany to make their homes in the Volga region. He apologised that as he had no records with him, we would have to make do with him singing us a song or two. Though his loudspeaker had an irritatingly scratchy quality, we had to admit that his voice was not all that bad. He sang beautiful Russian folk tunes, as well as old German peasant songs, some of them dating back to the Peasant Wars. In between songs, he announced that he would now have us peppered with a few mortar salvoes, which he did, and then he sang us a song about how lovely it is at home amongst one's loved ones. After the song he gave us another raking — and so it went on, and we could do nothing about it. What also was very disturbing was that much of his propaganda talk sounded true. We knew, of course, being in the middle of it all, that the Russians had completely turned the tables and were now beating us hands down, but we did not want salt rubbed into our wounds. We shouted over to him 'German bastard traitor!', but he only laughed and then gave us many precise details about lost battles and wiped-out Divisions and armies from all over the long front. He warned us that there was no chance for us ever to reach home again and see our loved ones, unless we laid down our weapons and stopped our barbaric crimes. He told us that his name was Georg Bauer, and that from the very beginning our officers had lied to us, and were still betraying us even now.

We were glad when we walked away from Georg Bauer, who had got very much on our nerves. The snow was about a foot deep and heavy to walk through, and the air was brittle with frost. Having no maps, we were surprised to come across a small collection of thatched cottages, in a hollow in front of us. Smoke was rising from the chimneys, and there was no sign of a military presence. Then Lindemann ordered some of us, including me, to go across and set fire to the huts. He had been told off a short while ago by a superior officer for not having carried out Hitler's 'scorched earth' policy, and he was now adamant that we should do it. Many of us found this a devilish order, especially as we knew about the horrible suffering of the Russian population.

We were each designated to burn a single hut. Walking round 'my' hut, I realized that there were people in it. When I tried the door, it gave way at once, and looking back I could see my mates with their rifles at the ready aiming at the door 'just in case'. There was much movement inside, but it was rather dark and I could see very little. At first nothing happened. Then I heard Lindemann call over, 'Move in, it's all right!' When I stepped through the door, I was hit by the heavy odour of human beings in distress. The single room was packed, there was no ceiling and above one could see the rafters and the straw of the thatch. Most of them were old people, but there were also younger women with children and babies. Apart from a ramshackle table, the odd chair and a sideboard, with perhaps a pretence of a bed, there was no other furniture. Parts of the earthen floor were covered with bundles of cloth, bits of cardboard and blankets. Everything looked in an unholy mess.

All of them just stood there, no one said a word, and even the babies must have sensed the tension. Some were lying or crouching on the floor, others sat on their haunches, stood in the middle, or were leaning against the walls or the warm stove. They were all ordinary peasant people. Then a young woman came forward from the back holding her baby towards me in a gesture. Everyone else seemed to be watching what effect that was having on me. I knew that I had not much time, as the *Kampfgruppe* was moving on and I had to catch up. When someone tried to shut the door behind me, things came to a head. I pulled it violently open again and shouted at them to get out, all of them, as I was going to burn their miserable hut down. As a result pandemonium broke out. Hands were stretched out to me, there was wailing and crying, and then everyone wanted to speak to me at the same time. They told me that they all had come a long way, that their villages had been burnt down and that they had lost everything. They said that they were starving right now, and I could see the truth of it in their faces. To stay in this hut, they claimed, was their only chance to survive the winter's hazards. All my shouting, my threats, my pistol waving had no effect. An old woman went down on her knees in front of me, she tried while praying to kiss my boots, when someone pushed me from the back and I toppled over her. That was all what I needed. Getting back on my feet, I held the pistol to the side of an old man's head who up to now had been standing there, saying nothing and holding the hand of a little girl. 'Out!' I shouted at them all, 'if you don't go, I will shoot him!' Everything was tumbled up in me, I did not know what to do any more, and I felt as if I was losing control of myself. But the old man showed no fear. He looked at me calmly without hatred, having only sadness in his eyes, and quietly said 'Shoot, go on', then looking down to the little girl, 'but please shoot her as well, as if you burn this hut of ours, it makes no difference.'

Lindemann came in, telling me that the *Kampfgruppe* was already ahead and that he had seen no smoke coming from my cottage. And when I told him that I simply could not move them out, he said something like 'that is their affair', and that the Führer's orders are the Führer's orders, that I had better watch my step and come out with him. The thatch, heavy with snow, reached down to chest level and he showed me what to do. The straw was dry at the inside of the thatch, he put a match to it, and so did I. The flames crackled lustily upwards, towards the inside of the hut. Then we simply walked away, hurrying to catch up with the *Kampfgruppe*, which was on the point of disappearing over the horizon.

I saw the door open, and they all tumbled out. I heard them crying and shouting and praying, the old people, the little children and the women with their babies. Lindemann and I just walked on. Then there was a soft but powerful thud. I looked back. The fire had broken through the snow cover of the roof from several places, and its vicious tongues were coming together to one torch-like stream reaching into the clear sky. Later, when I could no longer see the hut, I could still see brown-yellow smoke curling upwards.

A short time later we were absorbed into a large battle group which had a number of Panzers and other heavy weapons. I forget now which wide river it was that we were approaching, the Dnieper or the Bug; Russia has so many. From afar we had already seen the high west bank, rising out of the mist like a dirty white layer between the flat snowy waste and the grey sky above. The pale wintry sun, just slightly above the horizon, appeared to be tearing at the patches of mist which hung lazily above the river. With distances difficult to judge in the show, we were surprised how soon our column reached the river bank. While along both banks the ice was as smooth as a skating rink, towards the middle rough floes of broken ice had shifted on top of each other, forming grotesque, gigantic heaps which, we feared, could possibly prove impassable barriers for our Panzers and other vehicles. Then we noticed that several 8.8 cm Flak field pieces had been strategically positioned to protect the crossing area and we saw a couple of *Kübelwagen* jeeps driving towards the middle, blowing clouds of snow into the crisp air. Command cars from the other side had left to meet them and we were relieved when we saw them driving with apparent ease, though in zig-zag fashion, through the line of piled-up floes. Then a large green flag was waved from the centre and we received the order to cross. To reduce weight, especially in the middle, we spaced our Panzers, and though the ice creaked and groaned, it was a healthy creaking and we knew that we had made it again. 'God', as we so arrogantly liked to remind ourselves, 'was always on the side of the mighty who dared.'

Rumours and counter-rumours of the most bewildering variety had been chasing each other of late. They mainly centred around a secret new victory weapon, fresh Divisions arriving from France to relieve us, and heavily fortified defence lines waiting for us, from where we could make a stand. Sceptical as we were, we had not given up all hope, but there were many jokes about Goebbels' big tales to pep up our morale. In the case of this wide river we reasoned that if ever a stand was to be made to arrest what now had become a stampede out of Russia, it would be here by the river. But as soon as we had collected on the other side, and though many of us naturally were glad that we were continuing towards Germany, we actually carried straight on, which to us was an indication that our leadership had given up hope of stemming the Russians.

We arrived at a large village, and I was ordered to take over driving one of the Panzers again. Though there were problems in the bitter winter conditions, my new Panzer was in good shape. Petrol was scarce, and whenever possible when parking we drove backwards into haystacks etc. to save having to run them every hour. It was the general rule that drivers, especially those of Panzers, were not to stand guard on the first night anywhere. As I hated both driving a Panzer and standing on guard, my choice was always between the devil and the deep blue sea.

Our cottage was a comfortable one in the middle of the village. It was occupied by an elderly couple and their lodger, a female village teacher. There were two rooms, one a small annexe at the back into which we ordered our Russians. The large mud stove, though fuelled from our side, warmed their room as well.

Soon we were sitting around the table by candlelight in comfortable warmth and having our meal. We always made a point of eating together, and after the meal we often played cards or chess. However small a German crew, there is always at least one who can play the mouth organ, and our national repertoire alone is as good as inexhaustible.

There was often a slight disturbance when guards change duty at night. All too often, the woken-up guard would complain of having been woken up too early. When I heard a bit of commotion in the early hours one night, I took no notice, but when morning came, I heard of what had happened in the night.

An officer had introduced himself as Lieutenant Schmidt, and had said that he was liaising from a unit at the other end of the village. He had visited every single defence position and had had words with the guards. As far as it could be seen in the snowy night, he had worn a perfect German uniform under his white camouflage, and a hood over his helmet. His accent had been strong, but so was that of a number of officers and many men. As traditional discipline demands that no soldier has the right to question an officer, Lieutenant Schmidt had had no need to answer any questions. He only asked them. He had followed a very simple line of at first criticizing the guard for something not done correctly, and then settling down with them to have a friendly chat, offering cigarettes and sweets. In this way he had found out everything worthwhile about our food, personnel, petrol etc.

When morning came and it was clear that there simply was no other unit at the other end of the village, and certainly no Lieutenant Schmidt, it was of course all too late. It was suspected that he was still somewhere in the village, and our rough search of the cottages etc. and the careful questionings, especially of children, brought no result. Being in the mood we were in, most of us did not hide their respect for this man's obvious courage. Next night when I was on guard, I was ready for him, and hoped that he would first come to me. But, needless to say, he never came.

We stayed in the village for several days. Packs of T-34s were probing us all the time, but as we had heavy weapons and Panzers, they kept a respectful distance. Our three Russians in the cottage caused us no bother. Once we had got used to each other, they came into 'our' room in the evenings and sat with us, because it was the warmer of the two. The old woman was always busy with something, and the old man never refused our offer of tobacco; at that time we had plenty. He watched our every move with eagle eyes. I played chess with him several times, but had the impression that he lost on purpose because he probably thought that it would be unwise to beat a German soldier at chess.

Tanja, the teacher, was twenty-six years old and though of peasant stock, seemed a typical product of modern Soviet education. At the beginning of the war she had been sent to the village from Kiev University, and when our troops had overrun the area in the summer of 1941, she had remained throughout the occupation. She was heavily built and very buxom, had a pretty, rosy face and an engaging friendly smile. Her dark hair was tightly bound together at the back of her head. Her eyes were large and brown and she dressed in rough, unbecoming peasant clothes; unbecoming to our eyes, anyway, and it was perhaps because of that, that she did so. Tanja knew a fair amount of German, and liked to try it on me. As I was always eager to improve my Russian, it was perhaps natural that we often sat together in the evenings and talked.

There were still a few children in the village, whom Tanja collected together on odd days to teach. I don't know whether she had ever asked the German authorities for permission. We often talked about the beautiful city of Kiev which we both knew. Tanja was close to tears when I mentioned that it was badly destroyed. 'Beautiful Kiev', she said, 'and the Germans accuse the Soviets of being barbaric!' Even at that time, I still believed the Slavs and other eastern races to be less civilized and less intelligent than us Germans. During the many evenings together, Tanja taught me many lessons, and her wide-ranging knowledge and ability to interpret in Marxist terms every aspect of life astounded me.

Her main lesson to me, perhaps, was that one can look at events and things from quite different angles and come to different conclusions. Whenever I tried to steer her towards subject like politics, ideology or philosophy — and I tried many times — she always refused to be drawn. That she had her own firm opinions on these subjects was obvious to me, and at times I could discern an expression of contempt in her face about something I had said.

Two or three days later, Soviet tank columns threatened to get round our flanks and we had to move quickly. Everything ready, I gave my engine a good revving up, and while I watched our officers standing in a circle for the usual command discussion. A small detachment was set up by our Commander consisting of my Panzer and a personnel carrier with ten men to drive north for about twenty miles and blow up a river bridge, then turning west again to rejoin the *Kampfgruppe*. A young Lieutenant was in command. We got to the bridge without incident, tied two explosive charges underneath at each end and stood back to watch. There were two mighty bangs tearing the cold wintry air apart, and then came the crashing, bringing down the whole of the middle section on to the ice. The bridge had been a fairly new one, and had carried a single railway and a road.

Rolling west again, we came through a small industrial settlement with workers' three-storey blocks of flats right next to it. It surprised us to find a small SS and *Luftwaffe* unit which had made camp in one of the factory buildings. Hearing us coming, they had thought that we were Russians and had prepared to give us a mighty welcome of fire and steel. They were part of a larger *Kampfgruppe* which was on the move further north towards Poland, and for which they were providing flank security. After drinking some of their coffee and exchanging information, we drove on. It was bitterly cold even inside the Panzer with the engine running, and from time to time we heard the sound of cracking in the cold air. The low white sun pierced a layer of snow mist, creating a glare which hurt our eyes, and because we had no sun glasses, we pulled scarves around our faces and tilted the helmet right down so as to keep out the glaring light.

On the horizon we saw what looked like a collection of children's bricks, which had been plonked there at random. Coming closer, we recognized that they were the modern concrete buildings of an agricultural station. There were tractor sheds, work-shops, barns and other types of buildings. A section of the station was enclosed by rolls of barbed wire with a high wire fence behind it. Without having known of its existence, we had arrived at an Army Food Depot. A wide double gate barred our entrance, and behind it at the inside was a small guard cabin, out of which stepped a fully dressed and armed guard. We almost had to laugh, the whole set-up and performance seemed like one of Grimm's fairy tales. There was nothing for miles around, no bush, no hedge, no house, just flat white country, and right here in the middle of all the nothingness a guard steps out of his cabin as if it were the most natural thing in the world. Looking through the fence, we could see that the depot was stacked to the roof. What surprised us even more was that there was no obvious preparation for either moving the stocks or blowing the whole thing up. We knew that the Red Army would be here within days, possibly even hours. We all clambered out of our vehicles and, looking over at the rows of tins, cardboard-boxes, wooden drums full of food, we already started licking our lips in anticipation.

But the guard at the gate said not one word to us. His whole demeanour was sullen, as if we were all a great big nuisance to him. Being closer to forty than thirty, he seemed to us like an old man, and one of us tried to speed him up a bit: 'Come on, Pop, open the gates of heaven and let us in:' He slightly opened the gate but only just enough to let our Lieutenant through, and then quickly shut it again behind him. We were lost for words for once, we couldn't make it out, all this seemed to be beyond the limits of the ridiculous. To top it all, we heard him say to our Lieutenant that only food lorries with proper loading papers were allowed in. While all this was going on, a little self-assured officer in the greenish uniform of the *Wirtschaftsgruppe* (economic unit) with the rank of Major had arrived from the inside of the depot. He also looked in a grumpy mood, and in an unpleasant way asked the Lieutenant what he wanted. 'Loading up, of course!', we shouted from the outside of the gates. We heard him ask whether we had any loading papers. Not that again! 'Of course, we haven't', the Lieutenant bit back, 'we didn't even know of the existence of this dump before now'.

With all the problems of the retreat, we had not really had anything decent to eat for weeks, and now here right in front of our eyes was all this beautiful food and this green-clad Saint Peter refused us any of it because we had no loading papers.

At this point we heard motors approaching from the rear and at first we thought that the Russians had already arrived. Leaving the Lieutenant inside the gate, we jumped into our Panzer while all the others got into fighting positions with their machine guns etc. ready for anything. But then, to our great relief, we saw two lorries with distinct SS markings labouring out of a hollow right behind the fence at the back. Out of one of them climbed a troop of SS led by a Sergeant. We all had a good laugh and shook hands all round. They told us that they had got wind of this food depot and had come to load up before it was too late. 'Come on', they said, 'let's share the best between us! What are we waiting for?' With this their lorries nosed slowly up to the gate. 'Have you got loading papers?', we asked them. 'Have we got what?' They laughed loudly and thought we were telling them a good joke. 'Yes, our driver's got one, signed by Heinrich Himmler on a bit of cardboard.'

'No, no, really, no joke, that little green Saint Peter, the little Major, is telling us that he will only give us food if we have the proper loading papers!' But they kept laughing, obviously still believing that we were having them on good and proper. But while we were having that friendly banter, the guard had taken the precaution of chaining and padlocking the gates, and was sliding the key into his pocket.

'Hey', called the SS Sergeant, 'don't play about, enough is enough. Open the gates, we want to load up! It's German food, ours, not your personal property, and the Russkies are coming and will take what we can't carry, and if you resist them, they will castrate you into the bargain!' Some of them still kept laughing, obviously thinking that this pantomime surely could not be for real. To add to the whole comedy, another couple of elderly guards came rushing up with their rifles from somewhere behind, and the Major shouted at our Lieutenant that he had received strict orders from Army Headquarters not to release the tiniest tin of sardines without properly signed loading papers, that this was his final word on the matter and that he was sick and tired of our rudeness. By now all of us, more than a dozen, had lined up along the fence, witnessing something that seemed to be too stupid for our senses to accept as real. We were all talking at once, pushing our fists through the wire of the gate. Suddenly the Sergeant shouted at us all in a loud voice: 'Be quiet, the lot of you!', and then he turned round to the Major and said: 'Look here, funny comrade, enough of your jokes is enough. Stop your silly game, if you know what is good for you. We want that food and we want it right now; and to hell with your stupid talk about loading papers. And if you will not let us have it, we will cough on your permission and will take it ourselves without it. Now, open the gates, and I am telling you that this is an SS order!'

'Well,' I thought, 'this surely must be it now!' But I was wrong. I could hardly believe my own eyes when I saw Saint Peter step so close to the wire that he came almost face to face with the Sergeant. 'An SS order, did you say, Sergeant, what is that and who do you think you are?' And then he pulled out his pistol from the bolster of his belt and held it playfully in front of him. 'No, Sergeant', he snarled, 'for the last time, no! I am here in command on behalf of the highest authority of the Army — not of the SS nor anyone else. And now, will you all take yourselves off!' For a moment there was deep silence. But then I heard a clean, metallic click behind me and knew instantly that, apart from the Major's, there was another pistol on the loose; and then there was a loud bang coming close from the back near my ear. The Major staggered forward a step without saying one word, then fell flat on his face with his arms stretched forward and the pistol slithering away from him in the snow. The first reaction was disbelief. We all turned towards the centre, and I saw one of the SS men standing right behind me with his pistol in his hand. There was no reproach from his Sergeant, nor from anyone else. 'Just too idiotic to be true!', came slowly from his lips, 'the bastard got what he deserved!' With that he pushed me aside and stepped to the gate. 'And now, granddad, unlock it and be quick about it!' he icily called to the guard who, we knew, had the key in his pocket, who caused no further trouble and unlocked the gate with shaking hands.

Two of us had to step though to pull the body away first so that we could open the gates fully, and then we all drove in, the SS with their two lorries, me with my Panzer, and the personnel carrier. By now, probably alarmed by the shot and the revving of the engines, some more guards and Russian prisoners had arrived from the back, but once they had assessed the situation and one of us had called over in broken German that we were the Red Army in German uniforms and were going to liberate them from their food, they disappeared as quickly as they had come.

We smashed doors and locks when they barred our way, and informed each other of our discoveries. Most of us, being old campaigners, could not remember having had decent food like this for years. We looked at each other and grinned, this really was like heaven! Slaughtered parts of oxen, pig and lamb were hanging from hooks in a large hall. There was bread, mountains of it, large packs of butter, chocolate, honey, and buckets of marmalade. There was no end to our finds, and in one of the back stores, the lock of which we had to break with a cross-bar, we found boxes of cognac, champagne, all sorts of wines, vodka and schnapps. While the SS had it easy with their lorries, we had a severe loading problem. Every available gap, every niche was filled, with only the very best of the high quality stuff. We found ropes with which we tied meat and butter and other large packs to the turret, so that in the end we looked like an overloaded furniture van. The enemy from afar would never have believed that we were a fighting Panzer.

I saw our Lieutenant and the SS Sergeant standing amiably together, discussing what was, I suspected, some sort of 'gentlemen's agreement' while they were screwing up their faces, putting their upright fingers against their lips and chuckling dirty laughs. I later noticed the Sergeant go over to the guards and have a serious word with them.

Climbing through the packs into my driving seat, I realized that if we had needed to get into battle stations quickly, we would never have made it. As we drove through the gate, the pistol-packing SS man came running and signalled me to stop. Having had a few drops already, he wanted to shake hands with each of us again to assure us eternal friendship, and when he took mine, looking back in the direction of the body, he said: 'Keep your ears to the wind, Kamerad, who knows what will happen to us tomorrow!' He added, as a quiet afterthought, 'A good pair of boots he's got on, too good for the Russians to have. He was a fool, that's why he had to become a victim of the circumstances of his own making.'

While driving along, the *Jaegerbranntwein* (quality cognac) was passed from hand to hand, and when a bottle became empty, a full one was quickly substituted. Fortunately the terrain was flat and there were no ditches. I could see, and faintly realized why it was, that the personnel carrier in front of me was moving in a peculiar zig-zag fashion. Above the din of our engine arose the best German soldiers' songs. Every throat, including mine, gave its utmost. There was great merriment, no sadness, and certainly no regret. There was so much death around us that that of Saint Peter made no difference. After a few kilometres someone in the carrier signalled me to stop. I saw the Lieutenant climbing out. He gestured all of us to stand around, and then attempted to climb on to my Panzer to make a speech. After having slipped and fallen off several times, he gave it up as a bad job and made his speech from ground level. The gist of his slurred words was, as we all knew, that we had arrived at a German food depot which a Russian advance unit must have raided before our arrival, and we naturally had taken what we wanted from what was left over. Then he made the sensible aside that we all realized what would happen to us all if ever the truth was to come out. We all made as serious faces as we could, and nodded in comradely agreement. Even with our extremely befuddled brains, we understood only too well what he meant.

It was already conveniently dark when we rejoined our *Kampfgruppe*. There was some slight confusion when we approached, as none of us could remember the agreed colours and sequence of flares to be fired. Luckily everyone in our *Kampfgruppe* was sober and had recognized us long before we even saw them. During the night our officers had a great party. The singing went on until dawn broke. The cognac and all the other beautiful things were in great demand, and probably as a result of the party, not too many inconvenient questions were asked. In brandy terms, what was the price of a human life, especially at times like this?

When we broke camp next morning most of us felt awful. There was also a pang, not so much of conscience, but of concern arising, for what would happen should the depot guards ever catch up with our *Kampfgruppe*? But then Ivan settled that problem later on when his T-34s appeared over the horizon, beyond which, we knew, lay the depot. We silently hoped that no prisoners had escaped them. What a final twist of irony! I saw the Lieutenant that night. He carried a bottle in the large pocket of his greatcoat and offered me a generous gulp. He mentioned nothing about what had happened the day before, but said something thoughtful about the good snow which covers all evidence. He raised the bottle towards the east: 'Damn it all!' he said, 'Ivan, you devil, our heartfelt toast to you!' That gave me another chance to have a gulp, and then I held it high in the air and said, 'To Ivan — and the all-covering snow!' We both grinned knowingly at each other, and then had another gulp.

There was now little doubt that the overall situation had fallen to pieces, that we were on a headlong flight out of Russia and that only some wonder weapon Goebbels kept talking about back home, could save us. Every retreat was reported as a 'straightening of the front line' and every Division which was coming from France to stop the rot in the east, failed to arrive. Though generally discipline was still strong, we heard reports of mutineers and deserters being shot, and we were not at all surprised. On the whole we ordinary soldiers said very little because we had to be careful, but the resentment went deep and few were in doubt any more that we had been lied to for years.

The knowledge that with every day we were coming closer to the Polish border, gave all our actions a hard edge. The leaden sky, carrying wild snow showers driven by bitter winds merged with the snowy horizon. The only good thing about the weather was that it kept the enemy planes out of the sky.

It was already getting dark when we entered the village. It had become Army custom to give villages a German name for easier identification, and we called this one Nordhausen. In our arrogance we did not even want to know its Russian name. Finding at our entry that other small straggler units had already occupied many cottages, there was tension and confusion. No one knew what was what in this sort of situation, which made the proper placing of guards difficult and even dangerous.

We billeted ourselves in a small cottage which was already occupied by a signal unit. Though they did not want us at first, the signallers agreed to let us stay, reasoning perhaps that we might give them some protection in an unexpected emergency. Their radio set, a large, bulky grey box, had been placed on a low table in the middle of the room. The ceiling was so low that the taller ones of us had to crouch slightly, and with several candles in odd positions and a crackling fire in the stove there was an atmosphere approaching German *Gemütlichkeit* or snugness (although the precise meaning cannot really be translated into any other language). We were well aware, of course, that the Red Army was close at our heels, but as we had given them a bit of a bloody nose the day before, we were reasonably sure that they would not bother us too much for the next day or two.

I had been on guard duty until about midnight and had stamped up and down the village street, scanning the grey-white waste beyond for signs of the enemy. I knew, of course, how easily a white-clad figure could approach without being seen, but I had noticed nothing, finding the task boring, and was glad when my time was up and I could bed down in the warm signal cottage.

My four or five mates were sound asleep beside the stove, one was even lying on top of it, and although we had strict orders to sleep in full uniform, few took any notice of this. I took my jackboots off, and watched the two radio signallers. One was sitting on a low stool in front of the set with his earphones on, while his mate next to him drew lines and arrows and other signs and symbols on a map spread out in front of him. Apart from their quiet conversation, some bleeping and a bit of snoring at the back, there was nothing to disturb the peace.

Most of what was coming from the set seemed to me routine and repetitive stuff, and I took little interest in it. But then suddenly something alarming happened which made me sit up. The scribbler had been murmuring as he repeated the radio messages which he then put down on paper. He was saying something like 'enemy detachment of about a hundred men, some with skis, operating towards the vicinity of the village of so and so,' giving its Russian name instead of the German. As if in an afterthought, he then said quietly: 'they should have used the German name; by the way, what is the Russian name of this village?' They both glanced at the map then, and at the same time must have realized that it was our own village, Nordhausen, which the message was about and which the Russians were reported to be approaching!

As if stung by a scorpion they both jumped up from their stools, and so did I, quickly putting my boots back on, and grabbing my camouflage and rifle. And while my mates were in the process of waking up from the sudden noise, I was by the door and out, having already heard the first shots. I saw white camouflaged figures swishing past on skis, and threw myself into the snow right beside the door. What later happened to the signallers and my mates I never found out. The 'white ghosts' had made excellent use of the element of surprise and had placed a machine gun at either end of the street. Within a few minutes they had gained complete strategic control of the whole village, with all our units trapped in hopelessly.

Hardly daring to raise my head, I could see only total havoc being played out all around me. A mellow light fell across the snow towards me when the door of a cottage opposite opened with a bang and several of my mates came tumbling out; the Russians had been waiting for that, and none of them made it more than three yards beyond the threshold. More doors opened up and down the street, more shots were fired — and more lifeless bundles ended up in the snow. I heard the cries of agony, of pain and utter frustration.

Lying motionless in white in the snow, I had not yet been seen by anyone, but when some Russians swished past me only yards away, I knew that it was time to scramble — and scramble fast; I was also beginning to feel the penetrating cold. Shooting from where I was would have been tantamount to suicide, so I crawled on my stomach round the corner of the cottage to a small barn at the rear. Luckily not a soul was around, and I was able to run in a crouching position as fast as I could away from the row of the cottages and into the gloom of the white-dirty nothingness of the winter's night. My luck held, not one shot was fired after me. But now I was alone and frightened, and concentrated all my senses on everything around me. Walking away from the village I had a pang of conscience, realizing that the ski troops must already have been lying in wait outside while I was on guard duty.

After a short time, the firing in the village stopped. It meant that it was all over and that the Russians had achieved complete victory. I recognized the seriousness of my situation. The snow was about a foot high, I had no food and no idea where I was nor where I was going. It was snowing slightly, I had no compass and had totally lost my sense of direction. Then out of the all enshrouding gloom I was sure that I heard voices. They were coming towards me and I lay down in the snow and listened, feeling very frightened. But then when they were close enough, I was sure that they were German, and when I could make out their figures, I called to them in German. Their first reaction was to throw themselves into the snow, and it took us quite a while before we were sure that we were safe to introduce ourselves and tell our tales. There were nine of them, some from my unit, one was a Lieutenant, another a Sergeant. I did not tell them that I had been on guard duty just before the Russian attack. Luckily they had retrieved a flat-bottomed boat with some food, blankets, rifles and ammunition. They had had a similar experience to mine, only their cottage had lain back a bit and they had been able to get out unseen. They had heard no alarm at all, and were very angry about the guards. None of us had any doubt that all the Germans in the village, and there must have been well over a hundred, had been eliminated except for us.

The Lieutenant had a compass and a rough idea about the geography. We walked for many hours until the morning. Our mood was at its lowest ebb, and no one felt like talking. Then two of them started to quarrel. The argument was about our right to have come into Russia in the first place, and whether we were now getting what we deserved. One was a Nazi, still full of grandiose ideas, the other obviously not. And when the whole thing became so vicious that it threatened to develop into a fight, the Lieutenant had to step in and order them both to stop immediately.

When morning greyed in the east, we reached a village which seemed to rise out of the gloom in front of us. War had already swept over it in 1941, and all its three dozen or so cottages were burnt out and had fallen in on themselves. There was not a single living being in sight. We decided to stay the day, for at least we could have four, albeit roofless, walls around us as protection against the biting wind. And there were enough half-burnt timbers around for a good fire.

After a quick cook- and brew-up, my mates settled round the fire on blankets while I was the first guard on duty. Strolling around, I found behind one of the cottages several frozen human corpses, parts of which had been eaten by wild dogs. Walking on, I noticed smoke rising from one of the cottages down the street. Moving carefully, I came to a breach in the wall. An old couple were sitting on a beam with their backs to me, warming themselves in front of a fire. The man wore thickly-padded ragged clothes and a tattered fur cap with flaps hanging down at the sides. The woman was in a long, dark peasant coat, leaving only a small part of her face to be seen. They had just finished eating, as a pan, some tin plates and mugs with other utensils lay in the snow beside them. They were in the process of putting handfuls of snow into a small pot to melt it over the fire. The man looked positively ill, and they both looked sad, dishevelled and tired, and sat there in complete silence. When I stepped through the opening, they were startled, turning their heads in surprise, but they did not get up nor say a word. I could see that they had reached the lowest state of human deprivation, and could not sink any lower, and which must have made everything around them — even something as important as a German soldier's arrival — pointless.

I asked them what they were doing there. They told me they had come from their village, which had burnt down in the fighting, like this one. Most of their people had been killed, and now that they were old, they had lost everything that they had ever possessed. They explained that they had been walking for more than a week and that they were trying to get to their daughter, who was married and living in Kiev. I told them that they would never get there, as Kiev was several hundreds of kilometres away, with fighting armies in between. As Kiev and their daughter was probably their only hope, they looked at me with stony eyes, as if they did not want to understand. I noticed two sacks in the snow beside them, two dirty ordinary farm sacks. What was in them, I wanted to know. 'All that we have left!' said the old man.

'Open them!', I brusquely ordered him. He did so with an air of hopeless resignation. In one were cabbages, potatoes, beetroots and chunks of bread and cheese. All of it was untidily wrapped up in cabbage leaves, in peasant fashion. In the other was some rolled-up clothing, the odd tin cup and a pot. I told them to pick up their things and move on.

'But why?', they both wanted to know, they were doing no harm to anyone, besides, they were tired and had intended to stay the night. Then the old man beckoned me to come to the window hole and pointed out some displaced thatch down the road, out of which, they hoped, they could make themselves a sort of bed. I was just over twenty, and looking at them, I thought that they could have been my grandparents, standing there in their torn felt boots, so worn, so miserable. How must I have looked through their eyes, standing there all-powerful with my rifle?

I allowed them to go to their fallen-down thatch. The old woman asked me if I had some matches and I gave her some. They slung their awkward sacks onto their shoulders, helping each other while I stood by, doing nothing. I watched them walk slowly down the village street and noticed that they both found it hard to walk in the snow. 'Kiev', I thought, 'weak and old as they are — and the snow, — they will never make it.' I heard them being challenged further down the road by one of my mates. I called out to him to let them go, since I already had found them *in Ordnung*. I watched them reach the ruin with that bit of thatch, and begin to pull at the straw to make a bed for themselves.

I spent the rest of the day on a wide board tucked up in blankets close to the fire. The misery was overwhelming. Had I died there and then, I would not really have minded. When it was getting dark, we broke camp and left the village to move west through the night. One of my mates who had patrolled the village when I had been asleep told me that an old woman had come and had said to him that she thought that her husband was dying and she did not know what to do. Could he help, please. 'And so', I asked, 'did you go?'

'Of course not! What for? After all they are only Russians and so many of them, and also of us, have to die all the time?' And then we walked on through the snow in the night, wrapped up in our problems, and I did not give that old couple a further thought.

9
The conquerors are conquered

Da steh' ich nun
ich armer Tor
und bin so klug
als wie zuvor.

'There I stand,
poor fool
no more clever
than when I started out.'

Goethe, from *Faust*

We were driven before the advancing Russians across the old Polish border, from which three years ago we had set out full of hope to conquer the USSR. During the campaign I had been wounded several times but, luckily, only slightly. And then, it happened again. Not far from the River San and the large town of Przemysl I was hit by a shell fragment, which finally secured me a place on a Red Cross transport back home to Germany.

What a homecoming it was! We had heard, of course, about the Allied air attacks on the German cities. But what we saw from our windows was far beyond what we had expected. It shocked us to the core of our very being. Was this what we had been fighting for in the East for several years? And yet, there was still a hard core amongst us, when we were discussing the horrible spectacle, who could not see the connection between these ashes and what we had done in Russia. Breslau was very bad when we saw it, but no worse than Stalingrad had been.

As the wounded were now also being rushed into the Fatherland from the Western and Southern Fronts, all the hospital services were heavily overloaded. We came through Dresden, Leipzig, Halle, Magdeburg etc. Sometimes we went through air attacks, but our coaches had large Red Crosses on their roofs, and fortunately nothing happened to us. Finally we were unloaded at an emergency *Lazarett* at Gütersloh in Westphalia.

The faces of the civilians were grey and tired, and in some of them we could even see resentment, as if it was our fault that their homes had been destroyed and so many of their dear ones burnt to cinders. Smiling wryly, we reminded each other that Hitler himself had promised his soldiers that the gratitude of the Fatherland to them would be ensured forever. But we realized that these had merely been words, and the cold reality was quite different. Even so many of us expected some sort of reception committee, with flowers and speeches at the railway station. But when we arrived, there were only the porters, who had got used to these trains, and over-worked and harassed stretcher-bearers from the Hitler Youth, who dumped us as quickly as they could in the long corridors.

The medical and other care, though there was much pressure on the staff, was excellent. Leaving hospital, before moving on to garrison proper as was procedure, I joined a *Genesenden Kompanie* (convalescence company) which sent me to the Tyrol on the Austro-German border for a short stint of recuperation.

With Innsbruck, Garmisch and other famous Alpine resorts in close proximity and the war seemingly still far away, it all should have been like a dream. But it was not; the final collapse of our Reich was now only a question of time, and this dominated all the thinking of my waking hours. Though not daring to say to anyone, secretly I would have liked to have stayed medically unfit for war until the last shot was fired. But I was declared fit, and the thought of having to go back into that cauldron of fire touched all my emotions. When I joined my new battle unit in Schwetzingen garrison, not far from beautiful Heidelberg, and discovered that there was no one I knew from my Russia days, my mood plunged so low that I saw no sense in living any more.

By this time, with powerful enemy armies fighting on all sides of our Reich, even the most fanatical amongst us began to realize that our practical use as soldiers could now be no more than as cheap cannon fodder, to be carelessly sacrificed on an idiotic altar of glory. With everything so openly and obviously falling to pieces all around us, it was — and still is — a mystery to me why no revolt broke out anywhere amongst the suffering German population.

We were an odd collection of disillusioned survivors thrown together from once proud fighting Divisions. Our unit did not even have a name, only a meaningless number, and our equipment was ridiculous considering that we were going to do battle with General Patton's powerful tank army, which was now moving in from France. In marching order on foot, all the time looking out for marauding American Thunderbolt planes (which we called '*Jabos*', short for *Jagdbombers* or fighter-bombers) and carrying most of our equipment ourselves, we left our garrison at Schwetzinger and crossed the River Rhine at the old imperial town of Speyer. Ours was the last unit over the bridge. The sappers told us that they had been nervously awaiting our arrival, and shortly after we had crossed to the other side, they blew it up. What confidence our Headquarters must have had in the overall military situation and what fighting spirit therefore did they expect from us? When we asked our commanding officer about our operational priorities, he said; 'Defending the Reich, of course, as they always were.' And when we pointed out that the real Reich was on the other side of the river, and that with Patton's tank army approaching, we felt we were being sacrificed, he suggested, obviously not feeling all that happy about what would happen to his own skin, that we should be careful about making impertinent remarks.

I was now issued with a rifle with a 1917 stamp on it and a broken sight and a *Panzerfaust* bazooka which was heavy and awkward to carry. It was March, spring came early that year in the Rhine valley, and the weather was very pleasant but fate, we knew, was now on a knife's edge; whichever way it went, the war could not last very much longer, and it would be infinitely better to meet the end near Germany's Rhine than on the snowy plains of Russia. And all the time Josef Goebbels made big speeches from Berlin, talking about the secret weapons which would change the fortunes of war and bring about a *Götterdämmerung*, leading to final victory. But sullen and distrustful, few of us took any notice.

It was an early grey morning when, our songs down to a melancholy sad humming, we trudged past the famous Speyer Cathedral, like ghosts of a bygone age. Our orders were to dig-in in a field just outside the town, to the north. The farmer who owned it came over and asked us what we thought we were doing, messing up his field which only a few days before he had prepared for planting. As we had no answer to give him, he went over to our Viennese Captain, who sadly shrugged his shoulders and told him in his charming accent something about orders from above and defending the Fatherland. In both their faces we could see what they were thinking.

The Americans were not much more than ten kilometres away, but we had not seen any of their ground forces. Some civilians had already crossed the lines in both directions, and the rumours were that the *Amis*, as we called them, were behaving correctly towards the civilian population. This came as some relief, as nasty tongues had circulated the story that in the event of defeat the young male population would be castrated.

Together with five others I was sent to set up a listening and defence position in the town of Schifferstadt, which was about five kilometres to the north of Speyer. To the west was no man's land, and beyond, the enemy with his multitude of tanks. The town, a typical one of the Rhine valley, was widely spread out. We billeted ourselves with a family called Nagel. They were friendly and helpful, but obviously must have had their own thoughts about having a troop of soldiers in their home, with the enemy standing at the gates. We took over the cellar which, as in many houses in Germany, was sunk halfway into the earth. There was a table and some chairs, as well as a couple of old mattresses on which we made ourselves comfortable. There was a tap and a sink, and though we got our food every day from Speyer, Frau Nagel offered us the use of her cooker. Our job was to patrol the town, to keep a look-out for the enemy, and to report everything which had a bearing on the situation. Twice a day a messenger arrived from Speyer on a motorbike combination to bring food and mail and other necessities, and take back with him a written situation report, which it was my duty to write. He was also a very active manufacturer of wild rumours, most of which did not materialize.

After a few days the Sergeant who led our troop was recalled to Speyer and I, the next in rank, was given command. But as the other four were my friends and as there was nothing to command anyway, we continued our lives in undisturbed tranquillity. Close to our billet was a railway embankment from which we could conveniently look into no man's land with our binoculars. There was nothing to be seen really, everything was peaceful and undisturbed, with some peasants working in the fields or tending their animals as if nothing of importance had ever happened. We saw many American *Jabos*, but never one of their patrols. Had they been Russians, they would not have given us any rest. Psychologically, I found the drastic change from Russian conditions to this set-up very confusing.

The Viennese Captain came out to Schifferstadt to see what we were doing. He reminded us, probably being a music lover, that we should be proud to fight for our country which had produced a Beethoven, a Brahms, Bach, Liszt, Mozart and so on — but we never discussed what they probably would have said to this mess we had got ourselves into. I asked him what we should do, if and when the *Amis* moved against us. His answer was short and terse: 'Fight and defend Schifferstadt, of course, that's what you are here for!' I reminded him that we had five rifles, four bazookas, and nothing else, and he responded that, as I had been in Russia, I would surely find a way out. He added with a serious face 'There will be no retreat to Speyer!'

'*Jawohl, Herr Hauptmann*, no retreat to Speyer!' We looked at each other and I think we both 'understood'. Scrounging around the place, one of us found an abandoned Army BMW motorbike hidden by bales of straw in a barn, which, though it made plenty of noise and smoke, we managed to get going. Things looked up considerably, as I was now able to patrol the town from the relative comfort of two wheels.

It was around the tenth of March when our messenger brought the long-expected 'Secret Alarm Warning Code' which meant that Patton's Army was about to move against us. Why it should be secret, we did not know, and we told anyone who was interested. From now on we had to patrol the town in full battle uniform and carry our weapons with us. On one of these occasions I was stopped by a group of women who wanted to know what we were going to do when the Yanks arrived. They pointed out that their town was as yet undamaged and that they wanted it to stay that way. They begged me not to be silly and start fighting with the *Amis* in the streets, as it would only end in death and much unnecessary destruction. Deep down, of course, I agreed with them, but I made it clear that I was still a German soldier and that I would not take any lip from them. More women then gathered around us and I rested my bazooka in the entrance of a chemist's shop behind me. The mood was ugly and steadily rising against me and I was on my own. Some became rude, and when they openly laughed at me and I could not see what was so funny about it all, I simply had had enough and decided to move on. But when I turned round to pick up my bazooka, I realized what they had all been laughing about. My bazooka had gone — someone had pinched it while the rest had engaged me in argument. I had not observed my most fundamental soldier's rule, that of keeping my weapon safe; feeling humiliated and furious, I started to shout at them. But when that had no effect, I tried to reason: 'Please, give me my bazooka back, please, for if you don't, I will be in trouble!' But none took me seriously, many of them giggled and then simply started to walk away, leaving me standing alone in front of the chemist's without my bazooka. And when I trudged back to our cellar, I did a lot of hard thinking, because losing one's weapon could mean a court martial. I was therefore much relieved when all my mates agreed that I should report nothing and await things to come.

Then came the seventeenth of March 1945. A messenger arrived from Speyer in the very early hours of the morning to warn us that the *Amis* were about to move any minute. The sun had risen into a clear sky and it was a beautiful warm morning, when I came in at six from guard duty. The town was still asleep and everything seemed peaceful.

At seven o'clock I was woken up again. The guard had seen the American column advancing towards us on the open road. We all hurried to the embankment, and there they were, a grey, long untidy snake. The road they came on was a narrow one with cherry trees on either side. Heavy tanks, throwing up a cloud of dust were at the head, followed by lighter ones, and then came half-tracks, jeeps and lorries, pulling all kinds of artillery and cannons. The whole cavalcade looked like a Sunday outing. What a strange Army! At the sides, infantry was moving over the open fields, keeping in line with the tanks. And in a grinding and unsettling way the column and the line were coming closer and closer. They were still over a kilometre away, but one could already hear the humming and the clanking in the clear air, and the roar from the *Jabos* above.

When we reckoned that they were only about half an hour away, we decided to walk back to our cellar. In the houses on either side, we saw the first signs of popular surrender. There were sheets of white bed-linen hanging from open windows, just as the thousands of leaflets scattered from the air had advised. I wondered from how many of those windows the Swastika flag had been fluttering in the Nazi breeze not all that long ago. We called out to some that the *Amis* were on their way, and told them to get indoors, but they took little notice of us and I thought I detected an expression of relief on many of their faces.

Back in the cellar, we stood our weapons in the corner, brewed some coffee and sat around the table to discuss the situation and what we were to do. My friends were all younger than me, though I was not yet 23 years old, and I was the only one who had been in Russia. I felt responsible for coming up with some sort of a solution. To fight and die was out of the question, not one of us so much as mentioned it.

When we heard the first tanks over the cobblestones outside, I felt relieved, as their appearance had effectively taken the decision-making out of my hands. I looked down on my shiny medals, which had been given to me in the Russian campaign, and wondered what good they would do me now, and if it would not be wise to take them off. The cellar shook, and we could see the tracks through a dirty window below the ceiling. Though a tank man myself, I had never looked at them from this position, had never given a thought to how the Russian civilians must have felt when they saw us rolling into their towns and villages. After the tanks came all the other vehicles. They moved very slowly and not one shot was fired. And then we saw the walking legs, the infantry, the real occupiers of the town. Legs are legs, one would have thought, but these looked very different from ours, and strange. There were no jackboots with hard leather soles and iron nails, only brown boots, sometimes reaching above the ankles, and they all had rubber soles, slinking so unmilitarily over the pavement.

We agreed that we now had two choices, one to break out in the night, and the other to stay and decide in the morning. Never once did we dare to climb up the stairs and look out into the streets. To soothe our nerves we played end-less games of *Skat*, and it was only towards the evening that the Nagels came down to tell us about what they had heard was going on in town. The *Amis* had taken up positions in the parks and other open spaces, and had occupied all crossroads, bridges, the town hall, police station, waterworks and so on. Though the Mayor and other important figures had been taken into custody, no undue force had been used. We hung blankets in front of the window and put out candles after dark. Each of us wrote a letter or two, addressed to our next of kin, leaving them unsealed for the Nagels to add a few lines about our final fates, and asked them to mail them once the situation had settled down. None of us, I think, slept very well, I heard the shuffling of the American soldiers outside, and was fascinated by their strange language.

When morning came we took great care to wash and shave, as if preparing ourselves for an important event. An elderly man from across the road came to see us, and said that he had lost two sons on the Russian Front, and that we were welcome to their clothes to walk away in as civilians. While we were discussing the pros and cons of the offer, the young Nagel boy came down, looking very cheerful and eating chocolate, which few of us had seen for a long time. He told us that it had been given to him by *Ami* soldiers, who were very friendly and who had played football with him and others. In one of the parks was a soup kitchen, and everyone could go and get some ladled into a mess-tin. But then he told us that they also had put up many posters outside the town hall, and that one of them said that any soldier who was captured more than 24 hours after occupation of the town would lose the protection of the Geneva Convention, and be treated as a partisan or terrorist. Well, what were we going to do now? The twenty four hours were almost up, and by impart-ing the knowledge to my friends of what happened to partisans in Russia, I made up the minds of all of us. We thanked the old man, but did not want to know any more about walking away in civilian clothes. As all eyes were now on me to make a decision, I said: 'Right, that's it, we are going to sur-render and we are going to do it now.' No one expressed any objection. Stand-ing there and looking at them and thinking of my years in Russia, I never would have believed that one day it would all end like this in a German cellar.

Having been brought up near the port city of Hamburg, I had a very rough knowledge of English. From leaflets I knew what the word 'surrender' means, and how it is pronounced. I walked about in the cellar, rehearsing 'Surrender, surrender!' and my friends thought that it sounded good. We dressed up in full uniform, as if going on parade. My greatcoat, though I was almost six feet tall, was much too large for me and, reaching down to my ankles, made me look like a walking tent. Next I fixed a dirty-white towel to a broomstick, squeezed a loaf of bread under my arm 'just in case', and said goodbye to Frau Nagel and her family. It was about ten o'clock in the morning, the sun was shining brightly and it was pleasantly warm when, followed by my friends, I climbed up the cellar steps, opened the front door and stepped out into the street.

As it so happened, we had chosen the wrong moment. A group of chatting women stood on the opposite pavement, looked at us with mocking surprise and one of them said something about 'Hitler's last hope'. We looked up and down the street, but there was no American soldier anywhere. We decided to walk on, I in front with my dirty towel tied to a broomstick in that long coat; we must have looked like a procession of monks. When we arrived at the next crossroads we saw two American soldiers walking towards us from the left. They carried no weapons, had their hands in their pockets and whistled, and when I waved at them with my broomstick and shouted: 'Surrender, surrender!', they must have misunderstood and probably thought that we wanted them to surrender to us. In any case, they turned on their heels and ran as fast as their legs could carry them out of sight into some doorway. There we stood again in the middle of the street in broad daylight, a laughing stock to all who could see us, unable even to surrender. It was almost like an insult, I thought; having taken part in the battles of the Crimea, Stalingrad, Kursk and many others, and having received the Iron Cross and other medals for it — now it had come to this.

Whatever these two brave soldiers reported to their base, I will never know, but it must have been something hair-raising. For it did not take much longer than five minutes and we were as good as surrounded from all sides. There were several jeeps, an armoured car, and not much less than a platoon of infantry with machine guns positioned at each end of the street — and all that we had wanted was to surrender. All I could think of was to start my performance of waving my broomstick all over again, while my mates held their hands on top of their heads amongst all that awful loud shouting in a strange language. And then the first of the Americans, carefully holding his machine pistol at the ready, dared to come near us as if we were poisonous or loaded with dynamite or something. I was shouted at to drop my broomstick, and after I had done that, they were suddenly all over and around us and touched us down from head to jackboot, which made me lose my loaf of bread. A little fellow, I can still see in my mind his greedy gum-chewing face, tore off all my medals, which made gaping holes in my tunic, and then a hair-raising journey on the bonnet of a jeep followed. The road was rough and full of potholes, and the driver must have thought it was great fun to drive at high speed through them with me on the bonnet, trying to hang on for dear life but finding that there was nothing to hold on to. The windscreen behind me was folded down, with the co-driver's legs on the bonnet, and I felt the muzzle of his rifle in my back and could see that he had his finger close to the trigger. I wondered what would happen to me should I fall off the bonnet — apart from being run over.

We raced right into Speyer and stopped outside a fenced-in tennis court where a large number of prisoners were walking about in the sunshine. One of the guards opened the narrow gate, I felt a rough push from behind, stumbled over a door rail or something, and before I knew it, I was lying flat on my belly inside the court. When I got up and dusted myself down, everyone was laughing. I must have looked very funny in that long coat of mine, for someone called me 'Wigwam', a name which stuck with me for a long time, and when a year later I played football in the American PoW Camps, my name still appeared on the sheets as: 'Inside right-Wigwam'.

I had never really seen any black men from close up before, and there were two of them standing guard outside the door. They looked rather forbidding, and those of us who claimed to know the English language, could not understand what they were drawling. All the time, captured soldiers were brought in, sometimes on their own, sometimes in groups. Amongst one lot were three or four officers, looking even more forlorn than the rest; no one wanted to have much to do with them. There was much wild speculation going the rounds about what was going to happen to us. They ranged from being shot, to becoming plantation overseers in Red Indian Reservations. Many towns people were now walking about freely in the streets, though during the hours of darkness a curfew was in force.

A lorry arrived at the gate, loaded with cardboard boxes. We had to queue, and each of us received two tins, one was called 'K' and the other 'C' ration. In them we found meat, biscuits, ground coffee, powdered milk, sugar and sweets. It was as if manna from heaven was raining down on us. For the likes of us, real coffee had been unattainable for years. There was only one cold water tap inside the tennis court, we stirred our powder into it as well as we could, and walked around and drank it like that. We reckoned that with food and beverage of that quantity and quality, we could have conquered Europe and the world.

After dark the temperature dropped sharply, and in the early hours we had ground frost. We had been given cardboard for bedding, which we folded out along the fences. And all those who had to get up and keep walking did not laugh any more about my wigwam coat, in which I lay snugly rolled up. I thought about the coldest temperature I had encountered in Russia, minus 54 degrees centigrade. What did this little ground frost matter to me now?

Early next morning we were taken away by lorries. Most of the drivers were black, and they drove like devils. One lorry overturned, and was lying at the bottom of an embankment. We could hear the shouts and the cries and saw the prisoners crawl out from underneath like eels — those who could still crawl. What a way to die, a day or so after having escaped the war alive!

Our first destination was a farm near Baumholder, where we were herded through a tunnel entrance into a large yard with a dungheap in the middle, which was surrounded on all four sides by solid buildings. Shortly after, a couple of *Amis* arrived with spades, and ordered about a dozen of us, including myself, to dig a trench six feet deep, six feet wide and about twenty yards long. Many of us thought that fate had now finally caught up with us, as the measurements were those of a perfect mass grave. Everyone in the yard had become very quiet, except the guards who were driving us on with '*Schnell, schnell!*'. I noticed that a concentration of our lads was forming near the entrance, and kept a close eye on it. I had no doubt that it would be easy to overpower the guards and take their weapons from them, and was already measuring up the nearest of them and planning what to do with him. When we had dug about three feet deep, a lorry arrived with drums of chemicals — to be spread over the corpses, we thought — and wooden beams, which we thought could be for gallows. Cold panic had spread to everyone by the time a German-speaking *Ami* with hammers and a bucketful of long nails arrived, who asked for carpenters, and explained that he wanted a structure to be set up over the trench with two long beams running parallel to each other from end to end. It was only then that we suddenly understood what the trench and the beams were all about, and the word *Scheisshaus* went around like a spark; the guards looked puzzled as to why their strange German captives suddenly laughed loudly, and all had happy expressions on their faces.

I noticed a number of SS men sitting together in a corner of the yard, who were trying to remove the SS insignia from their uniforms. Their arrogance had completely gone, and they looked rather sheepishly at me. When I pointed out that their uniforms were after all a different cloth and colour and cut, they shrugged their shoulders, probably hoping that the Americans did not know. In the long run it did not do them any good as their bloodgroup was tattooed into their skin underneath their armpits, which no one could erase. German thoroughness in this case had backfired on them.

During the night many new prisoners were brought in, and in the morning there was standing room only. A large lorry convoy took us from there across the Belgian border to the garrison town of Stenay, where we were unloaded onto a broad meadow which stretched along a narrow river behind the old napoleonic barracks. On the field stood large round tents; in each of them the ground area was covered with large boulders. About twenty of us were ordered into each tent, and when we started to shift the boulders out we were stopped by the guards. We soon found that complaining was no good and that we just had to make the best of it. We had several horrible nights — none of us could stretch out on the ground, and we either curled up somehow around the boulders or sat on them all night. Nobody was allowed to go outside except to the lavatory, and we heard the guards laughing about us.

The next trek took us to the railway station, where a long train of open coal wagons was awaiting us behind a steam engine. We were lined up on the forecourt and ordered, as a last chance, to throw away all our weapons like pistols, knives, sticks, bottles and pieces of metal. I had decided to take a bottle of water with me, which I had hidden under my wigwam coat. After the last warning had been given, spot checks were made, and it was my luck that a big burly *Ami*, probably intrigued by the size of my coat, came straight for me, touched me down and found my bottle. He gave me one mighty blow to my face, which sent me reeling in the dust. I felt blood running out of my mouth and nose and my immediate reaction was wild fury and the urge to hit back. But when I turned in the dust and saw the legs of other *Amis* moving towards me, with their machine pistols at the ready, I very quickly cooled down. I realized that one quick movement could easily be my last, and very slowly picked myself up on to my feet, wiping the blood off my face and joining the ranks of my fellow prisoners. The *Amis* swore at me, which I really did not mind as I could only understand less than half anyway, but what I found hard to swallow were the angry reproaches from some of my mates, who accused me of having created a dangerous provocation which could have involved them all.

Between forty and fifty of us were loaded into each of the open wagons. As there was only space enough for some of us to sit down, most had to stand. Everything we touched was covered in coal dust. The journey lasted about two days and took us through some of the industrial regions of northern France. Not once were we allowed off the wagons. At times we got drenched from rain showers, and with the coal dust from the wagons and the spewing fire and ashes from the engine, we soon looked and felt like painted golliwogs. The whites of our eyes took on a pinkish look from the continuous rubbing. Our lavatory business became an acute problem, as we simply did not have any facilities. We solved the problem in the most simple way. We filled our food tins, and when we came to a crossing, where often a jeering crowd waited for the passing of our train, we emptied the contents over them. Their jeers then turned to furious howls once they realized what they had been covered with. They picked up everything they could lay their hands on, and bombarded our innocent mates, who were riding at the end of the train and did not realize what they were being punished for.

At Cherbourg we were unloaded at the main station, where our arrival platform had been barricaded off. It was about midday, and the sun was shining warmly. Our marching column was protected in the town by an American cordon on each side. It did not take long for trouble. The towns people, only recently subjected to German occupation, quickly realized that the boot was now on the other foot and decided to make the most of it. Having by now developed a thick skin, the jeers and the shouting did not hurt us much, but the hard objects they threw at us, did. I too was hit by some missile on the back of my head. Then one of the young Frenchmen made a terrible mistake; somehow he managed to break through the American cordon, and he must have thought that he could freely lash out at anyone in reach and get away with it. It was his bad luck that he was mistaken. Hardly a command was necessary for the action that followed. He was pulled into our column, and in barely a matter of seconds, while the *Amis* were helpless to intervene, bare fists settled the matter. When he was finally dragged away, the blood on the cobblestones bore witness to man's inhumanity to man. In a way I look at this as my last action of the war. Some of the guards were smoking, and whenever they threw a butt end on the ground some of us were diving for it, in what I thought a disgusting manner. There was still very much the Prussian militarist in me: I still believed in pointless honour.

The camp was right out of town on top of the cliffs, from where one could see the expanse of the English Channel. On our way we passed several now deserted Atlantic Wall bunkers. Next to me walked an old Sergeant who had defended them on D-Day, and he told me about the murderous bombardment he had endured, about the masses of ships which had suddenly appeared in the morning, and about the ensuing chaos, fear and death all around. Though one could still see the scars of battle on the bunkers, nature had been kind and had begun to cover them with fresh green growth. There was a refreshing soft breeze blowing in from the sea, and everything seemed so peaceful. The large camp was divided into several cages which were separated from each other by high fences and rolls of barbed wire. About twenty large tents stood in each cage, which each took about a hundred of us. We slept on the ground, but had ample supplies of cardboard to protect us from the damp and the cold earth.

Between the two rows of tents was open ground, the size of three tennis courts on which we played football and other games. We also organized chess and card competitions, and had lectures on all sorts of subjects. Each cage had a German leader and interpreter whose jobs were to carry out the American orders. Everything worked fairly smoothly. The food was excellent, probably the same as our captors were eating, and far better than we had received in our own army.

Each of us was given an American mess tin, which we had to rinse in special chemicals before and after using them. The *Amis* were very particular in all things which concerned safeguarding health. Lavatory and washing facilities were in a tent of their own, and good medical attention was available for all who asked for it. An attempt to delouse us was only partially effective though. Burly *Amis*, I think sadistic inclinations must have made them volunteer for the job, filled what looked like thick barrelled bicycle pumps with a white floury powder, which they pressure pumped into our flies and down our backs and fronts and trouser legs. The result was an awful stinging sensation, and on much coughing and spluttering. We looked like a collection of over-worked flour millers who had had no time to wash. At first there seemed a slight relief, but after a few days the eggs in the seams of our uniforms hatched again from the warmth of our bodies, and the lice came back with a vengeance. It was a matter of security, I suppose, that we were issued with spoons only. Even forks were considered to be too dangerous in our hands. But we quickly over-came that restriction by using stones as hammers and anvils, and tearing tins apart; and a few days later each of us had a complete set of cutlery.

There were church services almost every day, and as it was the only chance to get out of the cage, I took part in every single one, never mind which religion they were for. After one of the services we had a discussion which was led by a young American priest. He personally was prepared to forgive us all for what we had done in the war, but when someone suggested that we also should pray for our victims in Russia for those who had suffered from our deeds, the priest compared our eastern campaign with that of the Crusades in the Middle Ages, in which Christianity had defended itself against the Godless. Of course, we had heard all that before, it was exactly the line the Nazis had thrown out to justify our barbaric onslaught on the Russian people, and when we reminded the young priest of that, he was a little lost for words.

I think it was on the 12th of April when I noticed the Stars and Stripes at the main gate at half mast. 'Roosevelt has died', one of the guards told me, 'And that bastard Hitler is still among the living.' After about two weeks we were marched down to the port and loaded on to a ship. Given one blanket each, we bedded down in long rows on the iron floor of the holds. It seemed that the officer in charge did not like us much, for at the far end next to the iron ladder stood a huge oil drum with sharp edges which served us all, 500 or so, as the only lavatory. When it was full to the rim, no arrangement was made for having it emptied, and the contents kept slopping over, creating a hell of a stinking mess all round, until an American Army doctor made a round of inspection. We crossed the Channel to between the Isle of Wight and Southampton, from where we sailed west, close to the English coast, until we joined up with another large number of ships which must have come, I reasoned, from Bristol.

We had learnt at school that the slaves were taken from Bristol to America, and now we were lying in the holds to be taken on the same route, to work in America. Having skirted Ireland, we combined with another huge convoy, which must have set out from Liverpool, and all together we were now far more than a hundred ships. Being allowed on deck during all hours of daylight I found everything very fascinating to watch. The whole convoy sailed in a zig-zag fashion, and a number of destroyers darted in between and everywhere. We watched the dolphins and the flying fish, and after we had overcome the first bouts of seasickness, we enjoyed the good food and the experience as a whole.

One evening the sirens wailed and the ship's bells rang. The crew went into a slight state of panic and we were ordered on deck with our life vests. This was a U-Boat alarm, and we had to stand at the railings with our Army caps on, possibly so that we should be recognized as German soldiers. It struck me as a final swing of irony that, having fought in Russia for years, it could now be my fate to be sunk in an American Kayser ship in the middle of the Atlantic by a German U-Boat. But shortly after, the sirens howled again and life returned to normal. We had beautiful sunny days and calm seas, but also very rough days when we found it very difficult to walk with our nailed jack-boots on the iron decks.

After twenty-one days the call came through one morning that land was in sight. Those were magic words, and having scrambled up the steep iron ladder, we saw America rising on the horizon before us. We were greeted by the famous Statue of Liberty, which we had all seen photos of. Having sailed up a short stretch of the Hudson River, New York was there itself, with its mighty bridges, enormous sky scrapers, and the never-ending traffic along the quays. Soon we docked. America, we have arrived, what are you going to do with us?

We picked up our belongings and walked down the narrow gangway, at the bottom of which stood an officer with a counting machine. Next to him hovered someone who kept shouting: '*Schnell, schnell!*' Coming halfway down I saw that he had a pin in his hand which he poked into the bottoms of those he could catch. Of course, everyone tried to get past that little fellow as quickly as he could, and we heard later that never before had a troopship been emptied in such record time. How effective a small pin can be! We had arrived on the 8th of May 1945, and having no idea what was happening anywhere, we were a bit surprised when an *Ami* shouted to us while we were still in the holds that the sirens were howling all over New York because Hitler was dead and the war was over. We received the news with a strange and confused feeling. I did not quite know whether I should feel sad or shout 'hurrah'. We did not even feel like discussing it amongst ourselves, as the deadweight of the Nazi past was lying heavily on us. All us younger ones like myself could not really imagine a Germany without Hitler, and none of us had ever dared say anything adverse about our Führer while he was alive. We could not be all that sure that he was really dead now, anyway.

At the quayside we had to put every single piece of our belongings on the ground before us, and we were thoroughly searched. Since my last payday I had carried a wad of *Reichsmark* notes in my breast pocket, which the soldier searching me put into his own. Our troop train consisted of modern coaching stock, and we were surprised by the comfort of the soft seats. On them we found glossy brochures which dealt with German crimes in the concentration camps. The photos shocked us, and at first I believed that they were fakes. But when later on I had a second look, I could see that they were real and, reminding myself of so many events I had witnessed in Russia, the sheer enormity of the crime against humanity I had collectively partaken in, took a clearer conception in my mind. Germany, my Germany, what depth had you fallen to; I found it strange that none of us felt in the mood to even discuss what was in the brochures.

Leaving the dock area, we saw much seediness, but found the outlying districts more pleasant to look at. We were impressed and surprised by the many cars in factory and other car parks. Having in mind that almost no worker in Germany owned a car, we pondered how rich America must be. Workers having cars! We passed through Baltimore, Cincinatti, St Louis, Oklahoma City, Amarillo and El Paso, all names which to most of us had that touch of mystic. In Oklahoma the earth was red, and when we crossed the Rockies, pulled and pushed by three enormous oil-fired steam engines, we were much impressed. Rolling through the Texas plains, we saw the 'nodding horses', the oil derricks, and then came the Rio Grande River, which to our surprise was almost dried out and was no more than a trickle. On the other side was Mexico, a neutral country, and the fleeting thought occurred to me of a jump, a short run, and then freedom. But the train rolled on, and there were armed guards on each coach. And having come alive from the steppes of Russia to the Rio Grande, what was the point of risking one's life? After that came the semi-deserts of New Mexico and Arizona, with their enormous cactuses, and beautifully-shaped mountains with their distinct layers of sandy rock, which were often flat on the top.

All the lavatory doors had been removed, so that the guards were able to watch our every activity. The windows were shut all the time, and during the hot day the heating was fully on and we sweated like pigs, while it was turned off during the cold nights.

Travelling somewhere through Texas, a friendly American Captain came into our coach and told us that he had been to Germany before the war and had liked it very much. He asked us to sing for him *Stille Nacht*, the famous German Christmas song. As he seemed a nice man, we tried to please him, but with the sun shining down mercilessly, and all of us sweating profusely, we made a croaky start, and found that under the unusual conditions it was just impossible to do. The Captain understood.

We arrived at Florence Camp in the Arizona desert in the early hours of a cool night in the middle of May. Off the train, we were ordered to dump everything we had on, uniform, underwear, boots, caps, belts etc. on to one big heap, which was doused with petrol and then set alight. To watch it was very hurtful. It was like the cutting of the past from the present, in a very dramatic and symbolic way. There I stood in the grace of God, naked, thin, dirty, and forlorn in a strange country. All I had saved was my wristwatch, while photos and papers, like Army paybooks etc. had earlier been taken away from us and put into envelopes with our names on. We were marched into a large room in a barrack where two muscular soldiers in white coats stood on either side inside the door, grabbed us and pumped injection needles into our upper arms. I saw one of us pass out on the floor, and none of us really felt like laughing. We were passed on to a group of rough barbers who plonked us on to low stools and with electric shavers cut all the matted hair off our heads.

When we came out, we could hardly recognize each other — and when I looked into a mirror, I could hardly recognize myself. It was awful. From there we were shouted into shower rooms. When the warm soft water ran down over our heads and emaciated bodies, there came a most lovely feeling of complete relaxation which I had not known for years. It was as if all the nasty past, the hell I had been through, was washing away from me and running with a gurgling sound down into the grill beneath my feet. Even the soap was genuine, not the *ersatz* stuff which did not even foam, that had been our lot since the beginning of the war. We were each given a nice, clean towel but when I picked it up to dry myself, I found that someone had pinched my wristwatch from underneath it. The moment in my life had arrived when I possessed absolutely nothing, and in a strange way it gave me a feeling of freedom which never in my life had I felt before.

We lined up at a counter and were issued with underwear, socks, soft leather shoes and an American khaki uniform, all of which was brand new. After all the dirt I had endured and had become used to for years it was impossible to describe the feeling of fresh new clothes on the skin of my body. I stepped around, ran a few steps, shrugged my shoulders, bent over, threw my arms about and felt like a being newly reborn.

From there we crossed a dark square, up a few steps and entered a well-lit dining room. On either side along the walls were long, clean tables with benches attached, and we were asked to sit down when German prisoners appeared from a counter to serve us with a full warm meal. It was one of the loveliest I have ever tasted. Few if us felt like talking, and some one opposite asked me to give him a kick so that he could be sure that he was alive. Afterwards coffee was brought in from a large can, and real creamy milk and sugar, as much as we liked. And all this happened at about three o'clock in the morning! From there we were escorted into white wooden barracks. The floors creaked, everything was immaculately clean, the beds were spaciously arranged in rows and had soft mattresses with clean bed linen and eiderdowns. The smell, the feeling — and all this for us, the prisoners! I put my head on the clean, soft pillow, there was no conversation, only hushed words as every one was deep in his own thoughts.

Someone switched the lights off, and I could see the beams of a white moon playing on to the foot of my bed. There was utter peace. Tired as I was, I wanted to lie there for a while and think. My thoughts went home to my mother; if only she could see me now, and I did not even know how she had come through the bombings and the end of the war, and whether she was even alive. And then my thoughts went back to Russia, without which the whole thought of the war and me now lying here in Arizona had no meaning. It was all part of each other. Slowly dropping off into dreamland, I thought of Adjetz, walking with him down that pot-holed village street in Mankovo, of the old man in the hut, holding the hand of the little girl, of Anna and of Boris. What was the meaning of my life?

We stayed at Florence for a few weeks. Though in the beginning I did not feel well, probably from the injections and the unaccustomed heat, I soon became alive again. We had little to do but eat and sleep, and in between we played football and chess and walked around camp in the cool evenings, and talked about home. A fair German library had been set up in camp, probably provided by ex-compatriots living in the area, and I did a lot of reading. There were works by the great philosophers Kant, Schopenhauer, Hegel, Feuerbach, Nietzsche, and I struggled through many, though having to admit that because of my insufficient education I benefited little from their wisdom. Each afternoon 'Arizona', a sandstorm, arrived and blew all around us. When we heard its howling and saw its dustcloud coming in from the desert we quickly shut all the windows and doors. It never lasted more than a few minutes, but afterwards everything was covered with a thin layer of dust.

On our arrival the camp already contained several thousand prisoners, most of them from Rommel's *Afrika Korps*, and some of them were resentful towards us. They accused us of having thrown in the towel after the enemy had crossed into the Fatherland. I too had quarrels with some of them, but having fought in Russia, I could easily stand my ground against them in argument. Conveniently trying not to mention that they themselves after all had thrown in the towel in Tunisia, they were still living in the clouds, protected by their Nazi blinkers.

Although politically there had developed a splitting-off process, on the whole the Nazi elements still held sway. Habit, fear and a robot-like discipline were the reasons, rather than any intellectual conviction. Shortly before we arrived, the camp Nazis had hanged a fellow prisoner from a beam in the lavatory because he had dared to openly speak out against Hitler and fascism. I was shown the place of his execution, which made me rather cautious in what I said. It also went around that American intelligence was not as anti-fascist as it was anti-communist, and there had been attempts by them to draw on the expertise of some of our worst war criminals. Generally, SS prisoners had little to fear in America, or, as I later found out, in England. There was general pride amongst the patriots that there had been no rebellion against the government by the people, though the whole country of Germany was occupied by enemy troops. It was argued that it was a sign of our great racial maturity — but I could not agree with that any more, I thought, though did not dare say it, that the people should have revolted in the face of the crimes which in the end must have been clear to all who had eyes to see.

By that time Austria had become an independent country again, and one of the camp sections was reserved for Austrians only. A painted board had been placed at their camp entrance reading: *'Nur für Oesterreicher, Reichsdeutsche unerwünscht!'* (Only for Austrians, Germans not wanted.) Of course, it was an insult, and intended as such, and we assembled a troop every day and marched through their camp just to establish a point. After all, we were about ten thousand against their several hundred, and we loved to remind them that Hitler was an Austrian. That notwithstanding, however, the big camp event was the German versus Austria football match, which took place on a rough gravel pitch in the centre of the camp. Everyone came to that, and there was 'trouble on the terraces' before the match had even started.

In June about a thousand of us went by special train through Texas, along the eastern slopes of the Rockies through Colorado, and into the northern state of Montana. It was a very beautiful journey which took three days. Our camp was outside the town of Laurel by the side of the Yellowstone River, not far from the town of Billings. From the camp we could see the snow-covered peaks of the Yellowstone National Park. Every day we were taken out in working groups of about a dozen to hoe sugar beet plants on huge fields. Many of the farmers in that area were of German descent, and were still able to speak German. As the handles of our hoes were only a foot long, it was a backbreaking job, and the sugar company's officials who were in charge, tried by all sorts of tricks to make us work harder, while at the same time they introduced a ten-day working week and cut our rations. As a result, several of us collapsed on the fields, and only our determination to drastically cut our efficiency restored our rations to something like normal.

Once the hoeing was finished we were taken on a train journey across Idaho, along the Columbia River, across Oregon with its forests of Redwood trees into Central California to a camp near the town of Windsor, not far from Sacramento. The camp was beautifully situated amidst rolling green hills, and our square tents, sleeping six on mattressed beds, and which had a table and chairs in them, were very comfortable. The food was excellent in every respect, there was much too much to eat, and we worked well, picking hops and fruit in large plantations. With plenty of sport, music, drama, chess etc, we organized our own recreation, and received much help from the American YMCA for whom I have not lost my gratitude to this day.

Whenever there were days when we did not go out to work, there was trouble in the camp. We were all young, and probably had too much energy. Out of sheer boredom, I assume, an older friend with the name of Fischer had a marvellous idea. He wanted to escape. He reasoned that the port of San Francisco was not far away, and that ships would sail from there to Latin America where, he said, we Germans were welcome. Being also bored, three of us decided to go with him, and in our minds we already saw ourselves crossing the Andes from Chile into the Pampas of Argentina, just like that. All that Fischer had organized was a pair of wirecutters, which probably had given him the idea to escape in the first place.

The night of action arrived. With the American guards asleep, a couple of wires were quickly cut and the four of us were in freedom. Each of us carried a small bag with food, soap, toothbrush, towel etc. We walked for three or four miles, then dawn broke, and we decided to lie low and sleep in a hedge. This was a far cry from when I had slept rough about two and a half years earlier, to the west of Stalingrad. We assured each other what a great feeling it was to be free, and wondered why we had not thought about it before. We woke up about midday and decided to walk individually to a nearby settlement which we could see from our hedge, to find out the general situation. We left our bags in the hedge and, wearing workmen's clothes, no one took any notice of us. Strolling around, we all met each other but gave no sign of recognition. As none of us spoke any decent English, I think we were all at a loss at what we were supposed to find out in that settlement anyway.

It was very hot when I arrived back at the hedge, and when I parted the branches, there were two policemen sitting by our bags. They looked at me quite pleasantly, no even getting up, and invited me to sit down and join them. One by one the others arrived and received the same treatment. One of the policemen told us that children had found our bags, and when they had phoned the camp, the guards were not even sure whether we were missing. When we arrived back in the camp, everyone, Germans and Americans, laughed about us. Reporting to the Commandant, he did not even tell us off, but asked us whether we pleaded guilty to having stolen wirecutters and having cut two strands of wire which was government property. We got three days kalabush for that. The Andes and Argentina had to wait, and I saw to it not to get involved with Fischer again.

After the harvest in California was over, we travelled that same two-day journey back to Montana and went into camp near the town of Harding. In working parties we were taken by lorry as far as the Canadian border, and to the south into the state of Wyoming to harvest sugar beets. Our camp was not far from the Little Big Horn River where General Custer had made his last disastrous stand. At times we worked in Red Indian reservations, and all of us having read about Winnetou and Uncas, the last of the Mohicans, were rather disappointed at what we thought was the obvious degradation of the people. There was much drunkenness, bad housing, and cleanliness seemed sadly lacking.

Once the work had been done, we travelled back to the Mexican border and arrived at a small working camp near Casa Grande, a Spanish-looking place right in the wilderness of Arizona. The camp was surrounded by rugged mountains of grotesque shapes rising out of the flat dusty plain full of tall cactuses. From there, we went cotton picking, right down to the Rio Grande.

While racism had been a major ingredient in our theoretical upbringing, we had in fact very little practical experience of it. Where I had grown up there had only been poor white working-class people. At Casa Grande, we found that we were the only white cotton pickers, all the others were either black or Mexicans who had come over the border, and who often had trouble with the overseers and were badly underpaid.

Food and life for us was good; but suddenly we received a severe jolt. A new Camp Commandant arrived. He ordered the entire camp to line up on the big square, and made a speech in English which was translated into German sentence by sentence. He said that he was a Jew and proud of it. Several members of his family had suffered the worst in concentration camps, and he was now glad to be in a position to settle matters with us. He would see to it that we would receive the same quantity and quality of food which had been handed out in the concentration camps, and we would have to do the same work-load. There would be no more sport, musical instruments would be withdrawn, our payments would be stopped, the washrooms closed, and only one stand-pipe would be in operation for the whole of the camp. I could understand his attitude, and did not and do not complain. I just relate the facts.

His programme started the next morning. As breakfast we had a cup of black unsugared coffee, and a dry bread roll. The food going with us on the lorries was equally miserable, and when we came back in the evening, there was the same story. We had a chat-round and then a meeting. And next day on the cotton fields we picked no more than a tenth of what we normally did. The farmers, who probably had to pay the camp for our work, wanted to know what the matter was. After arriving back in camp, it was very late that night when the dinner bell gonged, but there was a big meal on offer and a very good one — and none of us saw the Jewish camp commandant ever again.

We celebrated Christmas at Casa Grande, and rigged up a tree with real candles, around which we sang our traditional Christmas songs. Many American motorists stopped on the lonely highway outside the camp to listen to our singing, and clapped and asked for more. The nights at that time were very cold and in the mornings the earth was covered with raw frost. We lit huge bonfires in the fields, around which we lazed in our thick coats until about ten. Minutes after, the sun had taken the frost off the cotton, and the farmers allowed us to start picking. Half an hour later our coats came off, and shortly after that the shirts as well.

From there we were taken back to the main camp at Florence, where we were engaged in boring routine Army camp work. One day, after he had chatted to me the day before, a friendly officer, a Lieutenant Hightower, asked me whether I would like to work in the PX (American Army shop and canteen), as he probably thought that my English was good enough for that. I would have agreed to anything which would take me out of camp. Next morning I reported to the gate and was taken by a guard to the PX. It was like a big department store, in which everything imaginable could be bought. I had anticipated that I would work in the stores or as a cleaner or general handyman, and was much surprised when I was taken into Lieutenant Hightower's office, where he asked me if I could type. I couldn't. 'You will have to learn then!' he said. 'Are you good at figures?'

'Reasonably', I replied. He then took me to a large writing desk in the corner by the window and told me that it was mine to work on. 'Well,' I thought, 'how about that?' Apart from me and Hightower, who had his desk behind a partition, there were two girls in the office who also had their own desks. They were about my age, made me very welcome from the first, and assured me of all the help I should need. I had little money myself, but they saw to it that in the breaks I had as many cakes and other goodies as they themselves had. Officially I was not allowed any alcohol but, thanks to the girls, I had beer every day. Never having worked in an office before, I felt bewildered in the beginning, but I soon learned to type and what to do with the filing cabinets, calculating machine, invoices, stamp machine and so on. I tried my hardest, because I wanted to do the job efficiently. When Hightower wanted me, he simply shouted 'Henry' from behind the partition and I rushed in, with 'Yes, Lootenant!' He often wrote rough letters by hand which I then had to type. I enjoyed work there tremendously, and hated the weekends when I could not go into the office. Apart from being his secretary, I also acted as his doorman. It happened sometimes that visitors without an appointment objected to being barred from coming into the office by a German prisoner. I lorded it all right when it suited me, and whenever there were complaints in that respect, Hightower, not to mention the girls, always backed me to the hilt. I worked in the office for about two months and regretted it a bit that the two girls were watching each other. They were both fine persons, we came to know each other very well, they helped me greatly and I repaid by covering up for them and taking the blame for the mistakes they sometimes made.

The announcement that we were going to leave Florence Camp was a hard blow for me. On my last day the girls arranged an office party in my honour, to which only Hightower and a few others were invited. The desk in the middle was covered with a white tablecloth and on it were cakes the girls had baked for me, and glasses and bottles, and Hightower, screwing his face a tiny bit at first, did not object. Everyone gave a little speech with a toast; and when it came to me, I was hardly able to say anything, because I had a great big lump in my throat. But my friends understood and came into my arms to hug and kiss me, and there were a few embarrassed tears, with Hightower again showing no objection. As a final act I had to hand in my gate permit card, and then both girls took me back to that ugly fence, snuggling lovingly against me. The gate guards did not like what they saw coming towards them, one of them was rude, but received a vicious lashing from the girls' tongues. It being a dark night, the guards shone the full power of the searchlight on to our parting scene. Once inside the camp, I walked along the barbed wire, while the girls walked parallel with me on the outside. We laughed and waved, threw kisses and gave all sorts of promises with hope for the future. Oh, how I hated that fence!

Once a week a re-educational meeting took place in the large canteen. Most of us went though attendance was not compulsory. A German-speaking American chairman opened up with a short introduction and then it was mainly up to us to discuss anything of interest or topical. Feelings often ran high in this attempt to introduce us to democratic values, and we were encouraged to speak our minds without fear, which was not an easy thing for us to do. As the war had been over now for quite some time, critical remarks about our own actions and policies now came slowly to the fore. What struck me was that the Nazis were always sitting at the back of the hall and though engaged in much heckling, seldom contributed anything thoughtful.

I never liked to stand up under all the eyes and say my part. But when one day an elderly prisoner urged the audience to be realistic and truthful and accept that horrible crimes against humanity had been committed by us, all hell broke loose at the back, with someone saying: 'Ah, well, that was war!' I raised my arm from sheer excitement, regretted it in an instant, but was called by the American chairman to speak. At first stuttering a bit, I challenged forcefully that if that were so, then we should think about the origins of war and not accept it unthinkingly without asking questions. We all knew, I claimed, that a war must have economic, financial, social and industrial roots and that enormous profits had been made out of it, while others had paid with their lives, and that if we truly wanted to stop another one from breaking out again, then we must look for those roots. There was much hissing from the back, but no one challenged me. But when I walked away afterwards, a group of Nazis stopped me and told me in no uncertain terms to shut my stupid trap in the future. Had I not been a member of the camp football team, they would have given me a good hiding there and then.

The next trip took us to the Californian Pacific coast. The transport was by road, and covered a distance of several hundred miles. While most of us travelled on the backs of lorries, I was lucky and travelled with two of my mates in a jeep driven by a Private, who after a short while simply announced that he would change over into another jeep to be with his friend and that I, who had told him that I could drive, was to drive this one. A German mate swapped over from the other jeep, and the four of us rolled along the smooth American highway. It did not take long before our convoy of about a hundred vehicles lost all cohesion. We were now as good as on our own, and I was the only one who could drive and also who could speak English. And all I knew was that I was to drive west into California to a place called March Camp. There was busy traffic, and soon we were leaving the flat desert and climbed on a winding road into the beauty of the border mountains. We observed a most marvellous golden sunset.

To my surprise when arriving at the border, there were customs officials, and all cars had to stop. The idea was that no one was allowed to take fruit across the border. When our official realized that he was dealing with a jeep-load of unguarded German PoWs, he ordered us to the side and called his superior. They made a few phone calls, scratched their heads, and then let us proceed on our journey west. Like this incident, I found much in America refreshingly uncomplicated, though not always very efficient. It was already pitch dark when we entered the wider Los Angeles region, and at one time we got hopelessly lost. A friendly American directed us in his car to an Army road sign to March Camp, and when we finally got there in the early hours of the morning, I was dead beat and all I wanted was to lie down and sleep.

The camp, of which the PoW cage was only a small part, was of enormous size, with its own airfield, hospital and what seemed like a town of its own. We were several thousand strong, and amongst us were well-known musicians, artists and others, and we had our own symphony orchestra which gave many good performances in a large festival hall to full houses, including many American servicemen and their families. All the work we were needed for was within the camp, and was boring. But food and sunshine was plentiful, and there was all kinds of sport, especially football, so we were getting into peak condition.

It troubled us greatly that we had had no news from Germany whatsoever, none of us. The war had been over for more than a year, and we were not allowed to write. In the summer of 1946 we each received a card, issued from the Vatican, which we filled in with our names only to show we were alive. But none of our relatives ever received them. On top of the card was the heading '*Ein Angehöriger der geschlagenen Armee sucht seine Angehörigen*' (a member of the beaten Army is looking for his relatives). It was only very much later, from England, that my mother, who had been officially informed that I had gone missing and was probably dead, received my first communication, after a dreadful time of worry. At about that time my war wounds, shrapnel in the leg, caught up with me, and caused much pain and high temperature. I was taken to a military hospital, received excellent treatment and all possible care, and recuperated after several weeks.

With winter at the door we left sunny California and travelled back to New York, crossing the whole of the North American continent in three days. It was cold and damp when we were unloaded at the huge Army complex of Camp Shanks. Our stay there lasted for several weeks, and being sure that we were now going home, all of us became rather impatient. When finally we walked up the gangway of the troopship, we were told by the officers that we would be taken to Bremerhaven, to be released from captivity. Compared with our westward crossing in convoy, this was almost luxurious, and took only one week. Everyone had his own comfortable bunk-bed and to a large extent the freedom of the ship throughout the 24 hours of the day. When we arrived at Liverpool, we naturally assumed that it would only be a port of call on our journey. But we were suddenly ordered to take all our belongings and line up on deck. Meanwhile a number of British personnel came on board, there was friendly handshaking with their American counterparts, and we were marched down the gangway, then boarded a train which took us through Manchester to Altrincham in Cheshire.

The war had been over for well over a year but when we were marched through the camp gates outside that town, we woke up to the fact that the Americans had sold us like slaves to the British. We were well over a thousand ordinary rank soldiers, and when we asked the German camp leadership to forward our complaint, they said that it was none of their business. Left on our own, we decided to make an official complaint to the British camp authority, and set up a committee for that purpose on to which I was elected. It was the first time in my life that I had taken part in a democratic procedure. The British quickly asked us to send a three-man delegation to meet them, and discuss the problem. As compared with the 'old' prisoners in camp, who had been captured by British Forces and wore British Army uniforms with patches on the trousers and jackets, we American arrivals were dressed in black, top and bottom, and when with my two mates I walked to the Nissen hut for that very important meeting, almost the whole of the 'American Black SS', as we were called, trooped with us to wait outside to give us moral support. After all, we were well aware that the outcome of it would mean the difference between going back home and staying prisoner in camp. We three were the first to arrive, apart from two British Sergeants who had to arrange the material preparations. A couple of long tables flanked by chairs on either side had been set up length-wise in the hut. The windows were high in the bent ceiling and the atmosphere, smelling of officialdom, gave me a gloomy foreboding. While we were offered tea and biscuits, and talked quietly with each other, our nerves were very much on edge — and we could hear the humming noise of our thousand mates out-side. Then, about five minutes late, the British delegation arrived. They had come in a car from outside the camp, all three were officers and one of them, who carried several books under his arm, was a lawyer. Behind them came a girl with a writing block, who sat down at the end of the table. It was all a bit overwhelming, as we had no books, no writing material, nothing, not even a prepared plan for anything.

The senior officer, a Colonel, opened up, they all introduced themselves and we did the same. Though they behaved correctly in every way, the whole stark difference of presentation made me feel as if we had walked into a lion's den. The Colonel said something about the weather and trusted that we had had a pleasant Atlantic crossing. He mentioned that he had recently been to Germany, and, that in his view conditions there were already improving. He asked which of us three was the leader. We had not even thought about that, perhaps assuming that democratic processes should mean that was unnecessary. While all of us were about 23 or 24 years old, our opposites were much more mature and experienced in things like this, and as my English was probably slightly better than that of my mates, we decided that I should be the leader.

'All right, *Obergefreiter*', said the Colonel, looking at me very sternly, 'what is it all about?'

'Well,' I said, 'Colonel, the Americans obviously have released us from cap-tivity. But they have done so in the wrong place, this is England and not Germany!'

'That's right! Thank you for reminding me of it. But what's wrong with it?'

'Everything, Colonel, the war is over for more than a year, not one of us thousand men has fought against you British. You just can't take us prisoners like that. It's peace time now. No one must do that!'

'Who says so?'

'I say so — and we all think so!'

'— and who are you?'

'*Obergefreiter* Metelmann of the German *Wehrmacht*!' Following that, he scratched his head, screwed up his face as if he was annoyed and looked over to the lawyer, asking him about the legal position of it all. The latter, who had been laughing, and seemed somewhat unprepared, cut his cackle short and started looking through one of his thick books. Then he seemed to have a bright idea.

'On what, *Obergefreiter*, do you base your contention?'

Of course, I had no idea, and looking at my mates, they did not seem to have one either. But then I shot out with the only thought I had and said: 'Geneva Convention!'

'Right,' the lawyer Major said, smiling all over his face and realizing probably that I had walked into the trap good and proper. 'what section and what article of the Convention are you referring to?' Well, I was conquered, and what was more, I knew it — and when I looked at my mates, I saw only empty faces.

'Well, that's it, then!', said the Colonel and he mumbled something about wasting valuable time for nothing. Directing his gaze at me, he said: 'and the next time you make an official complaint to which we are good enough to listen, please prepare it properly! If I were you, *Obergefreiter*, with your history behind you, I would not mention the Geneva Convention ever again!' All that I could do was stare back at him in defiance, and thought it better to let it be.

The meeting was now closed and we all filed out into the sunny morning. But now the 'Black SS' wanted to know: 'When are we going home? When are we going home?' My two mates, being crafty buggers, pointed to me to come out with the answer. Afterwards there was howling and shouting, some whistling and some nasty words, saying that it was all my fault. It was there and then on those steps of the Nissen hut that I decided never again to act as a democratic spokesman for anyone ever again.

Soon we were split up, and with about two or three hundred I was put on a train transport south, and arrived on a dark night in the town of Romsey in Hampshire. England from the train window had been interesting to observe, especially as we had come straight from America with Germany, France and Russia strong in our minds. In many ways England was a strange country. That narrow channel of water seemed to have made much difference over the centuries. Most things seemed small and old-fashioned. The rows and rows of houses in the towns, with their small backyards and gardens seemed cramped. The people were friendly enough, but strangely reserved, and life generally had an unhurried flow, so very different from America and the Continent of Europe. And yet, there was something likeable about it all.

From Romsey Camp we worked on farms all over Hampshire and beyond. We had accepted our fate now, worked hard and caused no trouble. Those who lived out on the farms had very good relations with the farming people, and on the whole were treated very well. From Romsey I was transferred to an outcamp in a beautiful old country house called Hazelhurst, near the village of Corhampton. It did me much psychological good, as it gave me a feeling of freedom which I had not had for many years. From Hazelhurst I was transferred to a camp near the small town of Bishops Waltham, and was employed to work in the garden of a family in the lovely village of West Meon, where I was treated with much understanding and friendliness. It made me especially happy to be with the children, who were always lovingly around me. From Bishops Waltham we were taken to a camp just outside Southampton in 1948, almost three years after the war had ended, and from there I was released from captivity shortly after.

From the age of 18 to 26, probably the most formative years of anyone's life, I had been a soldier and a prisoner, and there had been many moments when I wished that I had never been born. Suddenly I was set free like a bird, unused to it, and I found it difficult at first. In me was a great feeling of guilt, but also anger, frustration and disappointment. How was I to come to terms with all that?

A prisoner transport took me back to Germany. My parents were now both dead, everything we had, had been destroyed in the bombings. The clothes I stood up in and the blue American kitbag I carried on my shoulder were my only possessions. What was I now to do with my life? Before I left England, I had been assured by Colonel Courage, the brewer, for whom I had worked as a farm worker, that if I ever wanted to come back to England and work for him, he would welcome me back. Germany irritated me. There was no attempt even to talk about the war and what had happened and why. I had no home, there was much unemployment and I felt lost and alone. And when a close relative told me that the defeat of Germany was the fault of people like me who had had no faith in the Führer and who had not given their all in the struggle, I had had enough. I took my kitbag and went back to England, after only four weeks.

Working on Colonel Courage's farms near Crondall and Preston Candover and playing football for the Bentley village team, I slowly felt I was returning into the circle of humanity. Then the Colonel employed a lovely au pair girl from Switzerland. In those peaceful and beautiful surroundings in that Hampshire village, how could we help falling in love? We married in Switzerland in 1952. In '54 a son was born to us, and in '56 a girl. I started to work as a railway porter at Alton, became a signalman, and then stayed on until my recent retirement. My dear wife died in 1980.

The feeling of guilt for what in a collective way I have done to others, especially the people of Russia, lies very heavily on me. Coming to the evening of my life now, I sometimes wonder what it has been, a drama, a tragedy, a crime or a comedy. I cannot be quite sure. I have regrets for the suffering I have caused others, but no complaints about what others have done to me.

Epilogue

Nichts vom Vergänglichen,
wie's auch geschah!
Uns zu verewigen
sind wir ja da!

'Nothing from what has perished,
however it happened!
To make ourselves eternal,
that's what we are here for!'

Goethe, from a poem.

When I rummaged recently through old books and papers, I came upon a German Army prayer, which I instantly recognized as the one we had used constantly at our religious services in Russia.

Having a short time ago been on a tourists' holiday to Belorussia, where 209 out of 270 cities and towns, not to speak of the thousands of villages, were totally destroyed, I saw the inscription on a war memorial set up to honour a village population, including over 70 children, the youngest three months old, who were brutally put to death in an orgy of shooting, and burnt inside a barn.

As it is my own personal view, based on my own experiences, that by far the main and most important part of the Second World War was between Germany and Russia, I know of no better epilogue than these translations which to my mind, describe better than anything the vast gulf between the two ideologies, the West and the East, who were so fatally locked in that horrendous struggle a generation ago.

The German Army Prayer
Let us pray!
Your hand, oh God, rules over all empires and nations on this earth.
In Your goodness and strength bless our German nation
and infuse in our hearts love of our Fatherland.
May we be a generation of heroes,
worthy of those who went before us.
May we protect the faith of our fathers as a holy inheritance.
Bless the German Wehrmacht whose task it is
to secure peace and protect the home fires.
And give its members the strength
to make the supreme sacrifice for Fuehrer, Volk and Fatherland.
Especially bless our Fuehrer and Commander in Chief
in all the tasks which are laid upon him.
Let us all under his leadership
see in devotion to Volk and Fatherland a holy task,
so that through our faith, obedience and loyalty
we may find our everlasting home in Your kingdom of Your light and peace.
Amen!

The Russian War Memorial inscription
People of goodwill, remember, we loved life, our Motherland
and all of you dearly.
We were devoured by the flames of fire!
We appeal to all of you:
Let your sorrow and grief
turn into courage and strength
so that you can establish long lasting peace on our planet
so that nowhere and never
will life be devoured by the flames of fire again!

'Peace' and 'love' is all that is left for me to say. Judge me, condemn me, reader, perhaps try to understand and forgive me; but never, never forget what I have done, what seemingly normal human beings are capable of.

Index